LANGUAGE PROGRAM DIRECTION
DIRECTION
THEORY AND PRACTICE

LANGUAGE PROGRAM DIRECTION

THEORY AND PRACTICE

Gillian Lord
University of Florida

Series Editors
Judith Liskin-Gasparro
Manel Lacorte

PEARSON

Boston Columbus Indianapolis New York San Francisco Upper Saddle River
Amsterdam Cape Town Dubai London Madrid Milan Munich Paris Montréal Toronto
Delhi Mexico City São Paulo Sydney Hong Kong Seoul Singapore Taipei Tokyo

Editor in Chief: Bob Hemmer
Editorial Assistant: Jonathan Ortiz
Marketing Manager: Benjamin Zachs
Senior World Language Consultant: Denise Miller
Program Manager: Nancy Stevenson
Senior Vice President: Steve Debow
Production Manager: Fran Russello
Full Service Production: Murugesh Namasivayam/PreMediaGlobal
Art Director: Jayne Conte
Cover Designer: Bruce Kenselaar
Printer/Binder: RR Donnelley and Sons Company

Credits and acknowledgments borrowed from other sources and reproduced, with permission, in this textbook appear on the page number 185.

Library of Congress Cataloging-in-Publication Data
Lord, Gillian.
   Language program direction: theory and practice/Gillian Lord, University of Florida; Series Editors: Judith Liskin-Gasparro, Manel Lacorte.
       pages cm
   Includes bibliographical references and index.
   ISBN-13: 978-0-205-83784-7 (alk. paper)
   ISBN-10: 0-205-83784-0 (alk. paper)
  1. Language and languages—Study and teaching—United States.   I. Title.
   P57.U7L67 2013
   418.0071—dc23

                                                                      2013007381

2 2020

ISBN 10: 0-205-83784-0
ISBN 13: 978-0-205-83784-7

Dedicated with love

to

Resli, Lela, & Kennedy

TABLE OF CONTENTS

ACKNOWLEDGMENTS

I am grateful to so many people for their help and input on this project, either directly or tangentially.

First and foremost, I owe a debt of great gratitude to Bob Hemmer for believing that this was a worthwhile project, and to Bob, Manel Lacorte, and Judy Liskin-Gasparro for their insight, suggestions, and meticulous editing.

My research assistants, Lierra Longstreet and Maria I. Fionda, provided invaluable assistance in locating the sometimes arcane and sometimes elusive resources referenced within this volume. There is, actually, a good deal of very valuable research on program direction, but finding it was an ongoing challenge that I never would have surmounted if not for the dedication of these two young scholars.

My greatest respect and appreciation go to the talented supervisors under whose tutelage I worked as a graduate student at various institutions: Joan Clifford, Carmen García, John Gutiérrez, Donna Hankins, Edwin Lamboy, and Rafael Salaberry. When I became a program director myself, I would not have survived without the guidance and support of my fellow LPDs, coordinators, and colleagues who were and are eager to help and always up for a challenge: Theresa Antes, Joaquim Camps, Kathy Dwyer-Navajas, Antonio Gil, Stasie Harrington, Tammy Jandrey Hertel, Víctor Jordán, Su Ar Lee, Christina Overstreet, and Clara Sotelo. These colleagues have provided me with much needed mentoring and have always been there to bounce ideas off of, to share resources, and to offer guidance. Many of them have become invaluable friends in the process.

All the graduate students with whom I've worked and from whom I have learned so much over the years are present on every page of this book. They are too numerous to name, but without them, I would not be where I am and nor would this volume. *Gracias a todos.*

Lastly, very special thanks go to my husband, Harvey, for supporting this middle-of-the-night idea. When I said, "I wish there were something like a handbook to help me figure out what I'm supposed to be doing!" many would have responded by saying, "Sure, that would be great. Now go back to sleep." But he reacted with only enthusiastic encouragement and an unwavering belief in my knowledge and my skills, without which so much would be impossible.

CHAPTER 1

Introduction

A book such as this one raises many questions at the outset. Who is a language program director? What does she or he do? Do we need language program directors? Do we need this book? The list goes on, and I intend to address these, and other, questions in this volume. Before beginning, however, I start with a note on terminology. I have learned over the past decade that no single term is used for the person, usually a faculty member, who coordinates, directs, or supervises a department's or an institution's language program. *Language program director*, abbreviated *LPD*, is the term I've most commonly come across, and thus it is the term I use here. However, others refer to *coordinators*, *directors*, *supervisors*, *administrative heads*, and numerous other titles and terms. In some cases, the LPD is a tenure-track position and the coordinators are lecturer positions; in other cases, none are tenure-track positions. My use of the term *LPD* is based on the need for simplicity and streamlining. If you are responsible for maintaining, developing, implementing, or overseeing one or more language courses at your institution, this book is for you. If you may take on such a role in the future, or if you interact with LPDs in some other capacity, this book is also for you. Having said that, of course, the previous sentence in no way does justice to the multifaceted nature of our jobs. As Sadow (1989) so eloquently describes our role,

> Foreign language methodologists…are practical philosophers who identify problems and concoct solutions that must work for other people. They must be able to filter their intuitions of what might work through a lens of empirically obtained findings. They must be able to absorb material from many different sources and then decide what is possible in any foreign language classroom, not just their own. Moreover, they belong to a field that is international in scope, highly organized, and constantly reassessing itself. (p. 28)

I will return to this issue of who the LPD (or *methodologist* in Sadow's terminology) is and what she or he does after first dealing with some important
questions on the nature of this book.

1. WHY A HANDBOOK FOR LPDS?

One may ask why we need a book such as this one. Do LPDs need to be told
what to do or how to do it? In my experience, we do need guidance on how
to do the job effectively, because it is not second nature. Yet few of us received
specific training for the positions in which we now find ourselves. As a result,
many lessons are learned after the fact, and many insights come to us only after
a semester has ended. The motivation for this book is, therefore, to put into print
the tools I have used, the resources I have consulted, and the practical tips I have
come across, and to consolidate these things in one place. (To that end, the appendix to this chapter provides contact information for professional organizations
for language instructors and other helpful resources.) My intention is to help other
LPDs avoid the mistakes I have made and to help them be proactive and active
in their roles from the first day—whether they feel they have received sufficient
preparation for their positions or not. At the same time, in my experience as an
LPD, I find that I learn something new every term, and I always appreciate learning what other LPDs do in their programs. So for experienced LPDs, this book
may serve as a reference, a refresher, or an eye-opener. For experienced, novice,
or potential LPDs, it offers a space for reflection on their current or future situations and contexts, as well as a medium for articulating their beliefs and plans.

   This volume is not the first reference of its kind, nor will it be the last.
As universities have seen their language enrollments grow and the demand for
well-structured and well-organized programs increase, the position of LPD has
become more common. Twenty years ago, even the largest programs often made
do without coordinators, letting instructors design their own sections of multisection courses. Today, however, it is common to find institutional mandates for uniformity of content and pedagogical approaches, even in small programs and less
commonly taught languages. It seems the field has recognized the need for solid
pedagogical design and well-prepared instructors in language classes. As Moyer
and Gonglewski (1998) point out, in many cases the lower-division language
courses "provide budgetary sustenance for departments" and also "feed students
into upper-level literature or culture courses"—that is, they are profitable in terms
of revenue for an institution. They explain, "In extreme cases, the lower-division
foreign language program may justify the existence of the department. Thus, it is
understandable that foreign language departments are beginning to appreciate the
worth of a solid undergraduate language program" (p. 52). Different governance
structures in departments result in different approaches to overseeing the undergraduate language program. Nonetheless, in many language departments, particularly in those with large lower-division programs, the LPD does play a crucial role.

   The sample job announcement in Figure 1, adapted from a real ad placed
in the Modern Language Association (MLA) job list, illustrates how complex and
demanding LPD positions have become.

Department of Languages and Literatures

Director of the Spanish Basic Language Program

The Department of Languages and Literatures of University X seeks a Director of the Spanish Language Program at the rank of Clinical Assistant or Clinical Associate Professor. This is a full-time, renewable, non-tenure-track position to begin August 15, 2012. The successful candidate will direct and manage the growth and development of a large basic language program that offers over 65 language classes each semester, in the context of a vibrant interdisciplinary department with a wide range of undergraduate majors and minors. Responsibilities of the Director include, but are not limited to: development of curriculum and pedagogy in accordance with the goals of the department; ongoing textbook evaluation and selection; supervision of language instructors, including regular performance observations and evaluations; hiring of adjunct staff; training of graduate student language instructors and ongoing development and training of faculty in foreign language teaching methodologies; curricular planning, reform and design; scheduling of courses and staffing assignments; regular teaching in the program; student advisement. Requirements: Ph.D. or Ed.D in hand, with expertise in linguistics or applied linguistics desirable; proven excellence as a teacher, supervisor and administrator in a college-level language program; native or native-like fluency in English and Spanish; knowledge of Portuguese is a plus.

FIGURE 1 Sample LPD Job Description.

Note the many and varied responsibilities listed for the LPD: curriculum development, pedagogical development, faculty supervision, evaluation and hiring, education and training of graduate students, administrative planning and scheduling, teaching, and advising. Even an experienced LPD would find this job announcement intimidating; for a doctoral student on the job market for the first time, it could be overwhelming. The variety and nature of the tasks are notable given that future LPDs have rarely received training in all aspects of the job.

Therefore, it is somewhat surprising that relatively few works address the role of the LPD in language programs and departments, or offer assistance and training for those in this position. Over the last few decades, though, a small but important number of such publications have appeared, along with several articles that tend toward similar issues. I have consulted these works both throughout my learning process and while writing this book, and readers will see them cited in the following chapters. Additionally, a number of publications are listed at the end of each chapter in the suggestions for further reading. At the same time, however, many of these publications are somewhat narrower in scope than this volume, as they are geared only for ESL teachers, for example, or were written from a strictly theoretical (not practical) perspective, or are designed for an audience of graduate teaching assistants. Other reference works are now outdated and do not address all of the questions an LPD must consider today, from ethics to technology and everything in between. The intent of this book is to go a step further and a step broader than previous books have done. It is not intended to replace other works, but to supplement them. Taken as a whole, the chapters of this volume offer background, research, and practical insights into many issues facing LPDs today, from the roles and responsibilities of the LPD (and the various names and titles given to LPDs) to our position within our department, professional issues we face, and guidance on the tasks for which we are responsible.

What qualifies me to write this book? My experience has been in a Spanish program in a relatively large public university; I have coordinated the intermediate program as well as the entire lower division (elementary and intermediate) program. As a graduate student I had experience with similar programs at two other public universities, one quite large and the other mid-sized. My faculty appointment has always been in a language department, not a school of languages. I have always worked with Spanish, the most commonly taught language. And I have always been involved in programs that employ primarily graduate students as instructors, with some lecturers serving in teaching and level coordination roles. On only a few occasions have my supervisory duties involved overseeing tenured or tenure-track faculty.

I recognize that my experience represents only a small niche in the world of LPDs: large programs versus medium programs versus small programs; language schools versus language departments; public versus private institutions; two-year versus four-year institutions; staff of graduate students versus staff of faculty or outside adjuncts; commonly taught languages versus less commonly taught languages (LCTLs), and so forth. My place in a large commonly taught language program has given me flexibility and freedom to do things that might otherwise not have been possible:

> Program size also affects program design. A small program may have a few part-time teachers with only one administrator who is involved with teaching as well as administrative responsibilities. It is axiomatic that the smaller the program, the fewer the design options. (Davidson & Tesh, 1997, p. 182)

I would like to speak to all types of programs, to understand the issues that affect all LPDs regardless of program, department, size, language, or any other variable. For that reason, in the beginning stages of this project I conducted a survey of language program coordinators similar to those of Paesani and Barrette (2005), Katz and Watzinger-Tharp (2005), and Schulz (1980). This survey consisted of approximately 50 questions related to language program structure, administration, and experiences. In general, the questions asked about text selection, mission statements, levels of administration and support, syllabus design, and assessment. The survey, directed toward current LPDs at a variety of institutions, was administered online. A description of the survey and a request for input was disseminated widely via e-mails to e-mail lists and discussion groups, as well as by word of mouth. Unfortunately, given the nature of anonymous online surveys, fewer than 75 responses were registered.

Despite the limited number of responses, interesting trends are still evident. The issues remain largely the same across institutions, although the organization and terminologies may differ. Issues of teacher education and assessment, curricular design, and administrative hierarchies appear common to language programs, regardless of their size or structure. Therefore, there is general utility not only in my personal experience, but also in the lessons I have learned and want to share; similarly, reference is made to this survey and its results to expand the realm of the discussion of LPDs and their roles and tasks.

2. WHO IS THE LPD?

As mentioned at the beginning of this chapter, one of the most crucial, yet most complicated, questions to ask is *who* the LPD is. This question is challenging because it seems there is no universally agreed-upon answer. What are the duties and responsibilities of the LPD? Is the LPD an academic? A pedagogue? An administrator? All of the above? How does the LPD structure her or his program to fit in the organization of the overall department? What demands dictate the design of the language program? How is the LPD compensated? These issues are addressed in the following sections, but are also revisited throughout the book because they are topics that continue to present themselves in every aspect of our daily work.

Before addressing the specific roles and responsibilities of the LPD, we have to consider that just as there is no single term for the LPD, the duties of the LPD vary according to the institutional context. Sadow (1989, pp. 27–28) suggests that the LPD is, in essence, more than meets the eye: As LPDs, we must regularly make intellectual contributions in a field that is continually changing, and we must be aware of developments in related fields, such as second language acquisition, speech communication, anthropology, computer-assisted language learning, and cognitive science. Our commitment to our institutions requires that we produce ideas that "have direct, practical, and verifiable applications" (p. 28) and that are convincing to a broad range of people. We often author textbooks and other educational materials as a result of our practical and empirical work. For the most part, we are gifted teachers who put time and effort into learning and practicing the best methods, and sharing these methods with other educators and teachers-to-be.

In specific terms, the definition is more challenging. Factors such as the language or languages involved, the size and nature of the institution, and the makeup of the teaching staff cause programs to vary widely in their approaches and their administration. According to White, Hockley, van der Horst Jansen, and Laughner (2008, p. 33), these variables can be categorized as strategy, size, environment, and technology. Strategy refers to why the organization exists, and what its purpose is. Size, as discussed previously, relates to how large the organization is—be it the department, school, or language program. For example, although a smaller organization may be better suited to a more organic structure, larger organizations may require greater degrees of formalized structure and accountability. Environment refers to the location of the department or organization and the space it occupies; although intended literally, this issue can also be addressed figuratively, as we will shortly discuss where the LPD fits in the language department (and institution) as a whole. Finally, technology relates to how information is processed and shared and how communication takes place, as these aspects also can play a crucial role in how the organization works.

Although these variables will always come into play, some constancy and consistency is found across programs, particularly in terms of the key roles and responsibilities of the LPD. The following section summarizes these, keeping in mind that every organization is unique but trying to find the commonalities among them.

2.1 Roles and Responsibilities

A number of previous works related to language program direction have attempted to categorize the varied roles of the LPD. These are addressed here beginning with the more theoretical and moving toward the more practical. Later, other issues that can be related to program direction are introduced into the discussion. Worth noting is that particular institutions may require all or some of the duties described, as well as others that are not mentioned here. LPDs may be responsible for one course level, all lower-division language courses, or something in between. LPDs may be in charge of training all instructors or only a subset. They may have complete freedom when designing syllabi and curricula, or they may be constrained by external factors. The LPD's duties usually range from administrative to academic (e.g., Lee & Van Patten, 1991), from practical to pedagogical, and from managerial (e.g., White et al., 2008) to interpersonal. The specific needs of a program will determine for which of these roles an LPD is responsible and which take top priority at any given time.

Kaplan (1997, p. 10) breaks the LPD's job description into six primary duties, each with its specific tasks (see Table 1). As Kaplan notes, the roles of the LPD are "diverse indeed" (p. 9). Although Kaplan's summary is based on the roles of an Intensive English Program director, they are equally applicable to the language (second or foreign) program director as well.

Lee's (1989) practical guide to directing language programs and working with graduate teaching assistants offers a basic chronological (i.e., over one semester) description. With it, he notes that "the Director of Basic Language Instruction is the creative force behind basic language instruction and the administrator who keeps the bureaucratic mechanisms of the LP moving...and moving on time" (p. 12). While the brief summary that follows provides an overview, Lee (1987) has pointed out that "everything from the quality of the individual TA's instruction to the efficacy with which the office staff produces final exams is tied to the position of the Language Program Director" (p. 6), so the importance of these tasks, great and small, cannot be underestimated. Lee summarizes the primary duties of the LPD with the following list:

- Discuss course offerings
- Discuss the TA budget and projected new graduate student enrollment
- Organize and conduct the TA orientation
- Decide which courses each TA will teach
- Decide on grading criteria, teaching strategies, and book and material choices

TABLE 1 Summary of LPD Duties and Tasks (adapted from Kaplan, 1997)	
Primary Duties	**Tasks**
Academic content and assessment of these	• Curriculum design • Testing • Syllabus development • Student placement • Teacher evaluation • Articulation among levels • Test development and curriculum trialing • Teacher training
Administration of a large unit	• Operations • Policy development and implementation • Infrastructure planning • Long- and short-term budgets • Organizational planning • Staff development (in-service/pre-service) • Record keeping
Institutional linkages with academic and administrative units	• Liaison with higher-level administrators both within and beyond the department • Committees • Student/faculty advocacy
Political linkages in the external world	• Liaison with stake-holders • Institutional policy development • External professional organization involvement • Liaison with accrediting agency, funding agencies, sponsors, international agencies
Fiscal operation of the unit	• Budget development • Purchasing • Planned acquisition of office and instructional equipment • Grants and contracts
Intellectual management of the unit	• Staffing • Running meetings • Structuring committees • Hiring and firing • Dealing with grievances • Counseling • Engaging in legal action if necessary • Maintaining personnel records • Preserving personnel harmony

Source: Christison and Stoller (1997, p. 10)

- Deal with student complaints (of which, Lee notes, there are often many!)
- Edit exams written by supervisors
- Serve on departmental committees

As Lee points out, it is crucial that preparation for each semester begin well in advance, from one to two semesters ahead of time. This aspect alone makes the LPD's job unique in that there is never time to rest—there is always another semester to plan for. I have often joked with my colleagues that I would like to welcome the start of the new academic year with the luxury of a slow first week, when the main responsibilities are to prepare the syllabi for the classes I'm teaching, but LPDs do not have this option. In addition to the classes they teach, they are also training, writing other syllabi, preparing orientations, setting up online materials, and doing a good deal of troubleshooting.

Barrette and Paesani (2005) confirm the multiple aspects of the LPD's job description, as they discovered in their survey of LPDs that over half of their respondents took part in the following duties:

- Evaluate teaching performance of instructors
- Select textbooks
- Conduct coordination meetings
- Conduct preservice workshops
- Conduct class observations
- Develop course syllabi
- Schedule courses
- Teach methods courses
- Participate in the selection of graduate students
- Recruit graduate students
- Offer in-service development workshops
- Coordinate placement testing
- Develop achievement test for classes
- Develop websites for classes, program, or both

Some of these tasks may fall under the standard job description of the LPD. Others may come as a surprise to new LPDs. For example, I have found myself increasingly involved in recruiting and selecting graduate students for our program, as well as in creating and balancing the departmental budget as it relates to these teaching assistants. Barrette and Paesani (2005, p. 5) suggest that according to Guthrie (2001), the responsibilities of LPDs fall into three general categories: teaching and program direction; training and supervision; and professional engagement within and beyond the home institution (pp. 7–18). Although LPDs may begin their careers knowing that the first and second categories are expected, the third may come as a surprise.

What also often comes as a surprise, as in my case, is the scope of the LPD responsibilities. In addition to the more standard academic and administrative tasks, many (e.g., Leaver & Oxford, 2000) have noted additional facets of the position. For example, mentoring is an essential part of training and supervising instructors. Then in addition to carrying out the more tangible administrative, pedagogical, service, and scholarly duties outlined earlier, LPDs must also be proficient in the less tangible duty of understanding and managing the individual differences among participants in the language program.

To that end, White et al.'s (2008) book is a valuable resource, as it treats the management aspect of teaching organizations, although few LPDs may have thought of themselves as managers prior to accepting their first LPD position: "Management is something which is fundamental to the way any organization, including any [language teaching organization], operates, survives, and develops" (p. 8). These authors note that the job of a manager can be classified into four primary functions (p. 10):

1. **Planning**: deciding what has to happen in the future and producing plans to achieve intended goals
2. **Organizing**: making optimum use of the resources required to enable the successful carrying out of plans
3. **Leading/motivating**: employing skills in these areas for getting others to play an effective part in achieving plans and developing people's skills
4. **Controlling**: checking progress against plans, which may need modification based on feedback

What's more, LPDs are not just academic (i.e., curriculum, assessment, teaching, materials selection) managers; they are also expected to manage the program from the perspectives of business (i.e., volume, profitability, budgeting, meeting goals), resources (i.e., teaching materials, classroom equipment), and personnel (i.e., recruiting, assigning, training, motivating, problem solving).

It is clear, therefore, that LPDs have their hands full all year long and that they fill an important role in language departments. But we need to look a step further to better understand the nature of this position: not only who the LPD is, but also how the LPD fits into the bigger picture of the department as a whole. As Harris-Schenz (1993) points out, the position of the LPD is unique; as such, we need to consider all the facets of this job, from employment conditions to support for professional development and research, and the role of the LPD with respect to the other departmental faculty.

2.2 Position in the Department

The LPD has the potential to become a valuable, even indispensable, member of a language department, given the curricular expertise, institutional knowledge, and interpersonal skills that come with the position. In fact, I know of many cases—including my own—in which the LPD has taken on the chair or associate chair position in the department in which they serve or served as LPD. In many ways this is a logical progression for a tenure-track LPD, although if the position is not a tenure-track one, the options for administrative leadership may be institutionally limited. The LPD position is in many ways a position of value and honor.

At the same time, however, it is not always recognized as such, and often LPDs report that they feel undervalued by their colleagues. "To be sure, the primary challenge in running a successful language program is coping with the high level of responsibility demanded of an individual program director, which goes above and beyond what is expected of even the typically overtaxed junior faculty members of today" (Moyer & Gonglewski, 1998, p. 52). Given the responsibility and skill involved in executing the LPD position and the value of the LPD role in a language department, then why do we find this sense of disgruntlement?

For one, LPDs who have not been trained in pedagogy, language acquisition and teaching, or educational leadership may find themselves in a position for which they are unprepared and unenthusiastic. Other LPDs note that they are considered second-class citizens in their organizations, seen as administrators but not academics. Yet, others comment that few of their colleagues understand the extent of their responsibilities or the time these take. There is also the issue of rank or status in the department, as the LPD role seems to be increasingly non-tenure-track, which is dealt with in more detail in the next section.

Further, as Kramsch (1998) points out, the LPD position can exacerbate existing divides within a department, leading to the LPD feeling unappreciated or even unprotected:

> [LPDs] are in a particularly vulnerable position, because they are likely to be isolated on both sides of the foreign language department's language-literature divide...But it is vital for them not to lose sight of the unity of language and of the crucial role they can play in acting as intermediaries between the two halves of their department's curriculum. (p. 32)

This sense of being undervalued can also be a factor in the LPD's dealings with graduate students. When teaching the methodology course for our teaching assistants (TA), for example, I have often worked with graduate students who feel that they are merely biding their time teaching language, but will someday soon be teaching courses related to their research interests. It is difficult for some graduate students to realize or accept that the majority of them will work in departments where they will teach language courses. The foreign language profession as a whole has not yet succeeded in changing the perception of language teaching as a low-prestige activity; even some of our colleagues tend to consider good pedagogy the domain of lower-level language instruction only (Moyer & Gonglewski, 1998, p. 53). One approach to combat this attitude is perhaps to point out to all instructors, especially graduate students, that the percentage of graduating PhDs who secure tenure-track positions in Research I universities is small indeed, and that even teaching Cervantes, Goethe, or Proust requires solid pedagogical talent. (I often take copies of the latest MLA job list to my methodology course so the students can see the job openings for the current year.) Still, LPDs do often feel that they must fight for respect. Moyer and Gonglewski (1998) note this same issue as well: "In addition to running the program, LPDs are normally expected to train graduate instructors and continue their own scholarly pursuits—two integral parts of keeping the language program strong and their chances for tenure high. This extra burden would not pose such a problem if the amount of respect for this position were equally great" (p. 52).

One fairly obvious reason, but one that bears discussion, that many LPDs feel they must fight for respect is that, as mentioned earlier, many LPD positions are no longer tenure-track. In such cases, the individuals in charge of running language programs are in faculty ranks that are typically undervalued, such as lecturers, instructors, professors of the practice, and so on, in institutions that traditionally define themselves as research-oriented. Thus, the undervaluing of the faculty rank further aggravates the undervaluing of the LPD; these LPDs have a level of responsibility in the department that is equivalent to that of many senior faculty, but without the corresponding status. This mismatch between rank and responsibility is at the heart of the resentment that tends to characterize the lack of satisfaction LPDs may feel with their professional treatment.

Another issue is the sense that the LPD often feels overworked when compared to colleagues who do not have coordinating responsibilities. Is the LPD really required to do more work than others? At a typical research institution, the division of labor tends to be seen in thirds: one-third research, one-third teaching, one-third service, although others (e.g., Mancing, 1991, p. 49) claim that the distribution may be more along the lines of 40% teaching, 40% research, and 20% service. However, given the multifaceted nature of the LPD's responsibilities, many LPDs have noticed that workload distribution does indeed seem to be more along the lines of 40% teaching, 40% service, and 20% research (Harris-Schenz, 1993, pp. 45–50), assuming that LPD duties are considered service, which is not always the case. The categorization of the LPD responsibilities, as well as the issues of tenure requirements (in the case of tenure-track LPDs), are explored in the next section.

2.3 Compensation and Other Professional Issues

How the LPD is compensated in the department varies from institution to institution and within an institution, from department to department, depending on the size of the language program. The arrangements can be anything from reduced teaching loads to additional or summer pay to nothing at all. Tenure-track LPDs are typically granted reduced service or teaching assignments. At my institution, for example, coordinating a language program is considered "Other Instructional Activity," so it is included with responsibilities like serving on doctoral dissertation committees, but does not count as service to the department or the profession; for that the LPD has to serve on departmental and college committees. Most LPDs receive a reduced teaching load, although this reduction can occur every semester, once a year, or every other year. The benefits of this course reduction are sometimes more tangible than others, depending on the individual circumstances and the nature of the LPD's other assignments. Some LPDs have reported summer pay as compensation as well, which corresponds to continuing the coordinating duties in the summer, of course; but in many cases, the LPD is expected to keep things running smoothly in the summer, even without an official appointment or summer salary.

In their survey, Barrette and Paesani (2005) learned that most LPDs are untenured, and Katz and Watzinger-Tharp (2005) found that 58% are tenured or tenure-track, with 31% holding non-tenure-track positions. This situation raises the question of how these faculty members, given their LPD responsibilities, can prepare for tenure and promotion, and how their departments can help them. In the case of tenure-track professors serving as LPDs, modified requirements for tenure and promotion occasionally may be in place for the LPD, although these modifications seem to be rare. Given the difficulty involved in the day-to-day administration of a program on top of the demands of teaching, research, and service that the tenure and promotion process requires, LPDs seem to be at an inherent disadvantage. We probably all know of an LPD who, due to coordination demands, was unable to produce a sufficient amount of published research to qualify for tenure and promotion. It may be difficult for other faculty and especially for administrators to understand the nature of the LPD position and why it is an additional challenge to maintain an active research agenda. Books such as this one are intended to help our colleagues become better educated about the nature of the LPD position. What's more, even if LPDs are able to achieve tenure, the sense may remain that their "academic and intellectual legitimacy still has to be argued in comparison with that of colleagues in literary/cultural studies or in theoretical linguistics" (Kramsch, 2000, p. 320). To be sure, the dilemma of the LPD that Harris-Schenz (1993) pointed out over 20 years ago seems to still hold: "[LPDs] in most PhD-granting institutions across the country are in fact caught between a rock and a hard place, because they occupy a position that is frequently misunderstood, undervalued, and minimally staffed" (p. 45).

Add to this lack of understanding of the position the fact that because many "LPD positions are for junior faculty members, the workload itself presents another challenge, since few LPDs receive adequate preparation for such duties during their graduate careers" (Moyer & Gonglewski, 1998, p. 52). For example, in spite of my coordinating experience while a graduate student, I found myself unprepared for the demands of my new position. One can only imagine how challenging it would be for new junior faculty with no experience in language program coordination to make sense of their many duties and responsibilities. A survey by Teschner (1991) revealed that only 14.29% of LPDs had written dissertations in areas related to language teaching or acquisition, while almost 67% had come from a background in literature (p. 22). While those data are somewhat outdated by now and colleagues in literature being required to direct language programs are increasingly rare, the fact remains that few LPDs are trained for the position a priori. Again, one of the motivations for this book is to share what my fellow LPDs and I have learned through experience, trial and error, and the generous advice of mentors and friends, and to help provide the resources needed to be successful.

What kind of preparation and education LPDs receive prior to beginning their roles is an important issue, although not one that we tend to think of frequently. According to Barrette and Paesani's (2005) survey, LPDs more often than not are specialists in a subfield of linguistics. Yet the assumption that academic training in linguistics translates into preparation for the role of LPD simply is not true. The real academic preparation required for LPDs is in pedagogy, methodology, and management. Just because I work in second language acquisition, for example, does not mean that I am more qualified to discuss teaching approaches than anyone else. This common misconception, that linguistics equals teaching, is one that many LPDs struggle with, and it results in a constant process of educating our colleagues. This confusion is not new, but it has come to the forefront in the last two decades as language departments increase their offerings and in turn, discover the need for an administrative figure to coordinate them (e.g., Firth & Wagner, 1997; Kramsch, 2000; Lee, 1999).

The only explicit instruction I received that would have prepared me for my current responsibilities as LPD, albeit only tangentially, is the teaching methods course I took as a graduate student, and perhaps also a few electives I took in curriculum design. Increasingly, many universities are offering more specialized degrees in language acquisition and teaching (see the partial list in the appendix at the end of the chapter), some of which offer seminars on language program direction as well, which would be an invaluable preparatory resource for future LPDs. But at the same time, how many LPDs know as graduate students that their future employers will ask this of them? Many LPDs end up in their positions by default rather than by preference. Lee and Van Patten (1991, pp. 121–124) proposed a three-year plan for the gradual integration of new assistant professors into the LPD role while also growing as scholars, both to maintain the academic integrity of the LPD position and to foster the assistant professor's research agenda. Three years, though, may be an unrealistic training period, given the constant demands of the LPD position and the unstoppable tenure clock.

In spite of these challenges, there is a silver lining. To be sure, "filling the shoes of both junior faculty member and high-profile administrator creates a higher level of stress, but it also gives entry-level professors the opportunity to shape their programs from the ground up" (Moyer & Gonglewski, 1998, p. 53). While daunting, this opportunity to create programs is one many faculty members are not afforded, so the LPD should take advantage of it. With the proper tools, LPDs can and should be able to make the most of this chance to position themselves as vital and influential members of their departments. It is my hope that the following chapters can provide some of these tools.

3. CONCLUSION

Many issues have been addressed in this introduction. Because there are too many aspects of the LPD role to address in one volume, the focus in this one is the practical day-to-day running of a language program, including tips, techniques, and approaches that are relevant to many of the hats the LPD wears. The novice LPD will benefit from the volume in that it provides information that I would have liked to have received prior to taking on my role. But experienced LPDs can also gain insight from other programs, learn new ideas, and constantly reevaluate and modify their programs.

To that end, the remainder of this book is laid out as follows. Chapter 2 discusses the role of a mission statement, both practically and symbolically, and how to craft one for a language program. That chapter will examine mission statements in general, as well as issues related particularly to language programs. After discussing the resources available to consult while writing a mission statement, the chapter provides some sample mission statements as guidelines. In Chapter 3, course syllabi and other program materials are discussed. The topics included in this chapter range from the basic components of a syllabus to articulation across and within program levels. Chapter 4 addresses textbook selection and use, from the search process through possible complications with adoptions, and provides sample review forms for evaluating potential textbooks prior to adoption. In Chapter 5 the ever-important topic of hiring and training instructors is examined, with information on how to develop the right structure for a program, considerations for hires, and how to most effectively train and evaluate the instructors working in the program. Chapter 6 tackles the popular topic of technology and how to incorporate technological tools and innovations into program design, training, and course delivery. Chapter 7 discusses the process of assessing language programs, and it examines when, why, and how to make changes. That chapter also offers concluding thoughts on the future of language program direction. Each chapter includes questions for reflection and discussion as well as suggestions for further reading. These will help the readers assimilate the information presented and reflect on their own situations, while continuing to explore the topics on their own.

Questions for Reflection

1. Reconsider the lists of duties cited in the beginning portion of the chapter (e.g., Barrette & Paesani, 2005; Christison & Stoller, 1997; Lee, 1987). Compare the responsibilities discussed by the respective authors. What differences are there? What do you think might account for these differences? Thinking about LPD positions with which you are familiar, which are applicable and which are not?
2. Of the duties listed, which do you believe to be the most challenging, and why? (If you are not currently an LPD, consider what could make some of the tasks more difficult than others.) How could these tasks be made easier?
3. According to White et al. (2008, p. 205), the following are some of the roles the LPD can play:

   - Evaluator
   - Strategist
   - Manager
   - Executive officer
   - Diplomat
   - Publicist
   - Mentor
   - Educator
   - Advisor
   - Ambassador
   - Advocate

   Which of these describe the LPD positions with which you are familiar? In what ways does an LPD fulfill these various roles? Are there other roles that an LPD may be expected to carry out?

4. Consider the rank and status of LPD positions with which you are familiar.

   a. Are they tenure-track? What is expected in terms of research, teaching, professional development, service, and so forth?

   b. Are the LPDs compensated appropriately for their work in the language program? If not, what would be a more appropriate compensation plan? Is this work and compensation comparable to that of other colleagues?

   c. Do you believe that LPDs should educate their colleagues about their purpose and position in a department or organization? What do you think an LPD's colleagues should know about the position? How could this learning process be approached with colleagues, even those in different fields or specializations?

Suggestions for Further Reading

Katz, S., & Watzinger-Tharp, J. (2005). Toward an understanding of the role of applied linguists in foreign language departments. *The Modern Language Journal, 89*, 490–502.

> A useful and up-to-date analysis of the situation of LPDs in language departments today.

Kramsch, C. (2000). Second language acquisition, applied linguistics, and the teaching of foreign languages. *The Modern Language Journal, 84*, 311–326.

> An introduction to the relationship between the fields of SLA and applied linguistics and their relevance to the LPD.

Lee, J. (1987). Toward a professional model of language program direction. *ADFL Bulletin, 19*(1), 22–25.

> An overview of the increasing role of LPDs and suggestions for their incorporation in language departments.

APPENDIX

Resources for Foreign Language Teachers

ORGANIZATIONS

- American Association of University Supervisors and Coordinators (AAUSC): http://www.aausc.org
- American Council on the Teaching of Foreign Languages (ACTFL): http://www.actfl.org
- Central States Conference on the Teaching of Foreign Languages (CSC): http://www.csctfl.org
- Computer Assisted Language Instruction Consortium (CALICO): http://www.calico.org
- Foreign Language Teaching Forum (FLTeach): http://web.cortland.edu/flteach
- Modern Language Association (MLA): http://www.mla.org
- Northeast Conference on the Teaching of Foreign Languages (NECTFL): http://www.nectfl.org
- Pacific Northwest Council on Foreign Languages (PNCFL): http://www.pncfl.org
- Southern Conference on Language Teaching (SCOLT): http://scolt.webnode.com
- Southwest Conference on Language Teaching (SWCOLT): http://www.swcolt.org

American Association of University Supervisors and Coordinators (AAUSC) Annual Volumes

Allen, H. W., & Maxim, H. (Eds.). (2011). *Educating the future foreign language professorate for the 21st century.* Boston, MA: Heinle Cengage.

Barrette, C., & Paesani, K. (Eds.). (2005). *Language program articulation: Developing a theoretical foundation.* Boston, MA: Heinle Cengage.

Belz, J. A., & Thorne, S. L. (Eds.). (2006). *Internet-mediated intercultural foreign language education.* Boston, MA: Heinle Cengage.

Benseler, D. (Ed.). (1993). *The dynamics of language program direction.* Boston, MA: Heinle Cengage.

Blyth, C. (Ed.). (2003). *The sociolinguistics of foreign language classrooms: Contributions of the native, the near-native and the non-native speaker.* Boston, MA: Heinle Cengage.

Byrnes, H., & Maxim, H. (Eds.). (2004). *Advanced foreign-language instruction.* Boston, MA: Heinle Cengage.

Heilenman, K. (Ed.). (1999). *Research issues and language program direction.* Boston, MA: Heinle Cengage.

Katz, S., & Watzinger-Tharp, J. (Eds.). (2008). *Conceptions of L2 grammar: Theoretical approaches and their application in the l2 classroom.* Boston, MA: Heinle Cengage.

Klee, C. (Ed.). (1994). *Faces in a crowd: The individual learner in multisection courses.* Boston, MA: Heinle Cengage.

Kramsch, C. (Ed.). (1995). *Redefining the boundaries of language study.* Boston, MA: Heinle Cengage.

Lee, J. F., & Valdman, A. (Eds.). (2000). *Form and meaning: Multiple perspectives.* Boston, MA: Heinle Cengage.

Levine, G. S., & Phipps, A. (Eds.). (2010). *Critical and intercultural theory and language pedagogy.* Boston, MA: Heinle Cengage.

Liskin-Gasparro, J. (Ed.). (1996). *Patterns and policies: The changing demographics of foreign language instruction.* Boston, MA: Heinle Cengage.

Magnan, S. S. (Ed.). (1991). *Challenges in the 1990s for college foreign language programs.* Boston, MA: Heinle Cengage.

Muyskens, J. (Ed.). (1998). *New ways of learning and teaching: Focus on technology and foreign language education.* Boston, MA: Heinle Cengage.

Rifkin, B. (Ed.). (2001). *Mentoring foreign language teaching assistants, lecturers, and adjunct faculty.* Boston, MA: Heinle Cengage.

Scott, V. M. (2009). (Ed.). *Principles and practices of the Standards in college foreign language education.* Boston, MA: Heinle Cengage.

Scott, V. M., & Tucker, H. (Eds.). (2002). *SLA and the literature classroom: Fostering dialogues.* Boston, MA: Heinle Cengage.

Siskin, H. J. (Ed.). (2007). *From thought to action: Exploring beliefs and outcomes in the foreign language program.* Boston, MA: Heinle Cengage.

Teschner, R. (Ed.). (1991). *Assessing foreign language proficiency of undergraduates.* Boston, MA: Heinle Cengage.

Walz, J. (Ed.). (1992). *Development and supervision of teaching assistants in foreign languages.* Boston, MA: Heinle Cengage.

Graduate Programs with Specializations in Language Education/Teaching University of Arizona

Second Language Acquisition and Teaching

http://slat.arizona.edu

Georgetown University

Interdisciplinary focus on second language acquisition (SLA) with degrees in other departments

http://www8.georgetown.edu/departments/linguistics/sla/pages/degree%20 programs/degree_programs.htm

Indiana University

Second Language Studies (Department of Second Language Studies)

http://www.indiana.edu/~dsls/degrees

Michigan State University

Online Master of Arts in Foreign Language Teaching (Center for Language Teaching Advancement)

http://maflt.cal.msu.edu

*Offers course devoted to Language Program Administration

University of Iowa

Foreign Language Acquisition Research and Education (FLARE)

http://international.uiowa.edu/flare

University of Maryland

Second Language Education Graduate Program in TESOL or FLEd (Department of Curriculum and Instruction, College of Education)

http://www.education.umd.edu/EDCI/info/tesolfled.html

Hispanic Applied Linguistics

http://sllc.umd.edu/sites/sllc.umd.edu/files/Spanish%20Masters%20Flyer.pdf

University of Massachusetts Boston

Applied Linguistics/Foreign Language Pedagogy

http://www.umb.edu/academics/uc/degree/apling

University of Oxford

MSc in Applied Linguistics and Second Language Acquisition (Department of Education)

http://www.education.ox.ac.uk/courses/msc-applied-linguistics

University of Wisconsin–Madison

Second Language Acquisition (Language Institute)

http://www.sla.wisc.edu

CHAPTER 2

The Mission Statement

One may be wondering why the mission statement appears among the first topics in this book, especially considering that few language programs have one. Most universities and departments have a mission statement, and occasionally undergraduate programs do as well, but mission statements are not common among language programs. I have worked in a number of lower-division language programs at different institutions without ever seeing a mission statement or any other kind of statement of purpose for those programs. It seems that it is more common not to have any kind of guiding statement, even though almost all businesses, corporations, organizations, and institutions of higher education create such documents. Maxim (2005a), citing Byrnes (1998), explains the absence of mission statements in language programs by saying that "collegiate [foreign language] departments, despite sharing a common disciplinary focus, have traditionally not adopted a collective approach to teaching or learning" (p. 81). Thus while our departments or institutions may establish a course of study, "educational goals, pedagogical practices, and assessment procedures typically are course- rather than curriculum-dependent . . . without any true sense of curricular progression or trajectory" (p. 81).

However, after having gone through the process of developing a mission statement or a statement of purpose (I use the terms interchangeably), the value of this exercise becomes apparent, both for the language program director (LPD) and for all those involved in the program. To that end, this chapter examines what mission statements are and how they can be beneficial to the LPD and to language programs in general. Sample mission statements are provided at the end of the chapter.

1. WHAT IS A MISSION STATEMENT? . . . AND WHY SHOULD YOU HAVE ONE?

A mission statement is a declaration of an organization's primary purpose and focus, explaining to customers or clients the organization's values and priorities. (For definitions, see http://www.businessdictionary.com/definition/mission-statement.html or http://en.wikipedia.org/wiki/Mission_statement.[1]) Although in the business world mission statements and vision statements are different (the latter stresses what a company will do to accomplish the goals in its mission statement), in academia there is a tendency to collapse these two into a single statement. Therefore, throughout this chapter the term *mission statement* is used broadly, referring to what the organization wants to accomplish and what it will pursue to do so.

The goals of the mission statement are to guide the actions of an organization, explain the goal of the organization to its stakeholders or participants, facilitate decision making, and generally provide a sense of direction for those involved in fulfilling the organization's work. A well-written mission statement not only serves as a motivational force for those participating in the organization, but also attracts people to it. In terms of language programs, it may attract new students to language courses or motivate instructors to work as a team.

According to White et al. (2008), the mission statement involves "a pattern of beliefs, valued and learned ways of coping with experience that have been developed during the course of an organization's history, and which tend to be manifested in its material arrangements and in the behavior of its members" (pp. 34–35). These authors go on to argue that a mission statement, among other expressions of values, helps an organization develop a sense of its identity, enhances commitment to the organization's goals, and helps ensure that employees will act in a uniform and acceptable manner.

When examined from this angle, the question seems to be not why one should have a mission statement, but why everyone does not already have one. After all, "defining what your raison d'être is can not only be of value to your potential customers [i.e., students], but can also help ensure that the organization as a whole is pulling together to achieve a common goal" (White et al., 2008, p. 40). The corporate world has recognized the value of mission statements, although mission statements are often confused with pithy ad slogans and may result in memorable catchphrases rather than informational or meaningful statements. As we consider the value of creating and publicizing a mission statement for our programs, it is useful to consult other well-known

---

[1]Wikipedia is frequently scorned as an academic source and often for good reason. However, if we can confirm the validity and reliability of the information provided, I have found it to be a trustworthy and valuable reference. I make limited use of it here in some specific cases.

organizations to learn how they have expressed the mission that underlies their work. The following is a sampling of mission statements taken from varied organizations, ranging from the large and well known to the small and local:

- Google: "Google's mission is to organize the world's information and make it universally accessible and useful." (http://www.google.com/about/company)
- Wikimedia Foundation: "The mission of the Wikimedia Foundation is to empower and engage people around the world to collect and develop educational content under a free license or in the public domain, and to disseminate it effectively and globally." (http://wikimediafoundation.org/wiki/Mission_statement)
- North Carolina State Board of Education: "The guiding mission of the North Carolina State Board of Education is that every public school student will graduate from high school, globally competitive for work and post-secondary education and prepared for life in the 21st Century." (http://www.ncpublicschools.org/organization/mission)
- Aero Rental and Party Shoppe, Iowa City, Iowa: "Aero Rental exists to provide its diverse rental and party customers with the finest service, products and equipment available. [Our vision is] to be widely recognized as the finest rental and party supply store in the state of Iowa. If our people, our products, our service, and our attitude do not measure up, we will have missed our mark."

At the same time, it is important to remember that mission statements rarely exist in isolation. They are often followed—whether on a Web page or in a publication—by a list of goals or objectives and descriptions of how the organization or institution will achieve those goals. But the statement itself should offer a valuable insight into the organization's priorities, as can be seen in the preceding examples. The next section moves from general mission statements in these corporate or public sector contexts to crafting statements appropriate for language programs.

2. MISSION STATEMENTS IN LANGUAGE PROGRAMS

Although corporations tend to write their mission statements for the benefit of customers and we in academia tend to focus on students as the beneficiaries of our work, the principle can be the same: "Establishing leadership and presence and defining the expectations for one's job are the basis for what are ultimately the LPD's most significant and most daunting tasks: assessing the curriculum as it stands and taking responsibility for needed changes" (Moyer & Gonglewski, 1998, p. 56). The benefits described in the previous section are just as applicable to students and instructors as they are to companies, consumers, and patrons. Perhaps even more crucially, the process of writing a statement for a language program is invaluable for the LPD, as it helps the LPD solidify and verbalize what he or she sees as the main goals and purpose of the program, ranging from language skills to critical-thinking abilities: "Setting objectives and determining or measuring these objectives are key activities in exemplary professional development programs" (Peredo, 2000, par. 1).

2.1 What LPDs Are Doing

Only about one third of the respondents of my online survey indicated that their programs have mission statements. These statements were often written by the current or former LPD, although of those who indicated that they have a mission statement, a small portion were written by a committee rather than an individual. Of those programs that have mission statements, only about a third make those statements publicly available anywhere: They are occasionally placed in graduate student and teaching assistant (TA) handbooks or on course syllabi or the departmental website, but the majority indicated that their statements were not published. Further, more than half of the respondents with mission statements indicated that they would not be willing to share their program's statement. Some provided a reason—that it was old and outdated—but most did not say why. The phenomenon of mission statements that are not disseminated raises the question of why such statements are written if no use is made of them afterward.

Nonetheless, the vast majority of respondents (92%) indicated that they do believe in the value of a mission statement, regardless of whether their program has one or not. The reasons for their responses varied, but most believed that a mission statement would be useful for the following:

- Setting teaching and learning objectives
- Guiding textbook selection
- Informing other coordinators, instructors, or both about the program
- Educating colleagues in the department about the language program
- Training new instructors
- Evaluating instructor performance
- Informing students about the goals of the language program

According to the survey responses, topics addressed in language program mission statements have common ground. Most respondents whose programs have mission statements indicated that their statements include information on two broad topics: the value of knowing a second or foreign language and pedagogical approaches employed in the program. For example, many mission statements include mention of four-skills approaches, communicative language teaching, and the *Standards for Foreign Language Education in the 21st Century* (1999). Others, although fewer, mentioned group and paired work in class, technology use, expected use of the target language, and occasionally service learning or community involvement.

It seems that LPDs recognize the value of creating and maintaining mission statements to express their goals in terms of language behaviors and outcomes as well as processes and objectives. At the same time, many LPDs have not yet formulated these goals in a formal statement. Perhaps they do not know where to start. The remainder of this chapter discusses the value of mission statements with respect to language programs and offers suggestions for writing a mission statement. The chapter concludes with a sampling of mission statements from language programs in the United States and a list of resources.

2.2 Why Have a Mission Statement in a Language Program?

The first section of this chapter has laid out the value of a mission statement for language programs. In addition, there are specific aspects of language program direction that can benefit as well.

Klinghammer (1997) focuses on the benefits of strategic planning, which as discussed earlier is the process of creating and implementing a vision statement. As she points out, determining the long-term vision and goals of an enterprise and the means for fulfilling them (i.e., Bean, 1993) contributes to the success of the language program in numerous ways (Klinghammer, 1997, p. 62). For one, the process of defining a vision and a plan brings language program personnel together around common goals. Further, by solidifying the mission, all participants in the program are equipped with the knowledge needed to make smart decisions, think holistically, and plan for the future in accordance with agreed-upon goals. By engaging in the process of creating a mission statement, instructors develop professionally and may gain in leadership skills; this is especially valuable for graduate teaching assistants. Finally, the strategic planning process helps participants identify features of a program that differentiate it from other programs, which is valuable for recruiting students, undertaking program assessments, and complying with accreditation demands.

LPDs who do not currently have mission statements may balk at the idea of yet another task on top of their ongoing duties. Klinghammer (1997) recognizes that we often get "bogged down in the minutiae of daily operations" (p. 62); however, as she points out, "LPDs who engage themselves and their programs in the . . . process arm themselves with direction, a framework for decision making, and supportive personnel, making it easier for them to respond to the internal and external challenges faced by the program" (p. 62). This is important for LPDs to remember as they engage in the process, because the investment will pay off later as the language program becomes stronger.

This process may not be a simple one. For one thing, it requires that the LPD take on the roles of manager, strategist, and personnel administrator, tasks for which LPDs have not been trained, as was discussed in chapter 1. Most LPDs learn on the job how to serve in these roles. The LPD needs to understand not only the personnel in the program but also the institutional discourses that surround the program, as well as the ability to communicate skillfully across hierarchies and even cultures (Carkin, 1997, p. 51). We must keep in mind where our language programs are—and where we would like them to be—within the bigger picture of the college, university, or educational system. "A successful departmental administrator knows that to gain positions, equity, or equipment from a university, it is essential to frame one's departmental request with the institutional mission and the current administration's priorities in mind" (Carkin, 1997, p. 52). Finally, the LPD's knowledge has to extend beyond the institution as well. To be effective leaders and managers and to be well versed in what a language program should be, LPDs need to be "active inside and outside of [their] programs, keeping in personal contact with other professionals, attending meetings and conferences, and accepting positions in professional organizations" (Klinghammer, 1997, p. 72). Schultz (2005) also points out that the LPD must stay abreast of findings in applied linguistics as well as second language acquisition (SLA) theory to and use this knowledge to inform decision making in the language program. National and regional organizations provide information and resources of value to the LPD and to the mission statement. Many of these groups are listed in the appendix to Chapter 1.

3. CREATING A MISSION STATEMENT

After deciding that a mission statement will be a valuable document for a language program, the next step is the creation of the statement itself. The process of composing a mission statement, especially if one is starting from scratch, can be daunting. It requires focused energy and concentration on what the program aims to accomplish, as well as on the process of getting there. What follows are some guiding questions and tips to consider when writing a mission statement for a language program.

3.1 Who Is the Audience?

Whom does the program serve? Whom does the program not serve?

Be sure to keep your mission appropriately focused so that you are neither limiting your scope unnecessarily nor casting too large and unrealistic a net. Also consider who will read your mission statement. In my case, the primary audience is the instructors in the language program, but I share the mission statement with the students in our program, as well as with other faculty in my department and on occasion, with other administrators. So the statement needs to make sense to all populations and to inspire and inform them in different ways.

A case in point is that of heritage or bilingual speakers of the language you teach. Is your program designed for this population, as well as for the traditional foreign language learner? If so, how do you meet the differing needs of the two populations? If you do not have a policy in place, why not? Are other resources available for heritage speakers? Not all aspects of a program's operations can be included in the mission statement, but it is important to keep such questions in mind when crafting the statement.

3.2 What Does the Language Program Accomplish?

How does the program achieve its goals? What techniques are used, from the instructors' and students' perspectives?

Make it clear what the program hopes to accomplish, and how. It may help to pose the question in terms of your mission, vision, and values: "Articulating a teaching philosophy in this way can help clarify decisions relating to choice of classroom activities, materials, and teacher evaluation" (Richards, 2001, p. 16).

Another way to approach this process is to think in terms of Klinghammer's (1997) suggestions for developing a strategic plan, calling for the determination of vision, values, purpose, mission, and goals:

- *Vision:* A statement of direction and destination; long-term goals and what members want to accomplish (e.g., Collins & Lazier, 1992)
- *Values:* The principles that guide the conduct of a language program
- *Purpose:* The basic reason(s) for an organization's existence, giving meaning to the work of the language program
- *Mission:* A clear and compelling statement that "serves as a focal point of effort" (Collins & Lazier, 1992, p. 73)
- *Goals:* Time-bound steps that define the parameters of each arm of the mission

3.3 What Skills or Aspects Are Emphasized in the Program?

Does the program focus on a traditional four-skills approach to language teaching, or does the program view language learning from a different perspective?

As mentioned previously, of the LPDs who indicated that they had a mission statement, many use it to make reference to a traditional four-skills approach. Experts in language pedagogy have largely moved beyond this view, especially following the publication of the *Standards for Foreign Language Education in the 21st Century* (1999). This is not to say that we no longer teach the four skills (or, including culture, five); instead, it is how we conceive of these skills. The prevailing view, in line with the Standards, is that these skills are the building blocks, but our goals should reach beyond the acquisition of skills in reading, writing, speaking, and listening.

Accordingly, Bernhardt, Valdés, and Miano (2009) point out that the "inadequate nature of the popular four skills approach that was governing much of the language instructor's teaching and assessment" has led many of us to embrace the tripartite view of communication presented in the Standards (interpersonal, interpretive, and presentational), as this view motivates educators to "examine varying thematic content illustrating diverse sociolinguistic, stylistic, and structural features that would meet the Cs beyond communication" (p. 56). Just as we must stop seeing language teaching as teaching only skills, the Standards also make us consider the sequencing of course content. Phillips (2008) explains that "the five goal areas do not suggest a curriculum that builds communicative skills in early years and then layers on culture or literature or specialized content in more advanced courses"; rather, they envision that students will "engage in all these goals at all levels" (p. 94).

Phillips's point raises another issue that must be addressed in language programs, especially if we find ourselves falling back on the four-skills approaches: What role does the teaching of culture play in your program? Is culture an integral part of language education, a fifth skill to consider, or an add-on once the basics have been covered? Arens (2009) has lamented that we often view culture as a set of facts to memorize, although:

> the Standards suggest that culture may be profitably defined as a field of cultural practices, signifiers, and knowledge. In consequence, a curriculum may be developed stressing how learning a culture means not only acquiring its knowledge base but also the strategic competencies needed to function within it. (p. 160)

Many well-known and well-respected scholars and pedagogues have advocated this shift in mind-set. Phillips (2009) argues that using the communicative modes as the starting point for a solid base of cultural or interdisciplinary content, as modeled by the Standards, results in learning that has "strong intellectual content in the humanities rather than rote learning and manipulative language practice" (p. ix).

It may seem overly ambitious or even impossible to shift our thinking, and thus our curricula, from the traditional ways of viewing language to these recent approaches involving sociolinguistic and cultural competencies. For a motivating account of such a shift, see Bernhardt et al.'s (2009) description of their efforts to adopt a Standards-based curriculum at the Stanford Language Center. It took a number of years to transform their first- and second-year programs, beginning with evaluations and needs assessments and continuing with the intentional adoption of new goals and corresponding teaching approaches. They experienced some growing pains along the way, but ultimately were able to develop a program that they felt met the needs of their students and was in line with their beliefs about language teaching and learning. The changes they implemented would not have been possible had they not been able to articulate their vision for what a language program should be. The experiences they relay, as well as the resources they offer, will be of value to those who examine their own program's mission and approaches.

Another point to consider is why you have chosen the particular mission that you have, or if you need to make reference to any documents in articulating your goals. The value of referencing published documents is not only to validate one's mission statement, but also to offer external reference and additional information. In my mission statement, for example, I make reference to (and provide a copy of) the Standards as well as the ACTFL Proficiency Guidelines. Consulting other resources or documents not only helps you in formulating your mission statement, but also may lend credence to your goals. Nevertheless, references to external documents make sense only if they are relevant to your vision for your language program. My mission statement refers to these documents because I structure my courses and program with them in mind. Not every LPD follows a communicative approach or finds value in the Standards. Those who prefer other approaches may wish to make references to published documents that emerge from those approaches.

The implementation of any guiding construct, such as the Standards, is difficult to achieve, particularly on the program level. In discussing textbook selection and syllabus design, I approach this issue in more detail. But in constructing an overall mission statement to guide a program, it is important to contemplate how such a construct can help with the structure of that program. For example, of the five Cs of the Standards, it is most likely that the communication standard will be prevalent in lower-division language courses and probably the easiest to regularly incorporate, whereas others may be more difficult to integrate. Different courses or levels of study may choose to emphasize one area over another in order to, as a whole, reach the common mission. This should be spelled out in the mission statement.

3.4 What Are the Expectations?

What is expected of the participants in the language program? How will participants be assessed on their involvement in the program?

Someone reading the statement should be able to formulate a clear idea of what a typical classroom interaction looks like, what is expected of students and instructors, and what participating in this program would be like. This can include everything from student assessment in class to overall proficiency assessment, and can also include expectations and evaluations of instructors. Again, the focus will depend on the primary audience, but participants in the program should be able to read and make sense of the expectations. The course syllabi contain the details of grades and assessment, so the mission statement should express expectations in general terms. Differences in expectations across course levels may require a more general approach in the mission statement, or the LPD may decide to address some of the level-specific differences in expectations in separate sections of the statement. It is essential, however, to make clear how the levels fit together to work toward the unified mission of the whole language program.

3.5 Where to Seek Input?

Whose opinions should be considered when articulating the goals of the program? How can the input of the key participants be obtained?

Although the LPD alone may be responsible for the well-being of the lower-division language program, a mission statement created with others will be more beneficial than one created in isolation. Experience has shown that "if [the mission statement] is imposed from on high, it tends to be ignored and/or misunderstood" (White et al., 2008, p. 40). So the more input the LPD gets, the better. As you initiate the process of creating or revising the mission statement, ask for input from a variety of people, both those within the program (e.g., students, instructors) as well as those beyond (e.g., department chair, students not studying your language).

Input from multiple sources is especially important as you begin to share your vision. You may see things clearly from your perspective, and it is easy to forget that others may see things differently or prioritize differently. Be as open as possible to the feedback you get, while still maintaining the integrity of your core values and motivations. Remember that "if everybody . . . comes together to forge a commonly agreed-upon statement of purpose, then it can be genuinely inclusive, and it can really focus the direction of your program" (White et al., 2008, p. 40).

3.6 What Is the Bigger Picture?

What role does the program play in the department or institution? How do the courses in the language program relate to the overall course of study?

Another key aspect to consider in designing your mission statement is that of articulation between levels of the program, whether within the elementary and intermediate levels or between lower- and upper-division courses. Students who leave lower-division language courses and begin upper-level coursework in languages often find themselves unprepared for the rigors of those content courses, not necessarily linguistically but perhaps in terms of critical analysis or other skills: "Students who have received As in the basic language sequence cannot understand why they are suddenly unable to function in the next level course, which is actually several levels beyond them" (Harris-Schenz, 1993, pp. 45–50). This gap between lower- and upper-division courses is familiar to us and has been well documented (e.g., Maxim, 2005b; Schultz, 2005). It is symptomatic not of a curricular deficiency but rather of a lack of communication. In this respect, a mission statement that lays out and justifies the goals of the lower-division language courses can help both students and faculty at the upper levels know what to expect and hope for.

A full discussion of this phenomenon lies beyond the scope of this volume, but it is one that must be considered. The authors of the Modern Language Association's (2007) *Foreign Languages and Higher Education: New Structures for a Changed World* report also note the discrepancy between what often seem to be different factions of a department. They note that the existing structures in many departments "create a division between the language curriculum and the literature curriculum and between tenure-track literature professors and language instructors in non-tenure-track positions" (p. 2), a division that may result in conflict and misunderstanding. It would be naively optimistic to claim that by writing a well-thought-out mission statement the LPD can end these divisions; however, it is a step in the right direction to articulate our goals and how we see them fitting into the overall mission of the department housing our program. It is important to note these conflicts as we anticipate the needs and expectations of the participants in our program.

A mission statement need not necessarily address this division explicitly, but it is an important issue to keep in mind as you work with your colleagues to set realistic goals for the language program. Not only students, but also faculty colleagues should know what is expected and what is possible. Articulation, defined by Byrnes (1990, par. 1) as "the well-motivated and well-designed sequencing and coordination of instruction toward certain goals," is essential to the success of any program. As Moyer and Gonglewski (1998) advocate,

> a curriculum must be logically sequenced as a *continuum* of learning, with logical exit points along the way, and clearly defined learning objectives throughout. An articulated program specifies functionally and intellectually rich course content through sequenced levels of the entire program. (p. 56)

Even if you are responsible for a single course or level of instruction in your particular program, you must consider the larger context into which it fits.

3.7 Is the Length of the Statement Appropriate?

Is there anything that needs to be explained in more detail? Alternately, could the mission statement be shortened?

Most language program statements will be longer than the one-liners presented at the beginning of this chapter, but lengthy statements are not desirable. The right mission statement will be one that is brief enough to be easily read and understood by all participants—from students to faculty to administrators—but long enough to provide the important information. Finding the balance between those two factors is an issue of length as well as style: perhaps a bulleted list will work better in some situations than a few long paragraphs. Also keep in mind whether the mission statement will be followed by specific goals and objectives, have other supporting information, or if it will need to stand alone. The level of detail complexity of the statement will depend in large part on its contextualization.

3.8 How Will the Statement Be Disseminated?

How and when will the statement be implemented in the language program? How will the statement be made available to those involved?

For a mission statement to have a functional benefit to you, your program, and your department, it should be widely disseminated. Could it be published on a website? In syllabi? In the instructor handbook? The more people there are who read the statement, the more people there will be who understand your incentive and your purpose. It is only through that understanding that others—whether in your department or beyond—will come to respect your program.

The dissemination of the statement is important for longer-term considerations as well. Using the mission statement as a framework to plan your actions ensures that you stay on track with your goals and hold yourself and other participants accountable:

> Having determined your organization's mission, it is essential
> to use these as a basis for setting out goals and strategy. Strategic
> planning in this context means the act of outlining the goals and
> aims for the long-term future, perhaps the next three to five years.
> (White et al., 2008, p. 41)

Although a discussion of strategic planning and innovation is beyond the scope of this chapter (and will be discussed in Chapter 7), the mission statement is always at the heart of these considerations. When it comes time to establish specific learning outcome goals and plans for future development for a language program, that discussion will start with the mission statement.

3.9 Is the Mission Relevant and Up-to-Date?

Are the students' needs being met? Does the mission statement remain relevant with respect to the audience, the objectives, and the departmental and institutional contexts?

As your needs, those of your students, and your circumstances change, you will want to revise your mission statement so that it remains current. "An ongoing review enables the language program to revise goals and strategies as they are tried, thus minimizing unproductive endeavors and ensuring that the plan is being implemented" (Klinghammer, 1997, p. 66). For example, if students are entering your institution with more high school language preparation than previously, the mission and approach of the language program will need to adapt to meet their modified needs. Furthermore, as technologies change and resources become increasingly available to students and instructors, we can reconsider what is expected of students, both during class time and outside of class time. Although the overarching mission of a program may not change, the objectives and approaches we adopt to achieve our mission may change to keep pace with trends in education.

4 CONCLUSION

The purpose of this chapter has been to show that a mission statement is a valuable asset for a language program. The thoughts and discussions that go into its creation help solidify the LPD's goals and objectives, and having a mission statement aids in training and supervising instructors. From a broader perspective, such a statement helps the LPD engage in dialogue with administrators and articulate the importance of the program. The process of walking through the questions and topics in this chapter will offer LPDs, as well as instructors, administrators, and students, the chance to reflect on their values and priorities for the language program.

LPDs will also have to consider these issues in light of the larger structure in which they exist, whether the department, the institution, or the wider community. If there is no mission statement, then some fact finding will be necessary before beginning, especially considering issues like what is expected of the program, whose opinions need to be consulted, and how to disseminate the information. Not all questions may be relevant to all contexts, but the clearer the idea the LPD has of how they might be answered, the easier the task of articulating and implementing a mission statement will be.

With all this in mind, it is surprising that so few mission statements have been created for language programs and publicized on their institutional websites. An extensive search on Google for the term *mission* and the domain .edu revealed only a handful of mission statements for language departments, and only one for a language program—my own, which is published on my program's website. (Recall that only a handful of survey respondents replied that they had a mission statement for their language program; of those, only a few disseminated them publicly beyond a TA training manual or handout.) It is likely that many LPDs have gone through the process of considering the questions raised previously in this chapter as they write their syllabi, and design and administer their language programs. In fact, many syllabi include a statement about the mission of the language program. Although not a true mission statement, such statements imply that these LPDs have thought through their mission statement but simply have not formalized it as such. Further, reading between the lines, a good deal can be gleaned from a well-written syllabus, but this is not the same thing as having a true mission statement. A thoughtfully and collaboratively constructed mission statement is vital to the LPD and other members of the program. The process of creating my own program's mission statement was immensely helpful to me as I set out to establish my priorities and what I wanted instructors and students to know when they entered the program. I therefore suggest it as a worthwhile exercise for LPDs, which will be in turn beneficial to instructors, students, and the rest of the department.

Questions for Reflection

1. Of the sample statements provided in the appendix, which seems most beneficial? Which seems least beneficial? Why? Make a list of the strengths and weaknesses of the examples.
2. Does your language program have a mission statement? If so, who wrote it? When was it written? How is the mission statement currently disseminated and used? Determine the primary strengths and weaknesses of the mission statement.
3. Find the mission statements of your institution and your department. If your language program has a mission, to what extent does it conform to the goals of your department or institution? To what extent does your department fit in with the mission of your institution?

4. Imagine that you are developing a new language program and have been given the task of writing its mission statement. What points will you include? How will you justify those points to the departmental faculty or to a college committee that has to approve new programs? How will you convince them that your program is valid and necessary?

5. What are some ways to communicate the goals and vision of a language program to the people who need to understand them (students, faculty, administrators, parents, etc.)? Where and how should this information be available, and why?

Suggestions for Further Reading

Bean, W. C. (Ed.). (1993). *Strategic planning that makes things happen: Getting from where you are to where you want to be.* Amherst, MA: Human Resources Development Press.

> Overview of strategic planning techniques that are useful in any profession and especially for those new to administrative positions

Bernhardt, E., Valdés, G., & Miano, A. (2009). A chronicle of *Standards*-based curricular reform in a research university. In V. M. Scott (Ed.), *Principles and practices of the Standards in college foreign language education* (pp. 54–85). Boston, MA: Heinle Cengage.

> Discusses the process of revamping a language program based on adoption of the Standards.

Klinghammer, S. (1997). The strategic planner. In M.A. Christison & F. L. Stoller, (Eds.), *A handbook for language program administrators* (pp. 61–76). Burlingame, CA: Alta Book Center.

> Provides a useful and complete overview of the importance of planning and strategy, particularly with respect to language program administration.

Maxim, H. H. (2005b). Enhancing graduate student teacher development through curricular reform. *ADFL Bulletin, 36*(3), 15–21.

> Discusses the tradition divide between language and content courses, and suggests methods for remedying the situation in terms of teacher education as well as curricular design.

APPENDIX

Sample Mission Statements

In most cases, the mission statements provided here are for foreign language departments, as very few language programs have or make available mission statements. They are provided in alphabetical order according to institution name. Some have been slightly modified to include only the mission portion of the statement, leaving off other important but not directly relevant topics such as learning outcomes.

EXAMPLE 1: BUCKNELL UNIVERSITY, DEPARTMENT OF SPANISH

http://www.bucknell.edu/Documents/InstitutionalResearch/Spanish.pdf

The Department of Spanish at Bucknell University is committed to providing excellent instruction and learning opportunities that challenge majors and minors, other interested students, and members of the community, to develop to the maximum their language proficiency in Spanish as well as to know and understand the literature and cultures of the Spanish-speaking peoples of the world. We encourage our students to think critically, to question their cultural assumptions about the Hispanic world, and to seek to immerse themselves, as much as possible, in a Spanish-speaking community.

EXAMPLE 2: DAVIDSON COLLEGE, DEPARTMENT OF GERMAN AND RUSSIAN

http://www3.davidson.edu/cms/x18756.xml

The Department's primary academic mission comprises the following:

M1: To teach German or Russian to students at all levels of language competence and to move students toward fluency in the language;

M2: To expose beginning and intermediate language students to the literature and culture of the language they study;

M3: To expose all students to the literature and culture of German- or Russian-speaking groups;

M4: To expose advanced language students to complex issues in the literature and culture of the language they study;

M5: To afford students the opportunity to do advanced, independent research in German or Russian;

M6: To prepare students for graduate school and a variety of careers;

M7: To encourage and enable students to study abroad in German- or Russian-speaking countries;

M8: To enhance international awareness on campus;

M9: To expose in a public forum students and the community to issues pertaining to the study of German or Russian;

M10: To support interdisciplinary curricular offerings that pertain to the study of German or Russian;

M11: To seek continually to improve teaching on all levels;

M12: To enhance the articulation of foreign language programs in North Carolina in particular and the United States in general;

M13: To support the Trustees, the President, and the Vice-President of Academic Affairs by sharing in committee and advisory tasks;

M14: To support all administrative constituencies on campus in matters pertaining to the Department, its faculty, or its students;

M15: To undertake other customary activities expected of Davidson faculty, including research and other aspects of professional development, involvement in scholarly and other professional societies, service to the profession, and service to the local community.

EXAMPLE 3: DICKINSON COLLEGE, DEPARTMENT OF SPANISH AND PORTUGUESE

http://www.dickinson.edu/academics/programs/spanish-and-portuguese/content/Mission-Statement

The Department of Spanish and Portuguese provides the means for students to develop competence in literature, language and culture in multi-disciplinary contexts. . . . The Department of Spanish and Portuguese offers a wide range of courses, from beginning language instruction to advanced seminars in Iberian, Latin American and Latino literatures. At all levels, the department is committed to assisting students in learning to read, to write, and to speak about the Spanish and Portuguese speaking worlds with accuracy and insight. To achieve cultural and linguistic literacy, the curriculum encourages students to engage the literary, historical, cultural and global contexts in which Spanish and Portuguese are spoken.

EXAMPLE 4: ILLINOIS VALLEY COMMUNITY COLLEGE, WORLD LANGUAGES DEPARTMENT

http://www2.ivcc.edu/pietrolonardo/#IVCC_World_Languages_Mission_Statement

World Languages offers World Language Instruction for students with diverse learning styles to enhance global communication skills, develop cultural understanding, connect with other disciplines, compare and contrast languages and cultures to better understand ourselves and others, and to build communities of learners in a global society.

EXAMPLE 5: SAM HOUSTON STATE UNIVERSITY, DEPARTMENT OF FOREIGN LANGUAGES

http://www.shsu.edu/~fol_www/mission.html

As a citizen-department of the College of Humanities & Social Sciences, Foreign Languages espouses the mission of the College:

1. The College of Humanities and Social Sciences (CHSS) provides an essential component to a liberal arts education: understanding human beings in their diversity as expressed in their arts, literatures, histories, ideas, values, oral and written expressions, and behavior. By promoting analytic, interpretive, interpersonal, and communication skills, CHSS facilitates personal growth, competent professionalism, and responsible citizenship.
2. As an independent department, Foreign Languages supports the University and College missions. Therefore, the Department offers a broad and coherent undergraduate liberal arts approach to American Sign Language, Arabic, Chinese, French, German and Hispanic languages, arts and cultures, which prepares students for careers that will serve the human community and meet the global challenges which face our society.
3. The Department is committed to serving the greater community through programs in cooperation with other educational and cultural institutions. Similarly, the Faculty contributes to the intellectual life of the civic and academic communities through teaching, service, scholarship, and research.

EXAMPLE 6: UNIVERSITY OF FLORIDA, DEPARTMENT OF SPANISH AND PORTUGUESE STUDIES LOWER-DIVISION SPANISH PROGRAM (LDSP)

http://www.clas.ufl.edu/users/glord

Students completing the Lower-Division Spanish Program (LDSP) sequence should be able to communicate effectively in Spanish, understand the cultures of the Hispanic world, connect the study of foreign language with their other university studies and their world beyond the university, make informed comparisons of language and culture as a whole, and participate in a larger community of Spanish speakers.

EXAMPLE 7: UNIVERSITY OF SAN DIEGO, DEPARTMENT OF LANGUAGES AND LITERATURES

http://www.sandiego.edu/cas/languages/french/program.php

The mission of the French Program is the development of students' cross-cultural understanding and communicative proficiency in French through the study of current French society and culture.

EXAMPLE 8: UNIVERSITY OF WASHINGTON, DIVISION OF SPANISH AND PORTUGUESE STUDIES

http://depts.washington.edu/spanport/index.html

The Division of Spanish and Portuguese Studies is committed to the production and transmission of knowledge of the Spanish and Portuguese languages and the literatures and cultures of Spain, Portugal, Latin America, and US Latinos. We strive to fulfill this mission by providing University of Washington students the highest quality instruction, by pursuing imaginative and informed scholarship and publication, and by bringing to the university and the broader community cultural events that represent the richness and beauty of our areas of study. Our goal is to create knowledgeable and compassionate citizens, and foster in them tolerance, respect for cultural diversity, a capacity for critical thinking, and a sense of themselves as responsible members of a global community.

Additionally we strive to create a safe and secure environment for our students, administrative staff, and faculty.

EXAMPLE 9: WESTERN KENTUCKY UNIVERSITY, MODERN LANGUAGES DEPARTMENT

http://www.wku.edu/modernlanguages/index.php

Through coursework, experience abroad, and other cultural encounters, the Modern Languages Department cultivates communicative skills and cultural awareness that prepare students at Western Kentucky University to be more knowledgeable and sensitive citizens of the local, regional, and global communities. The Department's purpose is to deliver high-quality language instruction based on nationally recognized standards, and to contribute actively to cross-disciplinary international initiatives on campus. Our programs are designed to graduate majors and minors whose language skills provide them with enhanced opportunities for careers at the regional, national, and international levels and/or preparation for advanced study in language, literature, and culture.

CHAPTER 3

Program Design and Course Materials

The design of courses, from articulation to the nuts and bolts of the syllabus, is an essential aspect of a language program. Many of the decisions that underlie this design depend on prior decisions involving goals, mission, curriculum, and pedagogical approaches. Thus in consideration of the global issues raised in the preceding chapters is necessary before implementing decisions that affect individual courses.

This chapter addresses issues revolving around the design and structure of a language program, ranging from program structure to syllabus development and design. The first section deals with the overall articulation between elements of a program, as well as the structure of language programs, whereas the second section addresses the course syllabus, including its content and functions. The third section deals with both the options for designing a syllabus and the content of the syllabus. We then look at factors and issues to consider in creating syllabi. The next sections address programmatic, departmental, and administrative issues that come into play in syllabus design. The chapter concludes with an appendix that presents sample components of language syllabi.

1. PROGRAM ORGANIZATION

1.1 Articulation

The articulation of elements within a program (Barrette & Paesani, 2005; Byrnes, 2001; Lally, 2001) is an essential element when considering program structure and design at both the macro and micro levels. Articulation is relevant to virtually every aspect of the language program director (LPD)'s job. Although a full discussion of articulation is beyond the scope of this chapter, laying the framework for courses and determining the content of a syllabus requires an understanding of articulation. After all, "the characteristics of a program that allow it to work well in one educational setting may not yield success in another" (Paesani & Barrette, 2005, pp. 3–4), so the LPD should be aware of the needs and elements of the program in order to design the most effective syllabi for it. So what does the LPD need to consider when addressing general issues of program design? Paesani and Barrette (2005, p. 4) suggest four primary considerations as they relate to articulation within a program and by extension, how they contribute to the mission of the program. These can be seen as both horizontal (i.e., within a particular level of instruction) and vertical (i.e., across levels of instruction) articulation goals (see Lange, 1982):

1. Consider the program as a whole as well as the experiences and perspectives of the individuals in the program.
2. Develop a cohesive relationship among instruction, content, assessment, and goals.
3. View language as a process as well as a product, emphasizing that proficiency is one desired outcome of completing the program, but to achieve proficiency a program also needs to incorporate input, recycling, and expansion.
4. Facilitate the development of content knowledge and proficiency skills through curricular and instructional techniques.

With these considerations, the authors propose three axes of articulation that reoccur consistently throughout the published works relating to articulation: "a well-planned curriculum, coordinated instruction, and an awareness of the learner's experience and development" (p. 4).

Numerous factors influence program design and articulation, ranging from the relatively obvious (e.g., issues related to curriculum, such as course offerings, materials, and goals) to many that have already been addressed in this text (e.g., research findings related to second language acquisition). But others are undoubtedly questions we should ask ourselves when planning the content and design of a syllabus. For example, what characteristics of the institution and its culture could affect students, instructors, and classroom (research classification of university, commuter versus residential campus, demands on faculty, constraints of educational system, general education requirements, etc.)? Do most students stop after completing a language requirement (and is there a language requirement?), or do they go on? In other words, what motivates their language study? How are the students characterized in terms of their goals, needs, socioeconomic status, prior language experience, and so on? All these questions can impact the design of a course and the layout of content on a syllabus, as the LPD must consider not just the goals of an individual course, but often how that course fits into the mission of the greater language program, as well as the overall goals of the language department or institution.

Further, the LPD must consider multiple perspectives in course design and syllabus composing. First, the coordination of the curriculum across multisection courses is important, as is the extent to which the LPD requires uniformity; this is what Lange (1982, cited in Barrette & Paesani, 2005) terms horizontal articulation. The vertical articulation (also Lange's term) must also be kept in mind: that is, the continuity of the program across levels. We can consider as well the courses beyond the language program in addressing how our language program leads up to and prepares students for other coursework in the department. Lange also recommended consideration of interdisciplinary articulation, or the capability of the language program to interact with other disciplines. This final perspective may be somewhat beyond the purview of the LPD alone, although, as "often the lone departmental member with extensive expertise in applied linguistics and FL pedagogy, the [LPD] seems to be ideally suited to help coordinate departmental reform efforts" (Maxim 2005a, p. 84). Of course, developing a curriculum that spans an entire department or institution must be "based on consensus and commonality" and a shared responsibility among all parties (Maxim 2005a, p. 84). Nonetheless, the LPD can undoubtedly play a crucial role in setting the tone of the larger educational picture, which starts with issues such as textbook adoption and syllabus design.

1.2 Organizational Structures

The ways in which a program structure can differ from institution to institution or language to language have been tangentially mentioned earlier. For example, universities with large commonly taught language programs will have multiple sections and many different instructors to coordinate, whereas less commonly taught languages or smaller programs will have different staffing situations. The number and experience of the instructors may determine the hierarchy of responsibility within a program, as well as the education and professional development that are required (see Chapter 5). In that respect, the organization of a language program is relevant to its mission statement, to textbook selection, to teacher training, and to virtually all aspects of that program. But it becomes especially important to the current discussion when considering the division of labor, the roles of members in the program, and how the members of the program relate to each other.

Davidson and Tesh (1997, 177ff.) discuss two primary organizational structures, which we can consider as we design the flow of information. Their first model is the *mechanistic model*, adapted from Weber (1925/1947), which is a bureaucratic organizational structure that has, according to Weber, certain theoretical and practical advantages. The name comes from the model's machinelike efficiency used to accomplish its objectives. The mechanistic model is characterized by a strict, unbroken chain of command and by its impersonal nature, which in effect eliminates favoritism. The relationship among members of this model is impersonal and formal but efficient.

At the other end of the spectrum is what the authors term the *organic model*, based on work by Likert (1967, p. 47). This model is structured around the idea that productive organizations are flexible and adaptable, encourage trust and communication among members of the program, and maximize human motivation to achieve goals. In this model the flow of communication is both vertical and horizontal, crossing the chain of command that was unbroken in the mechanistic model. The organic model depends on teamwork and on a shared responsibility for decision making.

Davidson and Tesh (1997) note that "most optimally designed language programs . . . have features of both the organic and the mechanistic models. The particular mix in each case depends on administrative setting and size" (p. 182). Although the authors suggest that programs that depend on graduate teaching assistants and adjunct faculty tend to be based on the mechanistic model over the organic model, in my own experience the members of a language program react better to a more organic organization in which there is a free exchange of information and skills. Further, the opportunity for graduate students to work as language teachers is an excellent hands-on apprenticeship opportunity that prepares them for their futures in academia, as well as allows them insight into the administration of language programs and by extension, into relationships within academic structures. It is the LPD's responsibility to help graduate students make the most of that opportunity. Working together, sharing ideas, and maximizing professional development opportunities are the hallmarks of organic program design. That said, it is "not possible for all employees of [a language program] to report directly to the program supervisor [or LPD]; rather, it is necessary to construct some sort of reporting hierarchy that limits the number of individuals with whom the director interacts on a regular basis" (Kaplan, 1997, p. 10).

Most programs that I am familiar with and all of those represented in my online survey responses have a remarkably similar structure: The LPD supervises level coordinators, who in turn supervise the instructors, who range from graduate teaching assistants to lecturers to occasionally ranked faculty. Figure 1 provides a visual representation of the program that I direct, whose structure shares these features.

The general responsibilities for each member of the Lower-Division Spanish Program (LDSP) are explained in Figure 2.

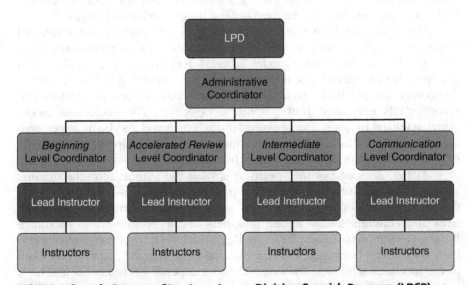

FIGURE 1 Sample Program Structure, Lower-Division Spanish Program (LDSP).

LDSP Director	Administrative Coordinator	Level Coordinators	Lead Instructors
• Select textbooks • Train instructors • Assign instructors to courses/levels • Design course syllabi • Observe and evaluate instructors	• Assign specific sections to instructors • Advise students on placement, registration, etc. • Order textbooks • Liaison with off-site copy center • Handle student problems and other issues • Arrange final exam location and logistics • Ensure instructors enter final grades on time and correctly	• Modify calendars as necessary each term • Set up online templates and sections • Establish deadlines for materials creation • Meet with instructors to create materials • Finalize/approve semester materials; transmit to admin. coordinator	• Assist level coordinators in materials creation • Keep track of dates and deadlines • Liaison with instructors

FIGURE 2 Responsibilities of LDSP Team Members

This multilayered system is common, although depending on the size of the program, there may be fewer levels of administration between the LPD and the instructors. Also worth noting, as is discussed in more detail later, is that the makeup of the various populations previously referenced will impact the duties assigned to each as well. For example, in the case of instructors who are graduate students, these should not be evaluated by their peers (serving in "lead instructor" positions). Although we can all learn from our friends and peers, it is unfair to put colleagues in a situation where one is asked to officially assess another, as this can create unnecessary anxiety and conflict. This kind of issue is discussed further in section 1.3.3.

> Anderson (1997) has observed that, we appear to have—whether we wish to call it that or not—a two-tiered curriculum, with language instruction at one level and literature at another, and we have largely two-tiered staffing patterns to match. In many of our programs, graduate students and temporary faculty members teach almost exclusively in the language sector, and tenure-track professors for the most part do not teach there at all. (pp. 20–21)

Such a division, whether warranted or not, complicates job descriptions, hierarchical structures, and hiring and training, as will be discussed later. Turning first to general job descriptions, the next subsections look at the players in a language program from coordinators to instructors. (As we have already examined the multitude of roles and responsibilities that define the LPD, there is no need to repeat that information here.) It is important to note, however, that even with the levels of responsibility described here, the LPD is ultimately the one accountable for the well-being of the program, and to that end she or he should be available to anyone involved at any level of the program.

1.3 Instructors and Positions

1.3.1 COORDINATORS AND SUPERVISORS

The job description of course (or level) coordinators or supervisors[1] can be as difficult to define as that of the LPD. These are liaison positions between the individual instructors, or teaching assistants (TAs), and the LPD. Some programs have coordinators for every course, whereas others have coordinators by level (e.g., first year, which consists of more than one course). As shown in Figure 1, my own program has a system of four level coordinators: one for the true beginner (two-semester) sequence, a second for the accelerated first-year review course (due to the large number of sections, instructors and students), a third for the two-semester intermediate sequence, and the fourth for the fifth-semester bridge-the-gap course, which is a conversation course that serves to prepare students to transition from the four-skills intermediate courses into the third-year grammar and composition courses that begin to form the coursework for the major and minor degrees.

The tasks these coordinators carry out vary according to a program's needs (see Lee, 1989, for another example) but can be generally summarized as in Table 1.

The coordinators should maintain contact with the LPD throughout the semester and are a vital source for disseminating information and getting input and feedback. At most institutions the coordinators are faculty (lecturers or junior ranked faculty); however, in some programs this task falls to advanced

TABLE 1 Level Coordinator Responsibilities	
Responsibilities	**Tasks**
1. Communication	• Make sure instructors are aware of policies. • Meet with students as needed to address concerns. • Report concerns or comments to LPD.
2. Supervision	• Meet regularly with instructor team. • Observe teaching; offer informational assessment to instructors to help improve their teaching. • Refer ongoing issues or concerns to LPD.
3. Assessment materials	• Assign instructors (individual or teams) to create exams, composition topics, oral exam topics, etc. • Review assessment materials with instructor team; forward to LPD for approval. • Create daily calendar for syllabus.

---

[1] I use the term *coordinator* from here on for the sake of simplicity, while recognizing that terminology varies.

graduate student instructors. Compensation for these positions thus varies according to rank, with course releases or increased stipends being the most common. In my program we have one additional coordinator position—an administrative coordinator who works with all these levels. As the title implies, this coordinator handles administrative (i.e., not pedagogical) issues ranging from textbook orders to unexcused absences to student complaints about teaching. Having a person in this position ensures the consistent and coherent implementation of program policies across sections and levels. In programs that do not have this position, the level coordinators generally handle these tasks, with the LPD as a final resource. Although there is undoubtedly value in having a consistent administrative resource to ensure uniformity and to protect the LPD's time to some degree, it is also desirable that the LPD maintain contact with the instructors and students of the courses in the language program. So it is important that she or he not be too overprotected. It would be wise for the LPD to seek out opportunities to talk to the instructors and coordinators regularly regarding the materials, the text, the administration of the program, and their satisfaction or suggestions for improvement, as well as to regularly observe classes (beyond the standard instructor evaluation) in order to get a feel for how the program is running.

1.3.2 Graduate Instructors

The elementary and intermediate courses in many language programs are taught exclusively or primarily by graduate student instructors, particularly in large research universities. There has been considerable debate regarding the effectiveness, practicality, and fairness of employing graduate students in this way. For example, Sammons (1976) opposes the use of TAs as a practice that is "unethical, educationally unsound, and increasingly disruptive of our welfare and purposes" (p. 8), whereas others, such as Schulz (1980), maintain that "a well-coordinated and -supervised TA program can provide valuable professional training—not otherwise available—for prospective foreign language educators" (p. 1). In today's language departments, few would agree with Sammons; the current conventional wisdom maintains that graduate education depends on support for students in the form of TA-ships, just as graduate students depend on their stipends in order to pursue their degrees. It has become a mutually beneficial arrangement. It does raise issues, however, that relate to how we structure our programs as well as to how we ensure the training and development of our instructors, because we cannot assume that they come to us able, or even always eager, to teach languages.

The role of the graduate instructors is important to define, especially since they are also taking courses and therefore need to manage their time carefully. Furthermore, in some institutions the graduate assistants are unionized and therefore protected by specific requirements about how much they are allowed to work in a given week. The first issue is that despite being commonly referred to as "teaching assistants," these graduate instructors are far more than assistants.

Even if they are not the official instructors of record, they are often the sole instructor of the class and are responsible for daily planning and administration of lessons, record keeping, assessment, and so on. Although overwhelming, fulfilling these duties provides an excellent training opportunity for these instructors: graduate students in the languages gain valuable experience in teaching and classroom management that their counterparts in other disciplines rarely get. As Lee (1989) tells his TAs, "being a TA means more than just working at a job in order to earn some needed income, you are an educator. You are there to contribute uniquely to [students'] general intellectual development" (p. 7).

Based on the responses I gathered in my survey and existing reports (e.g., Lee, 1989), most programs require their instructors to carry out a common set of pedagogical tasks. They are listed here from most to least common, according to my survey data and my experience, although they vary by institution:

- Develop lesson plans for daily lessons according to the course syllabus (which is usually provided to them)
- Hold regular office hours
- Evaluate student work
- Create additional teaching materials as needed
- Meet regularly with other instructors and coordinators
- Work with other instructors and coordinators to create evaluation materials

LPDs vary in the amount of guidance they give to their graduate instructors regarding these tasks, but some degree of independence is usually assumed and with it a corresponding degree of responsibility. For this reason all instructors, especially graduate student TAs, should receive professional development to prepare them to carry out their duties, a topic that is addressed in Chapter 5. The following subsections look at the other participants in a language program.

1.3.3 LEAD INSTRUCTORS

An additional element of the program structure that has become increasingly common in recent years is positions for advanced graduate students. These positions exist under a variety of names, such as "preceptor," "supervisor," "head TA," or "lead instructor," which is the term I use here. The tasks of the lead instructors vary by program and by institution, but the chief function is to provide a bridge between the level coordinator and the classroom instructors. Tasks commonly include meeting with the instructors to design teaching or evaluation materials, affording communication between the level coordinator and the other instructors, and carrying out unofficial teaching observations.

The selection of graduate students to fill these lead instructor positions can be carried out in a variety of ways, ranging from a direct invitation from the LPD to an application process. The size of the program as well as the makeup of the graduate instructor body will largely determine the most effective process for each program. In smaller programs a personal selection or invitation may work well, as the LPD will have an idea of who is most interested and best suited for the job. In larger programs, however, an application process may be best to ensure that all those who are interested have the opportunity to apply. Further, the application process itself can be seen as another opportunity for professional development and to engage in the valuable processes of writing a letter of interest and participating in an interview. The latter is the method I have adopted in my own program, for the reasons just mentioned, as well as to ensure fairness across the board. The application consists of a curriculum vitae and a letter of interest, followed by interviews with the applicants.

An additional purpose for having the lead instructor position is to offer further mentoring and professional development to graduate students who have shown a talent for and commitment to language program coordination. Through such a position, graduate students can learn decision-making, task-prioritizing, and interpersonal skills that will serve them well regardless of whether their future positions involve program direction or not, or whether their studies are in literature or linguistics. It is important that graduate students in languages prepare themselves to some degree to be generalists; this becomes increasingly true as the job market becomes more competitive and any skills or knowledge that can benefit a language department—independent of research expertise—are seen as a true bonus. The expertise and interest in language program design and direction that they can gain through such a position as lead instructor is one way to do this and can be an asset when they enter the job market.

There can, however, be complications inherent in having a peer serve in a "lead" position. Lee (1989) notes this potential conflict as well, in commenting that when lead instructors observe the teaching of other TAs, it "has the potential to place the supervisor in conflict with friends" (p. 10). However, there are ways to make the lead position successful while avoiding the potential complications. To begin with, as a matter of policy, there are a number of ways the lead instructor can benefit the program and assist with the workload without placing her- or himself in direct conflict with friends, as discussed previously. The most problematic situation, however, seems to be that of class observations—a time-consuming and important task for the LPD, and also a potentially valuable professional development opportunity for the lead instructor. Therefore, there should be clear policies governing this situation so there are no misunderstandings. For example, one very straightforward rule would be that lead instructors do not carry out official observations of other graduate student instructors, in order to remove the tension of the evaluation. At the same time, however, there should be a culture within the language program that encourages peers to engage in continual (nonsupervisory) class visitations. Everyone can always learn by observing others, but there is certainly a difference between observing for one's own benefit and observing to make an official evaluation. The distinction needs to be clear to both the instructor and the lead. (See Murphy [1992] for recommendations on approaching this kind of observation.)

If the program demands are such that lead instructors are needed to carry out supervisory observations, ensure that there is a strict hierarchy in place. For example, only a lead instructor who is a PhD student with at least 2 or more years of teaching experience can carry out such observations and can do so only of a first-year MA student. Alternately or additionally, the LPD can use the fall semester to engage in team visitations with the lead instructor, who uses that time to train the instructor in the observation process so that in subsequent semesters the lead instructor can act alone. Either way, however, the LPD should have to review, discuss and sign off on the observation report before it becomes an official part of the instructor's file.

1.4 Other Issues

1.4.1 PROFESSIONAL ISSUES

Language programs at institutions with graduate programs often follow the model previously outlined, employing graduate students as instructors. However, they are not the only instructors of language courses, as lecturers, adjuncts, and occasionally, ranked faculty also teach in language programs, especially in smaller programs. Increasingly, too, other positions are being created or are expanding to fill teaching needs, such as "Clinical Professor" (where the prefix *clinical* tends to denote appointments that provide practical instruction or application of practical knowledge) or "Teaching Associate" (i.e., a faculty member whose appointment is primarily in teaching and/or mentoring, but not research). (See, for example, the American Association of University Professors [AAUP]. 1993 statement and the Modern Language Association [MLA] 2003 statement on non-tenure-track faculty and their situation in academe.)

For example, in Spanish we tend to have a large number of graduate students who cover most of our lower-division classes, while ranked faculty and lecturers cover the upper-level courses; however, in the less commonly taught languages, fewer graduate students are available to serve as instructors and fewer upper-division courses are taught, resulting in lecturers and ranked faculty teaching at all levels. Furthermore, institutions that don't have a graduate student population obviously rely on lecturers, adjuncts, ranked faculty, or any combination of these to teach all their courses, including language courses. In these situations, all instructors are usually responsible for the duties outlined previously, although the administration is often trickier. It can be awkward to have a ranked faculty member reporting to the LPD, especially if the latter is not in a tenure-track line.

Compensation is another issue that is relevant to the discussion of these various structures and positions. While the compensation for the LPD position has already been discussed in Chapter 1, other members of the program, such as level coordinators, can receive compensation for their positions as well, which will usually take one of two forms: additional pay or teaching reduction. In many cases, compensation depends on the rank of the coordinator. Those serving in adjunct or lecturer positions may not be eligible for additional pay or for a reduced-course load, while tenure-track faculty may. As discussed in Chapter 1, it also depends on how work in the language program is considered within the institution as well. If it is considered as service, then legally a course release may not be a viable form of compensation, as it is in a different category (instructional versus service); in those cases, a reduction in other committee work may be the only viable form of compensation.

In those programs that employ graduate assistants as lead instructors, their compensation must also be addressed. The most common form of compensation for them is by reducing their course load by one per academic year (i.e., if their standard teaching load is 2:2, it is reduced to 2:1 or 1:2 depending on the department's needs and the students' preference). In all cases, faculty and student, these compensation plans must be approved by departmental and college administrators beforehand.

1.4.2 LOCAL PROGRAM ISSUES

Regardless of the system the LPD establishes for the program, it will involve a number of people working together for an ultimate shared goal. The LPD oversees the whole of the program and is responsible for its overall success, and given the different backgrounds and responsibilities in any organization, it falls largely on the LPD to know how to handle diverse populations with tact and professionalism. In many cases, this will involve, to some degree, knowing how to handle conflict within levels of a program.

Conflicts can arise in language programs in a variety of contexts, whether between students and instructors, instructors and the LPD, or between the LPD and other faculty members. Conflicts can relate to grading policy, dialectal uses of the target language, or to pedagogical, theoretical, or practical disagreements with respect to what or how to teach.

The way in which the LPD handles conflicts that arise in the program will naturally be determined by his or her own personality and relationship with other members of the program. Generally speaking, the LPD has to determine whether to decide or negotiate (Henry, 1997, pp. 82–84) or whether to use both approaches, depending on the situation. Negotiating entails engaging in a consultation process to reach an agreement and is never a solitary endeavor but always a group effort. Negotiation strives to bring together divergent perspectives and opinions, but doesn't necessarily result in any policy being set or precedent being established. On the other hand, deciding is settling an issue or a problem conclusively, either individually or in consultation with others. This decision results in a newly formed policy, which becomes consistently implemented. According to Henry (1997), "within a language program, an appropriate management strategy is to decide. When decisions are made, especially those that are determined by the group, they become policy" (p. 83).

Conflicts can arise, as we have seen, due to disconnects in the responsibility and ranks associated with certain positions. There is also the potential issue of seniority; for example, in my first year directing a language program I had faculty of varying ranks (from lecturers to associate professors) who had been at the institution for several years and had taught those same courses many times before. Some were open to my changes and leadership, but others had a more difficult time accepting that I was doing things differently or that they were now taking orders from someone new—particularly those who had been accustomed to doing things their own way and not having to seek approval from anyone else.

Whether the LPD has to work to establish authority from the outset or instead has to work on building a culture of collegiality, skill is needed to handle these situations. Success depends on establishing a clear mission and succinct goals from the beginning and to make the workflow plan as clear as possible. Whenever possible, the mission and goals should be developed through collaboration and communication among all involved parties so that everyone can be a part of the system.

In my own program, a specific procedure is stipulated in all program syllabi for addressing problems that arise. If instructors have conflicts or concerns, they report to their lead instructor, who then reports to the coordinator. The coordinator then comes to me if she or he feels it is something that I must address. Some instructors would rather come directly to me, while others may have conflicts with their supervisor or someone else who is higher up in the chain of command. Likewise, the university has similar policies for what students should do if they have a disagreement or a conflict with their instructor, and a similar procedure is followed. Regardless, it is important that all students and program members are aware that the LPD is always available to discuss concerns and other issues as needed. This openness has proven to be directly and inversely related to the concerns that come up: the more open and available I am, the less need there is for my intervention.

Of course, there will also be conflicts beyond the confines of the language program; after all, the program operates within the greater functioning of the department or institution as a whole. Although well beyond the scope of this volume, the functioning of the language program as part of a greater whole does merit some discussion. On one hand, there are institutional policies that all instructors must be aware of and abide by, such as university policies on conflict resolution (i.e., the role of the Office of the Ombuds), sexual harassment, or unsafe or unprofessional behavior. While the institution generally mandates training in these areas and thus it is not the purview of the LPD to provide that training, it is the responsibility of the LPD to ensure that the instructors are upholding the institutional policies and even more important, being protected in the classroom. If an instructor feels uncomfortable about a student or about anything that is going on inside or out of the classroom, it should be reported to the coordinator and the LPD.

These institutional and programmatic policies are an important piece of information that, along with others, must be conveyed in a clear and coherent manner to both instructors and students. The primary tool for making such information available is the course syllabus, which is examined in detail in the following sections.

2. THE COURSE SYLLABUS

Before delving into the details of the syllabus, we must consider the basic definition of this document. According to the *American Heritage Dictionary of the English Language*, a syllabus is "an outline or other brief statement of the main points of a discourse, the subjects of a course of lectures, the contents of a curriculum, etc." (http://www.dictionary.com). However, it is precisely the *etc.* in the definition that underlies the rationale for this chapter. While some syllabi include detailed information, others can offer hardly any information at all. What is right or wrong, correct or incorrect, may well depend on the program, the LPD, the instructors and quite often, institutional policies. Considerable research over the years has investigated this very issue, and although a full discussion of the history and legalities of the syllabus is not warranted here, a brief discussion of the principles guiding its design most definitely is.

A principle distinction to make here is that between curriculum and syllabus. It is generally assumed that the curriculum refers to the general method of how we teach what we teach, which can include a syllabus—the content of instruction—but not vice versa (e.g., Dubin & Olshtain, 1986); in other words, the syllabus is concerned with the content of instruction and less with the method (Krahnke, 1987, p. 1). At the same time, there are differing opinions as to the extent to which a syllabus is a theoretical or practical document.

Some consider that a syllabus is a "theoretical notion of the *types* of content involved in language teaching and the bases for the organization of language courses" (Krahnke, 1987, p. 73). Others have claimed that the language syllabus is ultimately "an expression of opinion on the nature of language and learning; it acts as a guide for both teacher and learner by providing some goals to be attained" (Rabbini, 2002, par. 3). Rabbini notes that these goals can be phrased as outcomes, as is more traditionally done in standard syllabi, but they can also include information on the process by which those outcomes will be achieved, as will be discussed further.

The more standard view of a syllabus, however, remains that of a legally binding or contractually mediating document. Afros and Schryer (2009) consider the syllabus a document that serves to mediate between instructors and students, and even between instructors and other colleagues. In that respect, it must be "balanced so that it can appeal to students, motivate and structure their learning, while, at the same time, can convince (senior) colleagues and external evaluators of the instructor's professionalism and the course quality" (p. 225).

Compared to these professional definitions, it is interesting to note what the users of syllabi consider this document to be. Lee (1989, p. 51) reports that he once asked his teaching assistants and instructors to define *syllabus* as they understood the term; he got a variety of responses, including the following:

- An external structuring of a course, arranged by topic in chronological order, including assignments, quiz and exam dates, and any pertinent references to texts
- The organized presentation of classroom activities over a period of time; usually goal-oriented
- A temporal organizational framework for the class
- An organizational plan/outline for a course that provides information about the requirements, calendar of events, and topics to be studied; it may include procedures to be followed

In spite of the differences, there were also some commonalities: the respondents agree that a syllabus should be informative, should provide an overview of and direction for the course, and that it should include chronological information for the course (pp. 51–52). As Lee points out, "a syllabus can have many functions, depending on the perspective adopted" (p. 52). For example, the instructor can view it as a guide for creating lesson plans. Students may see the syllabus as an explanation of what is expected of them, whereas the instructor uses the list of course components as the starting point for determining the assignments that contribute to the course grades. From the point of view of the LPD, the syllabus provides uniformity and perhaps accountability across multiple sections of a course. Other ways of viewing the syllabus might include as a guide to teaching methodology, an explanation of grading policies, rubrics for assessment, a contract between students and instructor, and a list of course and program policies. The LPD has to consider which viewpoint should be adopted in creating syllabi, because that will determine their content, organization and presentation.

2.1 Approaches to Syllabus Design

2.1.1 UNITS OF DESIGN

Robinson (2009) claims that the essential components of a syllabus are the *units* of classroom activity and the *sequence* in which they will be presented or performed (p. 294). In the case of languages, one might argue that both the unit and the sequence are, or should be, determined by research on language acquisition and learning, evidence of the rate and route of learning, what we know of language storage and processing, and so on. To a certain extent, this is indeed the case, at least insofar as the textbooks we use (see Chapter 4 of the current volume) are often largely informed by research in these areas. Robinson goes on to point out that the issue at the heart of language syllabus design comes down to "Is the L2 best learned explicitly, by understanding and practicing a series of formal units of language, however characterized, or is it best learned incidentally from exposure to the L2 during communicative activities and tasks" (p. 295)? Others had also previously noted this same essential question as at the very heart of our curricular and programmatic decisions. Long & Crookes (1992), for example, distinguish between Type A syllabi as synthetic, focusing on what is to be learned, that is, the language itself, while Type B syllabi are more analytic, focusing on how the language is to be learned (p. 29).

The answers to these questions determine the units of classroom activity (grammatical, lexical, task-based, etc.) as well as the order in which they are presented over the course of an academic term. For the most part, researchers and theorists have tended to agree on a handful of syllabus types, stemming from these input and sequence permutations. These are presented in the following sections.

2.1.2 TYPES OF SYLLABI

Various researchers working in language syllabus design have coincided in identifying several primary types of syllabi that are commonly employed in language classes (Krahnke, 1987; Lange & Crookes, 1992; Nunan, 1988, 2001; Rabbini, 2002; Rahimpour, 2010; Robinson, 2009). Table summarizes these main types, offering examples when relevant. The general progression noted is on a continuum from more structure- or form-focused to more meaning-focused.

TABLE 2 Syllabus Types, Descriptors, and Examples

Focus	Type of syllabus	Content of instruction	Content examples
FORM	Structural / Lexical*	Forms and structures of the language being taught / Frequently used words	Past tenses, question formation, subordinate clauses / Common words and phrases
	Notional / Functional	Functions that are performed when language is used; notions that language is used to express	Size, age, color, comparisons, time
	Situational	Real or imaginary situations in which language occurs or is used	Going to the doctor, ordering food in a restaurant
⇕	Skill-based	Specific abilities that may play a part in using a language (relatively independent of the situation)	Listening for the main idea, writing well-formed paragraphs, giving effective oral presentations
	Task-based	Series of complex and purposeful tasks that learners need to perform with the language being learned (more process- or outcome-oriented than situational)	Applying for a job, getting information on renting an apartment over the phone
MEANING	Content-based	Content or information unrelated to the language as a subject but rather using the language as a means to deliver the content	Science class taught in a foreign language

*Note that for the sake of simplicity I have grouped together the Structural and Lexical syllabus types, given that they share a defining characteristic that their unit of distinction is based on an element of the target language being learned, that is, a grammatical feature or a lexical component. There are, however, essential differences, as well. The structural approach to syllabi stems primarily from work by Ellis (1993, 1997) who claims that if timed properly grammatical instruction can influence the developing knowledge base of a learner; he also claims, though, that such instruction can serve other functions, from monitoring to noticing features in the input to awareness-raising. The lexical syllabus, on the other hand, comes from Willis (1990), who argued that rather than structurally determining the content of a syllabus, "we could lexically determine it, using corpora of language use to identify word frequency at the 700-word, the 1,500-word, and the 2,500-word levels. Words in the corpora are itemized as collocations exemplifying each word's typical patterns of use" (Robinson, 2009, p. 299).

While much work has documented the structural-to-procedure progression noted in the table, others have pointed out that this evolution is somewhat chronological, as well, as the more structural or synthetic approaches are considered the more traditional or old-fashioned, while the newer approaches tend to be those along the bottom range of the table. Diffey (1992) notes that the more recent focus on communicative teaching approaches has had an impact on course and material design, and thus on syllabus design as well. The things students are "likely to want to say, read, or write in the target language" (p. 208) must be considered alongside the more standard grammatical structures that drove curricular presentation prior to the advent of the communicative approach.

Nonetheless, others (e.g., Krahnke, 1987) are quick to point out that the most common language syllabus these days is often a mix of elements of two or more of the types presented earlier. Thus LPDs need not choose only one approach to their syllabi, but can opt for an eclectic syllabus design that is aligned with their program mission and their beliefs about language teaching and learning.

2.2 Other Considerations in Syllabus Design

As Schulz (1984) so rightly notes, "in order to make the crucial decisions necessary for sound syllabus design, educators in charge of devising and coordinating language instructional programs must be aware of the many factors that influence foreign language learning" (p. 6). As the LPD designs syllabi, a number of considerations should be kept in the forefront. Also worth noting is that every staffing change, even every academic year, necessitates a reevaluation of the syllabus and how well it achieves its goals. So these considerations are more than a one-time event, they are a part of the ongoing process of syllabus design and assessment.

2.2.1 PROGRAMMATIC PERSPECTIVE

From the perspective of the LPD or of the program, a number of questions are crucial to the very design of the syllabus (Krahnke, 1987; Rabbini, 2002). Of these, a number have been addressed previously, such as the goals and expectations of the program, the desire to have a product-oriented or process-oriented syllabus, the guiding methodology of the program or textbook used in the program, and the relative importance of structures, skills, situations, tasks, and so on in the program. The answers to these questions will in large part have determined the general type of syllabus that is most appropriate for a course or program.

Beyond those considerations, however, are other programmatic concerns to contend with. For example, the instructional resources available to those in the program may determine elements of the syllabus or flexibility within the syllabus. Likewise, if the program has systems in place for measuring outcomes and for holding students and instructors accountable for these outcomes, there is probably a greater chance that the syllabus will reflect these outcomes in some way. Although the subject of outcomes assessment is beyond the scope of a chapter on program structure and syllabus design, it is a topic worthy of investigation, and the interested reader is referred to Norris, Davis, Sinicrope, & Watanabe's (2009) volume on the subject.

As discussed earlier, another essential factor to consider is the basic administrative layout of the program: Are there multiple sections, different teachers, varying meeting days and times? The degree of detail provided in the syllabus may depend on some of these factors and on how much variability in day-to-day functioning across sections occurs in the program. Rahimpour (2010) also questions the role of the instructor in the design of the syllabus, a question that is particularly relevant in a multicourse program. Do instructors have free reign to design what they want, or are they, as Bell (1983) suggests, consumers of other designers' syllabi? Rahimpour (2010) ultimately advocates that "classroom teachers should be given appropriate training to be equipped with necessary skills and information to design their own syllabuses if they are to be successful teachers" and that simultaneously we should "regard the syllabus open and negotiable" (p. 1663). Of course, the degree to which the document is truly negotiable will depend on other factors, as was mentioned previously and will be addressed again in the next section. However, the issue of an instructor's involvement in the syllabus, both for her or his investment in the course and for her or his professional development, is an important one.

Along similar lines, Krahnke (1987) points out that one should not underestimate the potential power of the experience and beliefs that teachers bring to their own teaching endeavors. Teachers often teach the way they were taught and resort to tried-and-true techniques even if current research may not uphold those. Therefore, as the LPD designs a syllabus for a course and for a program, it is valuable to keep in mind who the teachers are that will be using that syllabus, and how well they will be able to adapt to it.

2.2.2 STUDENT PERSPECTIVE

The syllabus should also be considered from the perspective of the student (e.g., Krahnke, 1987). For example, one must consider the goals and expectations of the students taking the course and whether those match the goals and expectations of the instructor or LPD. There will likely not be perfect symmetry in all cases, but if there is continuous significant mismatch, then some aspects of the syllabus design should be reconsidered. Another relevant issue is class size: a class of 10 students will likely be able to engage in more one-to-one interaction during class time, and could benefit more from an entirely content-based syllabus than would a class of 35 or more students.

Along these same lines, Lee (1989) suggests that a syllabus can be considered student-oriented or teacher-oriented (p. 54), and various syllabus modifications have been proposed to lead to greater flexibility on the students' part. Breen and Candlin (1980), for example, discussed the idea of a *learner-led* syllabus, in which the learner is completely involved in the learning process and is consistently encouraged to play an active role in the design and implementation of course policy and procedure (see also Rabbini, 2002). In such a course, the official syllabus provides only the most basic of outlines, and the students fill in the rest—from due dates to policies, from grading rubrics to course content—as the term progresses. In a similar trend, Nunan (1988, 2001) discusses a *proportional* approach to syllabus design, in an effort to develop a more global competence. In this kind of syllabus, various elements are joined throughout units by a linking theme, which is chosen by the learners. The instructor has a greater role earlier on in the term and begins with more focus on form, but eventually progresses to a greater focus on interaction over time.

Zaro (1996) also ponders this same question of how to articulate the contents of a course into a clear, well-defined document and ultimately advocates that the syllabus be "more orientative than prescriptive, no matter what type (functional-notional, topic-based, task-based, etc.) is chosen. This can only be achieved by suggesting rather than imposing lists of contents" (p. 204). Many instructors would feel uncomfortable relinquishing their control in the classroom, especially when we consider that an LPD is necessarily taking the programmatic perspective. However, the greater flexibility offered by this kind of approach can be beneficial for students who might feel more invested in their own learning process, and these possibilities should be considered with the others.

Having taken into account the primary considerations of creating a syllabus, the LPD will by now have a fairly clear idea of what theoretical premises will underlie the design of that syllabus. Beyond those decisions are some fairly straightforward, essential components that should be included in all syllabi in one format or another, and these are the focus of the following section.

3. ESSENTIAL COMPONENTS OF THE SYLLABUS

As discussed, some syllabi include more or less information, depending on different variables. A useful way to approach syllabus creation is to start with the outline of the main components, filling in the information as needed. The information presented in Table 3 presents the essential components of a syllabus, although the specifics vary depending on the level, course, and institutional requirements.

The following sections discuss each of these areas in turn. The appendix at the end of this chapter contains examples of a variety of components of different syllabi.

3.1 Basic Information

3.1.1 COURSE INFORMATION

Course information can include everything from the course and section number to meeting days, times, and locations, as well as the goals and objectives of the course and its prerequisites. In sum, it should include, at a glance, everything students need to confirm that they are in the right place. It is also common

TABLE 3 Sample Components of the Syllabus

Basic course information	• Course
	    • Name, number, section number
	    • Meeting days and times
	    • Classrooms and locations
	• Prerequisites
	• Required, recommended materials
	• Instructor
	    • Name and contact information
	    • Office hours

Instructional and pedagogical information	• Materials
	• Goals and objectives
	• Evaluation
	    • Grade scale
	    • Components of grade, percentages
	    • Description of components
	• Comments on methodology used (e.g., expectations in a communicative classroom, use of technology)

Policies	• Course policies
	    • Late work
	    • Makeup work
	    • Attendance policy
	    • Use of cell phones, mp3 players, and so on during class
	    • Extra credit
	• Institutional policies
	    • Student accommodations
	    • Academic honesty
	    • How to handle conflicts
	    • Time commitment expected/required outside of class

Calendar information	• What material will be covered and when • Due dates for assignments • Test and assessment dates • Important academic dates and deadlines (drop/add period, deadline for pass/fail status, deadline for dropping or withdrawing, etc.)
Other information	• Necessary textbook or technology information (e.g., how to register for online components) • Additional resources (books, Web pages) • Sample of grading rubrics • Tips for success

to include information on the teaching methodology and language policies (e.g., class is conducted exclusively in the target language) for the course and what students can expect. Because class time in a communicative language course is spent differently from the lecturer courses may be more familiar with (i.e., conversing with a partner, carrying out group activities) and because class participation is active, rather than receptive intake of information, students should receive this information from the outset. The structure of hybrid courses, which consist of face-to-face meetings plus online work, may be new to students, and the syllabus should include information about the rationale for hybrid instruction, the structure of the course, and how students can be successful in this type of course. (See Chapter 6 for a discussion on the role of technology in language programs.)

3.1.2 INSTRUCTOR INFORMATION

A syllabus should include all the relevant instructor information, from the full name to contact information: email address, phone number, office location, office hours, and website. This section can also contain information about how and when the instructor prefers to be contacted. In multisection courses with a level coordinator or director and different instructors, contact information for both should be included; but in this case it is wise to also include specific directions about the chain of command and who should be contacted, for what reasons, and when.

3.2 Instructional and Pedagogical Information

3.2.1 MATERIALS

Students will need to know what textbooks are required for the course and how or where to purchase them. If you require a certain edition or format, be sure to specify that information. Students who wish to purchase their textbooks online will not be able to do so if your program has a custom package of the textbook, and it is important that they understand that not all versions of a textbook are the same. This section is also a good place to include recommended materials, such as a specific dictionary or links to useful online resources.

3.2.2 GOALS AND OBJECTIVES

It is important that both the goals and the objectives be stated clearly and succinctly on the course syllabus. The goals and objectives of an individual language course, although directly related to the mission of the overall program, should be designed with the rest of the syllabus components in mind. For example, if a large portion of class time is devoted to oral communication and a great percentage of the final grade is dependent on students' abilities to communicate effectively in spoken dialogues, then this emphasis should be reflected in the statement of the course goals. Windham (2008) reports on the effect of designing language programs with specific educational objectives in mind, in this case levels of speaking proficiency on the ACTFL scale, but "with modifications that allow for student achievements that go beyond being able to communicate" (p. 35). Windham found that such "guidelines are useful precisely when they focus our attention on student learning outcomes" (p. 31), and this premise can be applicable to any language program, whether using the proficiency guidelines, the Standards, or any other framework to elaborate the program goals.

3.2.3 GRADING AND ASSESSMENT INFORMATION

The information on how a student will be assessed is of paramount importance, and every component of the student's grade needs to be explained in the syllabus. This is, after all, the part that is most interesting to the students in their eternal concern for their grades. This information is what is labeled "Evaluation" in Table 3: policy statements that can affect students' grades; statements about attendance, homework, makeups and late work; course materials; grading scale; and components of the grade. I try to give as detailed a description of each component as possible, spelling out the expectations, criteria, due dates, and so on whenever possible. (This will result in some duplication across the syllabus, although that is acceptable to me, as the main point is making sure the information is understood.)

3.2.4 COMMENTS ON METHODOLOGY USED

As needed, it may be useful to offer additional information on the types of methodological approaches used in the course and why they are used, such as the expectations for paired or group work in class, use of the target language during class time, and the like. Nunan (2001, see Table 4) discusses different types of language practice that can take place in classes, and it may be beneficial to explain to students which of these they can expect to participate in and why.

This section will help students understand the justification behind what they do in the course, and it will help them see the connections between what they do with their time and how it will help them achieve the course goals.

3.3 Policies and Institutional Information

Most programs have policies that apply to all courses in their language sequence, and most institutions have standard policies that must be included in course syllabi. This section is divided into these two broad categories, and although not all programs or institutions will have the same requirements, these can serve as a general reference.

3.3.1 COURSE POLICIES

Attendance   The attendance policy should be explained fully in the syllabus, including the number of absences allowed before they affect the course grade, documentation of absences, and the distinction (if relevant to your program) between excused and unexcused absences. Must justifiable absences be documented? If so, how and with whom (instructor only or coordinator/

TABLE 4 Types of Language Practice, Adapted from Nunan (2001)

Practice type	Description
Real-world or target task	Communicative act achieved through language beyond the classroom
Pedagogical tasks	Classroom work involving learners in comprehending, manipulating, producing or interacting in the language; attention is primarily focused on meaning rather than forms; outcome is nonlinguistic outcome
Rehearsal task	Classroom work in which learners rehearse a communicative act they will carry out beyond the class
Activation task	Classroom work involving communicative interaction, but not one that entails rehearsing for out-of-class communication; designed instead to activate the acquisition process
Enabling skills	Mastery of language systems such as grammar, pronunciation, vocabulary, and so on, which permit ("enable") learners to carry out communicative tasks
Language exercise	Classroom work focusing on a particular aspect of the linguistic system, such as grammar practice
Communication activity	Classroom work focusing on a particular linguistic feature but also involving the genuine exchange of meaning, such as true communication

director)? The policy on late arrivals or early departures from class should be spelled out as well.

Late work   What time are assignments due on the due date? Will instructors accept late work? If so, under what circumstances? If late work is not accepted, does it automatically receive a grade of 0?

Makeup work   Is makeup work allowed? If so, what kinds of assignments (homework, tests, compositions, etc.)? And if so, under what circumstances? (See preceding questions.)

Extra credit   It is useful to establish a programwide policy on extra credit to avoid dealing with individual requests. Some institutions require that extra-credit policies apply to all sections of a multisection course. To hold students accountable for the work of the course, some LPDs prefer to allow no extra credit at all.

Use of cell phones or other technology   It is advisable to establish a policy for the use of cell phones, laptops, and other electronic devices in class. The most common policy in language programs is to prohibit their use except when directed by the instructor for an activity. The consequences for violating this policy should be spelled out, such as a zero for participation that day or being asked to leave the class.

3.3.2 INSTITUTIONAL POLICIES

Academic honesty   Most institutions have published policies on academic honesty and plagiarism, and some departments or programs have their own additional information. For example, my university has a policy, but the language program includes additional information with respect to the use of online translators, asking others for help with compositions, and so on. Whenever possible, provide a link to the institutional policy.

Students needing accommodations   By law, all institutions have policies to provide access and accommodation to all students. This policy should be included in the syllabus as well. Where can students go for help? How can they certify a need, such as a learning disability or the need for accommodation for a visual or auditory disability? By law, an instructor cannot offer accommodations that have not been requested, and most institutions have a central office that handles student requests for accommodations and works directly with the LPD to arrange for them. Making it clear to students in the syllabus that we cannot proceed without official documentation from the appropriate university office will avoid potentially delicate personal situations.

How to handle conflicts   It is also important to include in the syllabus the procedures for students to follow if they have a complaint about the course or their instructor. Students with concerns should know that procedures are in place, have easy access to the contact information for the people they should talk to, and be assured that they will suffer no negative consequences for expressing a concern.

It is true that with all these policies that need to be explained, included, and linked to further online policies, it can seem that "the contemporary syllabus is becoming more like a legal document, full of all manner of exhortations, proscriptions, and enunciations of class and institutional policy, often in minute detail that seems more appropriate for a courtroom than a classroom" (Wasley, 2008, par. 4). But more often than not, problems could have been avoided by having policies that were clearer or better explained from the beginning. Legal experts involved in academic disputes "say that when things go wrong in the classroom, fuzzy expectations are almost always to blame" (Wasley, 2008, par. 8). Furthermore, administrators—including LPDs, one would imagine—also tend to favor a comprehensive syllabus over a less detailed one. When student complaints arise, often the very first thing that the chair, "dean or ombudsman asks is whether there is a policy in the syllabus that covers the complaint" (Wasley, 2008, par. 32). The challenge is striking the harmonic balance between the right amount of information without stifling creativity, learning, or enjoyment of the course.

Additionally, most institutions have policies stipulating what information must appear on course syllabi, and often with specific wording and stipulations regarding where and how course syllabi must be made publicly available—although instructors are often unaware of them. Who determines such policies can vary from institution to institution, but usually they originate in the office of the provost, the academic senate, the board of trustees or similar governing board, the institution's undergraduate studies office or the office of legal affairs, or even the regional organizations that develop policies about academic affairs and are responsible for academic accreditation (e.g., the Middle States Association of Colleges and Schools; the New England Association of Schools and Colleges; the North Central Association of Colleges and Schools; the Northwest Commission on Colleges and Universities; the Western Association of Schools and Colleges; and the Southern Association of Colleges and Schools). Many provide tips for writing and developing syllabi, as well as considerations for class design. A number of institutions gave sample syllabus templates or example syllabi along with their guidelines

The motivation behind establishing such policies seems to be, first and foremost, to facilitate effective communication between instructors and students by putting into clear language what the class is and what will be necessary. Additionally, establishing policies and guidelines helps faculty define their expectations of students for a given course. Crucially, setting forth common policies beforehand and making them available to students from the beginning of the semester helps avoid potential problems later on. Finally, the information provided through these policies gives the students the tools they need to succeed in the course.

3.3.3 CALENDAR INFORMATION

The calendar is a crucial element of the syllabus as well, and students consult it frequently to know what homework to do for each class. In many ways, the calendar is the least creative portion of the syllabus in that its primary function is to move the course from Point A to Point B, to progress through the material (chapters, textbook, etc.) in the specified amount of time. In that respect, the most basic of decisions for a syllabus calendar are mathematical: How many days of class are there? How many chapters or units must be covered? How many days can be allotted for each chapter or unit then? Subsequent questions follow, of course, as time needs to be allotted for holidays, testing, and other assessments or activities. Beyond those purely logical calculations, however, more subtle issues come into play at the programmatic and policy levels. The decisions the LPD makes in these areas reflect administrative and professional needs as well as the LPD's attitudes and approaches toward classroom administration. The primary issue to deal with in creating the calendar is the balance between detail and flexibility, which can also be viewed as a trade-off between LPD control and instructor autonomy.

On one end of the spectrum, consider a syllabus for a multisection language course, often taught by many different instructors with varying degrees of experience, and coordinated by a level coordinator. Given this great variability, an LPD might opt in this case for a very controlled and detailed calendar in order to ensure uniformity across all sections. A number of calendar approaches, such as *categorical* or *calendarist* (e.g., Lee, 1989, pp. 52–55) deliver this level of detail, providing specific page numbers and assignment information for every day or every class period. (See the appendix for examples of different calendars.) Under such an approach, perhaps instructors are given less leeway in terms of what they do in any given class period, but the LPD can use this schedule to maximize the uniformity of her or his expectations and of the content of daily lesson plans. As such, she or he can be more confident that all sections will be proceed at the same pace, and all will be prepared to take the assessments on the scheduled days. In my own program, this is the sort of calendar we use for beginning level courses, given the number of students and instructors, and the need to maintain uniformity across all sections.

On the other end of the spectrum, we might find a calendar that instead maximizes instructor autonomy, providing less detail for students and in doing so, offering less guidance for instructors. These *minimalist* calendars (Lee, 1989, p. 52) are characterized by showing how much time is spent on each chapter, but not specifying what pages or activities are covered on each day, nor what is expected in terms of preparation outside of class. In such cases, the instructor would have to inform students periodically (i.e., every class period, or with a daily e-mail reminder) of the specific assignments for upcoming classes. In a smaller program with fewer sections of the same course, this can be an attractive option, especially if instructors are experienced and able to work without the lockstep guidance of a day-to-day plan. Some of our higher-level language classes (e.g., fourth or fifth semester courses), of which we often offer fewer sections and which are usually taught by lecturers and advanced experienced graduate student instructors, have taken this approach successfully. It requires constant upkeep and contact from the instructor, as well as monitoring from the LPD, but serves as valuable professional development experience for graduate instructors who one day will be responsible for planning the courses they teach entirely on their own.

There are also options between these two extremes. The challenge for the LPD is establishing the balance between uniformity and autonomy, and finding the calendar that strikes such a balance for each course. As with the other topics seen in this chapter, it may be most effective to use elements of different designs to create the most appropriate calendar for the needs of a specific course or program. For example, in some classes I have used the categorical column approach but only partially filled in some information, allowing individual instructors to complete the rest as best benefits their classes. Thus as with the general syllabus design, an eclectic approach may be the most beneficial.

3.3.4 OTHER INFORMATION

Finally, other information may need to be included as part of or in addition to a syllabus. This section could provide technology-related information, such as how to register for an online course component, links to the institution's course management system, or troubleshooting advice, and so on. Likewise, a syllabus could offer additional resources such as tips for successful performance in language classes, suggested readings, useful Web pages, cultural or grammatical references, and the like. Finally, many syllabi offer further pedagogical resources, such as error correction codes used in evaluating written work or the rubrics used in assessment of class participation, oral exams, or compositions. The challenge remains, however, in finding the balance of information: enough to be useful and informative, without being overwhelming or off-putting. A syllabus that is not read by students or instructors is no longer a valuable resource.

4 CONCLUSION

The main goal of program materials is to provide the essential information to students and instructors in as clear and concise a manner as possible. What each LPD, and even each instructor, deems essential will naturally vary by course, by setting, and by student population, but this information needs to be included in the syllabus. The importance of developing a coherent and accessible syllabus cannot be underestimated; it is the opportunity to provide concrete, necessary, and useful information to students and instructors in a format that is easy to follow.

Questions for Reflection

1. How integrated and articulated are the different levels of instruction at the institutions where you have studied and/or taught language? What would you like changed, if anything, and how might you make those changes?
2. What are the advantages and disadvantages to having uniform syllabi for multisection courses? Are there ways to minimize the disadvantages without jeopardizing the advantages?
3. Examine the suggestions for what to include on syllabi that were provided in section 3.3. Select three features that you would like to incorporate into your own syllabi, and explain why and how you would do so. Do you see anything problematic about those sample syllabi?
4. Investigate whether your institution (where you study or teach) has a policy on information that must be included on course syllabi. If so, what information is required? How do these requirements compare to the information suggested in this chapter? If you are unable to locate one, come up with draft of a policy for your institution.
5. A recurrent problem is that students often fail to read, or read closely, the syllabus. How can we encourage them to do so and hold them accountable for knowing that information?

Suggestions for Further Reading

Davidson, J., & Tesh, J. (1997). Theory and practice in language program organization and design. In M. A. Christison & F. Stoller (Eds.), *A handbook for language program administrators* (pp. 177–198). Burlingame, CA: Alta Book Center.

> Discusses advantages and disadvantages to different organizational structures in language programs.

Harris-Schenz, B. (1993). Between a rock and a hard place: The position of the language program coordinator. *ADFL Bulletin, 24*(2), 45–50.

> Relevant to many chapters, but particularly of interest here is her discussion of possible sources of conflict between the LPD and her or his colleagues, as well as between the LPD and the instructors in the language program.

Norris, J. M., Davis, J. McE., Sinicrope, C., & Watanabe, Y. (Eds.) (2009). *Toward useful program evaluation in college foreign language education*. Manoa, HI: University of Hawaii, National Foreign Language Resource Center.

> Provides a comprehensive analysis of how program assessment is currently conceived and offers concrete examples for carrying out evaluation and improvement; describes theories and experiences related to the Foreign Language Program Evaluation Project (FLPEP) at the University of Hawaii.

Robinson, P. (2009). Syllabus design. In M. H. Long & C. H. Doughty (Eds.), *Handbook of language teaching* (pp. 294–310). Malden, MA: Wiley-Blackwell.

> A summary of seminal and recent work on syllabus design theory and practice in language classes.

APPENDIX

Sample Syllabus Components

1. STATEMENTS OF GOALS, OBJECTIVES, AND LEARNING OUTCOMES

EXAMPLE 1: LYNCHBURG COLLEGE—INTERMEDIATE SPANISH

The five overarching goals for education at Lynchburg College are to "inquire," "explore," "conclude," "persuade" and "engage." With that in mind, students in this course will be encouraged to "inquire," asking questions about linguistic and cultural issues related to readings and topics of discussion. Students will "explore" by comprehending written and aural sources about Hispanic cultures, investigating and examining a variety of issues from global perspectives, and gathering information for presentations, compositions, and class discussions. Students will "conclude" by pulling together information from a variety of sources to complete written essays, engage in class discussions/debates, and perform class presentations. For the goal of "persuade" students will participate in class debates and write essays and persuasive journal entries. For the final goal of "engage," students will constantly interact and cooperate with classmates to achieve shared goals, and through attendance at *Mesa hispánica* or other extracurricular activities, will value culture and language learning beyond the classroom.

EXAMPLE 2: MICHIGAN STATE UNIVERSITY—INTERMEDIATE GERMAN

The course goal is to assist you in achieving an American Council of Teaching of Foreign Languages Intermediate or Common European Framework A2 level. This means that by the end of the course sequence (201 and 202), you should be able to:

- Understand sentences and frequently used expressions related to areas of most immediate relevance (personal and family information, local geography, employment, shopping, etc.)
- Communicate in routine situations requiring a simple and direct exchange of information on familiar matters
- Describe in simple terms aspects of your background and immediate environment and matters of immediate need

EXAMPLE 3: UNIVERSITY OF FLORIDA—BEGINNING SPANISH

The primary goal of the Beginning Spanish courses is to offer students an introduction to basic communicative skills in Spanish while developing an awareness and appreciation of Hispanic/Latino cultures. The courses take their goals from the *Standards for Foreign Language Learning in the 21st Century*, also known as the five Cs, which focus on five general areas:

- *Communicating* in Spanish
- *Gaining* knowledge and understanding of *cultures* of the Hispanic world

- *Connecting* with other disciplines and acquiring new information
- *Developing* awareness of similarities and differences (*comparisons*) among language and culture systems around the world
- *Using* Spanish to participate in *communities* at home and around the world

EXAMPLE 4: UNIVERSITY OF FLORIDA—INTERMEDIATE SPANISH

The primary objective of this course is to prepare the students for higher-level Spanish courses, particularly in their communicative skills. The course stimulates oral comprehension through varied activities such as oral presentations on the part of the professor, dictations, videos and songs, etc. The course also provides the students with extensive practice in developing their reading skills. Finally, we foment speaking skills by incorporating student discussions, role plays, debates, and presentations into the class. The following table explains the specific skills students will develop over the course of the semester.

Linguistic	Learn vocabulary and basic idiomatic expressions; expanded sophisticated vocabulary; reinforce and increase use of relevant grammatical points.
Sociocultural	Understand the differences among Hispanic countries with respect to history, customs, traditions and other cultural aspects.
Discursive	Understand written and spoken speech in a variety of genres and from a variety of backgrounds. Recognize tone, perspective, and main theme of a text and be able to contextualize it. Express, support, explain, and defend an opinion. Disagree respectfully. Make presentations, dialogue, investigate, interview. Connect new information with old.
Strategic	Use techniques to compensate for linguistic deficiencies such as contextual clues, circumlocution, semiotic information, etc. Expand and increase strategies for learning and using language.

EXAMPLE 5: UNIVERSITY OF KANSAS—INTERMEDIATE SPANISH

Students enrolled in each section of [Intermediate Spanish] share a common syllabus, complete common assignments, and take common exams that are evaluated using the same grading scales. In short, all sections of the course share a common philosophy toward teaching and learning. Our approach to language teaching and learning (discussed in detail below) offers you a unique opportunity to become a proficient speaker of Spanish. After successful completion of fourth-semester Spanish, you will be able to understand spoken and written Spanish and be able to express yourself both verbally and in writing. Whether you realize it or not, this skill will be very valuable to you in the future, regardless of the profession that you choose. We will also focus on developing cultural awareness and understanding through the examination of our own beliefs and practices juxtaposed with the great variety of beliefs and practices of the many unique communities that share Spanish as a common language. We hope that this experience will prepare you to be an informed citizen and a more effective member of the global community in which we all live.

EXAMPLE 6: UNIVERSITY OF NORTH TEXAS—BEGINNING SPANISH

This is a beginning course designed for students who have no prior knowledge of Spanish.

At the end of this course the successful student:

- Will be able to use Spanish to negotiate meaning in basic contexts
- Will be able to interact with basic Spanish texts
- Will have attained awareness of and sensitivity to language in general
- Will have attained understanding of some of the significant social, cultural, historical, and political aspects of Spanish-speaking communities

EXAMPLE 7: UNIVERSITY OF SOUTH CAROLINA—BEGINNING FRENCH

Students who successfully complete this course should be able to do the following:

1. *Communication*
   - Demonstrate an understanding of the main ideas and many supporting details of written and spoken communication in the present time frame on topics of one's immediate environment, background, friends, family, pastimes, travel, etc.
   - Engage in oral and written exchanges with a focus on providing and obtaining basic information, expressing feelings and preferences, describing and narrating, giving directions, and exchanging opinions on topics of personal interest such those mentioned above.
2. *Cultures*
   - Demonstrate an understanding of cultural information and relationships between cultural perspectives, products, and practices, especially as they relate to the Francophone countries featured in the text.
   - Use appropriate cultural behavior in social and survival situations
3. *Connections*
   - Use the French language to reinforce and learn new information in academic areas such as history, geography, art, anthropology, and literature.
4. *Comparisons*
   - Develop insights into their own language and culture through readings, listening, and classroom activities which deal with Francophone speakers in the students' community and abroad.
5. *Communities*
   - Be made aware of opportunities to practice and hear the French language outside of the classroom in activities such as concerts, movies, lectures, exhibits, festivals, and conversational exchanges with Francophones.

EXAMPLE 8: UNIVERSITY OF SOUTH CAROLINA— BEGINNING GERMAN

German 109 is the first course in a three-semester sequence for beginning students of German (109, 110, 122). All four foreign language skills (reading, writing, speaking, and listening) will be addressed to help you acquire a reasonable level of proficiency in the German language. With your active participation and cooperation, upon completion of this course you should be able to:

- Demonstrate the ability to speak and comprehend German with a reasonable degree of accuracy when dealing with specific topics. Topics include introductions and greetings, personal interests, housing, family, telling time, and your daily schedule.
- Demonstrate that you have acquired reading strategies in German enabling you to understand and analyze different kinds of texts with limited dictionary use.
- To write short messages, postcards, letters, summaries, take notes, compose coherent paragraphs dealing with the topics mentioned above.
- Demonstrate the ability to use correct basic grammatical and syntactic structures and patterns, which underlie all communication in the language, through speaking and writing tasks.
- Analyze the products, practices, and perspectives as they relate to the culture of German-speaking countries.

2. ASSESSMENT CRITERIA

EXAMPLE 1: LYNCHBURG COLLEGE—INTERMEDIATE SPANISH

Tests (2)	30%
Final Exam	15%
Class Participation	10%
Compositions (3)	15%
Group Oral Presentations (3)	15%
Homework & Quizzes	10%
Mesa hispánica	5 %

EXAMPLE 2: MICHIGAN STATE UNIVERSITY—INTERMEDIATE GERMAN

Category	Weight
Attendance, preparation and participation (assessed through self-evaluation; 5 times during the semester)	10%
Project: oral group multimedia presentation (10%) and reflective essay (5%)	15%
Essays: each essay will be submitted in two drafts (2 × 2 × 5%)	20%
Regular On-line, In-class Activities and Homework Assignments (e.g. Quia, quizzes, oral exercises, short writing assignments, oral presentations)	25%
2 Exams (Midterm 10% and Final 20%)	30%
Co-curricular activities (replace up to 5 grades of daily activities or 3 self-evaluation)	substitutions
TOTAL	100%

EXAMPLE 3: UNIVERSITY OF KANSAS—INTERMEDIATE SPANISH

Preparation in *Acceso* [online text]	10%
Participation in Class Activities	10%
MySpanishLab	20%
Unit 1 Quiz	5%
Midterm Exam	15%
Blogs	15%
Oral Evaluation	10%
Final Exam	15%

EXAMPLE 4: UNIVERSITY OF NORTH TEXAS—INTERMEDIATE SPANISH

Evaluation procedure	Weight	Notes
Attendance	5%	See rubric below. Graded every exam period.
Participation	5%	See rubric below. Graded every exam period.
Oral Interview	8%	At the end of the semester.
Compositions	10%	First Draft (in class) at 5% and Final Copy at 5%
In-class Tasks	15%	10 total.
Portfolio*	12%	2 at 6% each.
MySpanishLab Activities	15%	See Schedule.
Exams	15%	Three total.
Final Exam	15%	Comprehensive.

*Sample portfolio cover page

Actividad	Descripción	Puntos
Películas	*Cine club*—authorized movies only Submit commentary using *Hoja de Preguntas.* 75 words in Spanish 10 pts/film Maximum 20 points/portfolio	
Lectura: periódico o revista	Printed or virtual—published on or after June 1, 2010 A copy of the article must be submitted. Submit commentary using *Hoja de Actividades.* 75 words in Spanish 10 points/reading Maximum 20 points/portfolio	

Actividad	Descripción	Puntos
Interacción cultural	Attend a Hispanic festival or a religious service in Spanish, visit the Latino Cultural Center of Dallas, or other activity approved by your instructor Submit commentary using *Hoja de Actividades* 75 words in Spanish 10 points/activity (minimum 30-minute encounter) Maximum 20 points/portfolio	
Interacción por Internet	Interaction (written/oral/visual) with native speakers over the Internet through Live Mocha Submit commentary using *Hoja de Actividades* 75 words in Spanish 10 points/20 minute encounter Maximum 30 points/portfolio	
Expresión creativa	Express yourself in Spanish. Write a poem, song or story. (minimum 1 page, must represent significant effort at self-expression) 10 points/portfolio	
Tertulia	Meet with other Spanish students and instructors to converse in Spanish Wednesdays 3:00–4:00 pm in LANG 410 Submit commentary using *Hoja de Actividades* 75 words in Spanish 10 points/Tertulia (minimum 30-minute encounter) Maximum 30 points/portfolio	
Aprende ayudando	Participate in Service Learning program: *Success for Life through Reading* or *America Reads* Submit commentary using *Hoja de Actividades* 75 words in Spanish or submit copies of materials created 10 points/hour Maximum 40 points/portfolio	
Puntos sumados	Total Portfolio Points Determined by Instructor	/50

EXAMPLE 5: UNIVERSITY OF SOUTH CAROLINA— BEGINNING GERMAN

Homework	10%
Journals	10%
Participation/contributions to class	10%
Quizzes	20%
3 Chapter Tests	30%
2 Interviews	10%
Final Exam	10%

EXAMPLE 6: WESTERN MICHIGAN UNIVERSITY— BEGINNING SPANISH

Class Participation	10%
Homework	16%
Compositions	16%
Quizzes	15%
Midterm Exam	15%
Final Written Exam	18%
Oral Exam	10%

3. CALENDAR LAYOUTS

Notes:

- Examples here are chosen to display different formats, and only excerpts of select days or weeks are provided.
- Although not reproduced here, at some point in this section of the syllabus most include a disclaimer of sorts, indicating that the schedule is subject to change, and often how and when such changes will be publicized or made available.

EXAMPLE 1: MICHIGAN STATE UNIVERSITY— BEGINNING GERMAN

Woche	Datum	Thema	Aufgaben
5	Di. 28.10	Stationen 64–73 Oktoberfestbesuch Teil 2	
5	Do. 30.10	Projektvorstellungen	Projekte Teil 1
6	Di. 5.10	Stationen 75–85 Heidelberg, Hannah Arendt, Studentenleben, Das Imperfekt	
6	Do. 7.10	Stationen 85–96 Belegen ist Belügen, Videoblog, Wortschatz, als, wenn, wann, Redemittel zum Diskutieren	Selbstbewertung 2
7	Di. 12.10	Stationen 96–106 Das Plusquamperfekt, Freunde	
7	Do. 14.10	Wiederholung	
8	Di. 19.10		Midterm

EXAMPLE 2: UNIVERSITY OF IOWA—BEGINNING SPANISH

Week 2 Aug. 31 M	**Submit Quiz #0** (about the Course description). The quiz is on ICON Study: M, p. 16 (Los meses del ano y . . .), p. 18 (La hura), p. 19 (El tiempo) **SAM: P-42**	M:P-22 to P-27 P-17, P-22, P-29
Sep. 1 T	Studv: M. p. 23. p. 24 (A primera vista] Write: M,~p 23 (A vista de pajaro) SAM: 01-01	Exchange information about classes M: A vista de pajaro and A primera vista M: 1-1 to 1-4 SAM: 16
2 **W**	Study: M, p. 27 (La universidad), p. 28 (las actividades de lus . . .), p. 29 (En la libreriaj Write: 1-6 SAM: 01-08	identify locations at the university M: 1-5 to 1-10 SAM: 1-10 (if time allows)
3 Th	Studv: M. pp. 32-33 fFunciones v formas) Write: M. p. 32. Pienselo Watch: M, p. 31 (En acccion) SAM: 01-16	Talking about academic life and daily occurrences M: En **accion:** 1-14, 1-15,1-16 M: p. 32 (Pienselo), 1-17, 1-18
4 **F**	Study: M, p. 47 (A conversar: Estrategia)	**Talking** about academic life and daily occurrences M:l-19, 1-20,1-21 M: **SITUACIONES,** p. 35

EXAMPLE 3: UNIVERSITY OF NORTH TEXAS— BEGINNING SPANISH

Week	Day	Objective	Pages in Textbook	Student Activities Manual
5	14	**Capítulo 7:** ¡A comer!	278–283	7-46, 7-47, 7-49
	15	**Chapter 7 exam**		
	16	**Capítulo 8:** ¿Qué te pones?	284–291	8-1 – 8-5, 8-7, 8-12
	17	**Capítulo 8:** ¿Qué te pones?	292–297	8-14 – 8-16, 8-17 – 8-19
6 Sept. 27 – Oct. 1	18	**Capítulo 8:** ¿Qué te pones?	298–302	8-21 – 8-24
	19	**Capítulo 8:** ¿Qué te pones?	302–305	8-26 – 8-29
	20	**Capítulo 8:** ¿Qué te pones? **COMPOSITION 1 DUE**	306–309	8-32, 8-34 – 8-37
	21	**Capítulo 8:** ¿Qué te pones?	310–311	8-40 – 8-42
	52	Review		

EXAMPLE 4: UNIVERSITY OF SOUTH CAROLINA—BEGINNING FRENCH

Week	Chapter/ Lesson	In Class	HOMEWORK *specific assignments will be given by your instructor
ABBREVIATIONS: PD = Points de départ ; VC = Vie et culture ; SL = Sons et lettres ; FF = Formes et fonctions ; CP = Chapitre préliminaire ; C1 (C2, C3, etc.) = Chapitre 1 (2, 3, etc.); L1 (L2, L3, etc.) = Leçon 1 (2, 3, etc.) ; VCN = Venez chez nous !			
Feb. 1	CP/C1	**CP/C1 Exam**	
3	C2.L1	**Textbook:** PD, VC (Activities 2-1 to 2-3; Video) SL (Activities 2-4 to 2-5) FF1 (Activities 2-6 to 2-8)	
6	C2.L1	**Textbook:** FF2 (Activities 2-9 to 2-12) Lisons (Activity 2-13)	
8	C2.L2	**Textbook:** PD, VC (Activities 2-14 to 2-17)	
10	C2.L2	**Textbook:** SL (Activities 2-18 to 2-19) FF1, FF2 (Activities 2-20 to 2-24) Écoutons (Activity 2-25)	

EXAMPLE 5: WESTERN MICHIGAN UNIVERSITY—BEGINNING SPANISH

Week 9 (Mar. 12–16)	
Textbook pages & topics:	*MSL homework & compositions due:*

• Chapter 7: pp. 228–236
  • *Perfiles*
  • *Los deportes y las actividades deportivas*
  • *Letras y sonidos*
  • Irregular verbs in the preterit (III): more strong preterits
	• *The following are all due Sun., Mar. 18th:*
	 → MSL (7-30, 7-31)
	 → MSL (7-33, 7-34)
	 → MSL (7-38)

Week 10 (Mar. 19–23)	
• *Mon., Mar. 19: LAST DAY TO WITHDRAW FROM COURSES*	
Textbook pages & topics:	*MSL homework & compositions due:*

• Chapter 7: pp. 237–243
  • Double object pronouns
  • REVIEW: *¿Cuánto saben?*
  • *Observaciones: ¡Pura Vida!* Episodio 7
  • *Nuestro Mundo: Panoramas*
	• *The following are all due Sun., Mar. 25th:*
	 → MSL (7-42)
	 → MSL CS P2 (7-46, 7-47, 7-48); MSL *Práctica* oral (7-2); MSL Game (7-1)
	 → MSL PV (do 7-49; (re)view video while completing 7-50; then complete 7-51)
	 • *4th 50-minute session:* **FIRST DRAFT OF COMPOSITION 2**

4. SAMPLE TIPS FOR STUDENTS AND NOTES ON CLASSROOM PRACTICES

EXAMPLE 1: MICHIGAN STATE UNIVERSITY— INTERMEDIATE GERMAN

Learning a language is time- and work-intensive and requires daily practice and preparation. Some of you may have studied abroad, many have not. Some of you may have had a more grammar-focused language learning experience, others a more communicative one. Some may have begun German in high school, others in college. This means that everyone will bring a different level of language expertise and expectations to this class. Don't get discouraged— language learning is a long process, and the little steps are often not noticeable when you are in the middle of it. Since it's hard to catch up, don't get behind. If you have questions or concerns or need help or extra practice, you are always more than welcome to come by office hours or set up an appointment for another time. Seek help if you need it!

EXAMPLE 2: UNIVERSITY OF FLORIDA—BEGINNING SPANISH

All 1000-level SPN classes in the Department of Spanish and Portuguese Studies are taught in hybrid format. Hybrid courses are defined as classes in which instruction takes place in a traditional classroom setting augmented by computer-based or online activities which can replace classroom seat time. These types of courses are common in higher education in the United States, and even in language classes. While we maintain that human interaction is absolutely essential in learning and using a language, we also believe that advances in technologies have enabled us to reach a point where students can accomplish a great deal working on their own, reserving class time for true communication and interactive learning. These classes are five-credit courses but meet only three days a week, with supplemental instructional activities to be done at home to constitute the other two credits. Although the course requires reduced face-to-face class time, your success and learning require substantial commitment and study both in and out of class. The level of proficiency you attain will depend largely on what you put into your learning. This course requires self-discipline and time. Please be sure to read the "Methodology and Activities" section of this document for tips on succeeding in a hybrid learning format.

EXAMPLE 3: UNIVERSITY OF NORTH TEXAS—BEGINNING SPANISH

This is a four-credit course that meets four times a week. In addition, students are required to register for a lab class that meets one hour per week. Because exposure to and practice in Spanish is essential to successful acquisition of the language, these courses will be conducted mostly in Spanish. Although you are not expected to understand every word, through repeated exposure, study, and practice you will find that you understand increasingly more as the semester progresses. So relax, and make every effort to use only Spanish in the classroom. Please note: The role of the instructor in the classroom is that of "communication facilitator," and students will work extensively in group and partner on various, mostly communicative activities. Your instructor will not provide extensive grammar or vocabulary instruction during class time. This is the role of the text, electronic student activities, and other technology and your interaction with it. If you feel you need additional help with the material, consult your instructor during office hours, and take advantage of departmentally provided resources such as free tutoring.

CHAPTER 4

Choosing Textbooks

When the topic of this chapter came up in conversation with my colleagues, one commented that textbooks are more trouble than they are worth: they are overpriced and overvalued, he said, and we should just teach without them. This comment raises an interesting question: Do we need a textbook? Traditionally, language curricula have followed what is called the "coverage model" (Chaffee, 1992), which is driven in large part by the scope and sequence of a textbook. Through this model, the process of language learning is viewed as the passive transfer of information (Allen, 2002). In spite of recent emphasis on proficiency, task-based instruction, and a Standards-oriented approach to teaching language, as opposed to a curriculum of lexical and structural items, Bragger and Rice (2000) found that textbooks still play a key role in language classrooms, and other recent research (e.g., Aski, 2003; Fernández, 2011; Rubio, Passey, & Campbell, 2004) confirms that second language acquisition (SLA) theory informs textbook design less than it probably should.

Many instructors recognize the limitations of textbooks, as we are aware that they can go only so far in terms of presentation and cannot guarantee communication, interaction, or any of the correlates recommended by the Standards. This is not new. More than three decades ago, Allwright (1981) noted that

> there is a limit to what teaching materials can be expected to do for us. The whole business of the management of language learning is far too complex to be satisfactorily catered for by a pre-packaged set of decisions embodied in teaching materials. (p. 9; see also Crawford, 2002; Dalby, 2009)

Ansary and Babaii (2002) note that there are three main opinions when it comes to textbooks: (1) we need textbooks, (2) we do not need textbooks, and (3) we choose the best text possible and then supplement with additional resources as necessary (p. 2). These authors go on to propose a number of reasons for using a textbook, such as to encourage students to take their learning seriously, to provide a framework and focus to a course, and to offer a useful aid to the teacher, especially in the case of novice teachers. As Williams (1983) notes, novice teachers are those "who rely most heavily on the textbook," yet they "are the ones least qualified to interpret its intentions or evaluate its content and method" (p. 251).

The textbooks used in a language program more often than not play a central role in shaping the program as a whole. Richards (n.d.) summarizes the importance of the textbook as follows:

> Textbooks are a key component in most language programs. In some situations they serve as the basis for much of the language input learners receive and the language practice that occurs in the classroom. They may provide the basis for the content of the lessons, the balance of skills taught and the kinds of language practice the students take part in. In other situations, the textbook may serve primarily to supplement the teacher's instruction. For learners, the textbook may provide the major source of contact they have with the language apart from input provided by the teacher. In the case of inexperienced teachers, textbooks may also serve as a form of teacher training–they provide ideas on how to plan and teach lessons as well as formats that teachers can use. (p. 1)

Our textbooks are often the driving force that "states curricular goals, lays out material to be taught, and suggests ways of teaching it" (Byrnes, 1998, p. 271, cited in Schultz, 2005, p. 64). Thus the process of choosing a textbook for a language program is a crucial one.

1. THE TEXTBOOK SELECTION PROCESS

Considering the central role that the textbook plays in the development and implementation of foreign language courses, it is surprising to find relatively little in the way of published work regarding this process (although see Blyth, 2009; McGrath, 2002; Paradowski, 2010; Richards, n.d.). In the area of teaching English as a second (ESL) or foreign language (EFL), scholars and instructors have recognized the value of work in this area. (See e.g., the comprehensive bibliography at http://www.denisesantos.com/research.htm.) Although the issues involved in teaching English to speakers of other languages in the United States and those involved in teaching foreign languages can be different, when it comes to textbook design there is a good deal of common ground. Because the lion's share of the work on foreign language textbook selection comes from the ESL/EFL field, many of the references in this chapter come from work done in English language teaching.

Although I refer throughout this chapter to textbooks, I recognize that the term *textbook* has become shorthand for *textbook program*. Most textbooks now include a large array of ancillary materials and various options for packaging. (See Blyth, 2009, for a discussion of the changing nature of textbook design in light of technological developments.) With multiple materials available in these programs, our selection of pedagogical materials can have a great impact on the shape and direction of our program. Nonetheless, language program directors (LPDs) often carry out this task on their own. The goal of this chapter is to provide resources, options, and assistance to LPDs as they undertake the daunting process of evaluating and selecting a textbook.

As LPDs initiate this process, they confront the reality that no textbook is perfect, nor can any book be perfectly suited to the needs of all learners and all instructors. Additionally, instructors may find themselves locked into a rigid calendar or curriculum when they must closely follow a textbook (Williams, 1983, p. 251). LPDs often develop their language curricula around the chosen textbook, thus awarding the text an overly prominent position in their vision of their programs (Byrnes, 1998; Lange, 1994; Richards, n.d.).

Experienced instructors advise using any teaching material, textbooks included, with caution and judgment. Although we know that "the textbook does not, in and of itself, constitute the curriculum" and that no text alone guarantees successful language learning, because "only the students and the teacher can determine how effective the course will be in enhancing language proficiency" (Omaggio Hadley, 2001, pp. 459–460), we must remember that the textbook does constitute an important and valuable component of our programs. So care must be taken in considering the options, and instructors—and especially LPDs—must learn how to effectively assess these options. Williams (1983) points out that "the teacher takes over where the textbook leaves off, and he or she must be able to assess its strengths and weaknesses" (p. 254). Furthermore, in large programs with multisection courses, the textbook is a valuable tool for the LPD, helping to ensure uniformity across sections and thus enabling a common set of objectives and activities, as well as assessment procedures.

The current chapter proceeds from this perspective. While recognizing that the text is only one component of a language program, we also accept that it plays a vital role in shaping our vision. Therefore, the process of evaluating textbooks is crucial. The next section examines when and how an LPD might carry out text evaluations, followed by a discussion of factors to consider when engaging in such assessment. The final section of the chapter discusses the creation and implementation of evaluation checklists or rubrics, accompanied by samples.

1.1 When and How to Evaluate

The decision of when to evaluate a textbook program is just as important as knowing what to evaluate. We generally think of looking at prospective textbooks when a new edition of our current text will be published or if we are dissatisfied with our current book. However, there are other times to consider the evaluation process.

Mukundan (2004, 2007) draws a distinction between the *predictive* and *retrospective* evaluations of teaching materials. As the name implies, a predictive assessment is undertaken prior to using a textbook; this is the kind of evaluation to adopt when designing a language program and making the initial textbook selection. Such an adoption could take place, for example, when a new LPD arrives to a language program or when major revisions are being made to an existing program. Mukundan further defines two types of predictive evaluation, implicit and explicit. "The implicit model, also known as the fuzzy model, is . . . based on impressions and aptly named the impressionistic model. This method of evaluation depends very much on teacher intuitions" (2007, p. 80). Although implicit or impressionistic textbook assessment can be effective if carried out by knowledgeable and experienced educators, it is prone to personal bias. Furthermore, such assessment excludes opinions other than those of the primary evaluator; a team of instructors sharing their respective impressions can be difficult to manage and unlikely to result in consensus.

In contrast, explicit evaluation can be used by teams of educators, and it allows for multiple sources of input:

> Explicit evaluation is done using an evaluation instrument which is usually in the form of a checklist. Instruments come in very many forms, some have open-ended questions as items while others may resemble the Likert-style checklist which are in the form of a rating scale. (Mukundan, 2007, p. 81)

Explicit evaluation seems more scientific, and being less impressionistic, it is perhaps less susceptible to individual whims or unsubstantiated personal preferences. In general, LPDs are encouraged to engage in explicit evaluation whenever possible, especially when working in large programs.

Explicit evaluation takes more time and expertise, as it necessitates the creation or adaptation of a rubric and possibly the involvement of other team members. Whereas we could probably impressionistically evaluate a textbook or two in a few hours, explicit predictive evaluation can take weeks, so LPDs must allow ample time for this process. "Complex problems, such as setting up a new course or introducing or changing coursebooks, cannot be dealt with quickly" (White et al., 2008, p. 243).

The issue of timelines brings up the other type of evaluation, which Mukundan (2004, 2007) terms *retrospective evaluation*, that is, the ongoing assessment of material in use, as well as at the end of the semester or year: "Retrospective evaluation . . . involves continuous evaluation of the textbook after it is selected and while it is used" (Mukundan, 2007, p. 82). Retrospective evaluation brings numerous benefits to the instructor, the program, and the LPD, because it allows us to continually assess the effectiveness of the materials for our needs and offers us the opportunity to make a text more productive, valuable, or useful. It also enables us to make changes to the program in a timely fashion. Unfortunately, claims Mukundan (2007), "most teachers are not even aware of retrospective evaluation" (p. 80); after making the initial decision, which can undoubtedly be an arduous and tiring task, we may forget that continual assessment of all aspects of the program is in everyone's best interest.

1.2 The Evaluation Process

Having established the need to carry out both predictive and retrospective evaluations of current and future teaching materials, the next question is how to do so. Even accepting the superiority of explicit over implicit assessment and the need for a systematic tool for assessment, such as a rubric or checklist, many questions still remain. Who should be involved in the evaluation and decision processes? What elements of a textbook should be considered? What external factors should or should not play a role in the evaluation or selection of textbooks? These issues are addressed in the subsections that follow.

1.2.1 WHO IS INVOLVED

Although it is expected that the LPD will be responsible for the text selection process, there are other potential contributors to the process, and working in a team will not only lessen the workload of each individual but also produce more favorable and more reliable results. Unfortunately, research (e.g., Braggar & Rice, 2000) has found that instructors themselves do not often have an active role in textbook selection, and when they are involved, it is superficially at best. This section discusses the different participants who can—and should—be involved in evaluating and selecting textbooks for a language program, beginning of course with the LPD, but also considering coordinators, instructors, and publishing companies.

Many LPDs approach the text-selection task alone, and for some that may be the best decision. The LPD establishes the vision for the program and directs the implementation of that vision: "We design or oversee the development of all course syllabi and examinations; we are actively involved in programmatic planning (i.e., selection of textbooks, materials) and the establishment of methodologies for classroom language teaching" (Harris-Schenz, 1993). The respondents to my online survey indicated, almost unanimously, that the LPD was the person primarily responsible for selecting textbooks. But the LPD alone "cannot design, implement, and administer a language program" (Lee, Binkowski, & Binkowski, 1993, p. 227) single-handedly. There is value in giving language program participants the opportunity to participate in the process so that the ultimate decision reflects the will of the majority, thereby diminishing the possibility—and strength—of disagreement with the final outcome. And there is power in collective wisdom. To that end, it is not only logical but also advisable that as many people as possible participate in text evaluation (e.g., Chambers, 1997). If a program has course coordinators in addition to the LPD, these individuals would be involved. Depending on the size of the program and the direct involvement of the LPD in all aspects, the level coordinators may be more familiar with the day-to-day needs of a given course than the LPD. What's more, in the case of teaching assistants (TAs), this process offers them an excellent opportunity for professional development in a task that most of them will have to carry out on their own in the future. Just over half of the respondents in my survey indicated that they do, in fact, consult with others in the textbook evaluation and selection process. Those consulted range from coordinators and other instructors to other faculty, and even to department chairs, in a few cases.

There is also value in inviting instructors to participate in the textbook evaluation process. Many of these instructors may not have reviewed or even seen other textbooks, but they may compensate for their lack of training or experience with their ability to see the practical sides of issues. They may also see clearly what will or will not work well in their classrooms. Again, their opinions must be tempered by those of contributors with more teaching and administrative experience, but the unique perspective they offer is valuable.

The more people who are involved in the reviewing process, the greater the chance for disagreement. There is no doubt that "teachers, students, and administers . . . may have conflicting views about what a good/standard textbook is" (Ansary & Babaii, 2002, p. 3), and these conflicting views will inevitably lead to different opinions regarding the value of a proposed textbook. But as Moyer and Gonglewski (1998) point out, "balancing perspectives on teaching and opinions on materials to fit certain courses" is a necessary part of language program direction. Subsumed in these perspectives are greater issues that we will also need to confront to a certain degree, such as "differences in teachers' personalities, work styles, and pedagogical convictions" (p. 54). In situations in which a variety of program members contribute their opinions, it is important to establish beforehand what weight or authority each person will carry with their contribution. For example, what is the relationship between advising and deciding for those involved? In other words, does everyone have a voice but only some a vote? Or does everyone who participates get a vote as well? Or do the opinions of some participants carry more weight than others? For example, in some cases the perspective of the coordinators may be more relevant or essential to the ultimate program design than those of the instructors. Finally, how does the selection process ultimately take place? Is there a committee that decides the process, or is everyone equally involved? Each LPD will consider different options depending on the design and structure of the program, but these are the considerations they must take into account in the process.

The textbook publishers can serve as a valuable source of information as well, if used wisely. After all, by adopting a textbook, the LPD essentially enters into a relationship with the company that publishes that book. The extent to which she or he develops that relationship is a personal decision, but knowing in advance what the publisher can do to help in the selection process and beyond is crucial. Just as crucial, though, is knowing what the publisher cannot or should not do in this process.

On one hand, publishers seem to be an obvious source to turn to, as they are the experts on what makes a text special or valuable. So LPDs should rely on publishers and their representatives to highlight the features of a text under consideration, give pricing information, share the names of other schools or programs that use their text, introduce other books for different levels of instruction, and provide instruction on their technologies and ancillaries. These bits of information are all necessary considerations for any textbook.

On the other hand, of course, we have to remember that they, too, come to the situation with a distinct agenda. "Obviously whatever the publishers claim the book can do are based on biased, non-objective evaluations of the book. They are in fact . . . marketing strategies to help sell the book" (Mukundan, 2007, p. 81). The publishers cannot decide for the LPD what textbook is most appropriate for a program, or even reliably compare their own product to the competitors' products. For these things, the LPD requires expert judgment that comes from experience and training.

The respondents to my survey largely ignore this potential source of information, however, and only about 25% indicated that they work closely or somewhat closely with the textbook publishers in the text selection process, and several (20%) said they never meet or consult with representatives from the publishing companies. The general impression is, as Mukundan (2007) stated, that publishers cannot be trusted to represent their materials fairly or in the most realistic light. This is not to say, however, that opinions of the publishers should be discarded. A valuable first step in the search for a new textbook is to consult the various textbook representatives to ask what texts are new, what texts are most popular in similar programs, or even what texts they would recommend for the LPD's specific program. Sharing the program's mission statement with textbook companies can help the representatives tailor their recommendations and presentations to the needs of the program. Having the textbook companies help the LPD narrow down the initial options can save a great deal of time. Further, the textbook publishers can provide evaluation copies for all members of the evaluation team, and can give presentations on the merits of certain programs. As with any one opinion, we have to consider the source and temper the information with our own opinions and perspectives, but this is still useful information.

Also important to remember is the fact that many textbook companies, more and more in recent years, will create custom texts for a specific program— adding or deleting material, reorganizing or reformatting, packaging different elements together, and so on. Although not a part of the evaluation per se, it is important to keep in mind that the textbook companies should also be available for trainings with instructors after you adopt their book— whether to introduce the elements of the text, to train them on technology-related ancillaries, or anything in between.

1.2.2 WHAT TO CONSIDER

Having discussed who has a role in the selection process, it is also, of course, of primary importance to decide what factors to take into consideration. What follows are a series of considerations that should come into play in the process of evaluating and ultimately adopting a text. Things to keep in mind are what theories of language learning and teaching guide the text and how they are evidenced in the layout of the text itself, what support is provided for teachers and

students, what materials accompany the text, and how the text can accommodate different semesters or articulations. These considerations are by no means
the only ones to consider, and each program, language, or institution will have
to consider their specific situations. But by asking these questions, the LPD will
be sure to have considered the most essential facets of a textbook program.

What theory, methodology, or premise drives the text?   Of paramount
importance is the underlying theory or methodological premise of the text, and
whether the theory and methodology are not only current but also aligned with
your program's mission and style (e.g., Williams, 1983) and with the teaching
approaches favored by the LPD and instructors. The reality is that most introductory, and even intermediate to some extent, textbooks cover the same basic
grammar and vocabulary; so what becomes most important for the LPD is finding a book "whose approach is compatible with the orientation of the student
body, corps of instructors, and departmental philosophy" (Schultz, 2005, p. 64).
In this respect, the LPD's task is to determine the texts that do match with the
philosophy of the language program and then to select from among them,
using a clear set of criteria.

It is possible to approach the new textbook adoption process as an
opportunity to embrace a change and to move toward a new philosophical
approach to language teaching. This can often be the case when an LPD is
hired into an existing program and would like to make some basic changes in
how language instruction in the classroom works. Such a change in direction
is possible with a new text, but the LPD needs to recognize that in these cases
the adjustment to the new book may require more time and should be accompanied by professional development opportunities for the teaching staff, as well
as an additional time commitment for the LPD, who may simultaneously be
working towards tenure or other promotion benchmarks.

It can be difficult to find a text that meets every aspect of a program's
mission. It can also be difficult, depending on the text, to identify its underlying approach. The theoretical background of a text should be clearly stated in
the preface and evident in every chapter: How is material presented? How is
it practiced? How are students encouraged to interact? If these questions cannot be readily answered, it is possible that the text is not based on a coherent
theory of language learning and teaching, which may affect the decision to
adopt the text.

That said, however, most current textbook programs claim to be communicative in their philosophy and approach to second language teaching and
learning. Of course, the term *communicative* has come to mean so many different things that such claims may not provide much guidance to the underlying
approach of a textbook. It used to be the case that *communicative* meant that
it adopted a Natural Approach (e.g., Krashen & Terrell, 1983), but over time
the phrase evolved to mean that a text was proficiency oriented, and currently
it seems to mean simply that there are activities in which students speak to
each other. Such an interpretation covers most textbooks these days, so relying
simply on a *communicative* label for a text does not necessarily offer much

information. And it can make it hard to ascertain, from this perspective, what makes textbooks stand out from each other.

Another common approach to classifying texts in the last decade or so has been to claim that they are based on or follow the Standards, and work to incorporate the five Cs throughout. At the same time, however, the extent to which a text is truly organized around the Standards—versus adding in notes about how certain sections could comply with certain elements of the Standards—is often not as readily determinable. Many recent textbooks do focus on language in context and integrate connections with other academic disciplines (Shrum & Glisan, 2005; Shrum & Glisan, 2010; Terry, 2009), so these may represent a step in the right direction for those language programs that focus on the Standards. Regardless of whether it is the Standards, the Proficiency Guidelines, or some other guiding framework that informs the underlying theory of the text, the driving force should be clear.

How does the text present language as it is used? While we expect that all textbooks will present a basic combination of vocabulary and grammar, most would hope for a book that can present these linguistic elements as they are used in natural situations. As just discussed, most current textbooks do claim to present language as it is used, including variations in linguistic use, information on sociocultural norms, and other pragmatically relevant material so that students are equipped with appropriate cultural sensitivity and awareness. Again, the extent to which this is true is debatable, as is the extent to which this is truly realistic or possible in an introductory text. In light of such potential complications, LPDs should consider pragmatic goals for their programs, and ideally these would be clearly stated in the mission statement. For example, perhaps at introductory levels awareness and understanding of pragmatic and cultural norms is a sufficient goal, while productive skills in these areas are more logical for an intermediate program. With some beforehand consideration of what LPDs expect students to know and be able to do, the evaluation of this element of a textbook program can be carried out in a logical and sensible way.

Who will teach from the text and how? The earlier sections of this chapter addressed who should be involved in the process of evaluating and selecting textbooks for a language program. It is also important to consider the other side of the equation: Who will be using the textbook? Some texts may be easier to use than others because of a highly formulaic structure that includes a predictable scope and sequence, as well as predictable activity types in each chapter. Others may be more appealing to novice instructors because they offer a great deal of instructor annotations to help with lesson planning. Such books may have advantages for programs where the instructors are primarily adjuncts or inexperienced TAs with little opportunity for mentoring. On the other hand, in a program that relies on more experienced instructors, the LPD can be comfortable knowing that such instructors are often capable of supplementing the text as needed or of judging what portions of a text might require more or less class time. In the latter situation, the need for structured support in a text could be less significant a consideration than in the former situation. Similarly, native speakers and non-native speakers of the language being taught may have different needs when it comes to knowing how to explain the language and grammar (e.g., Canagarajah, 1999; Ferguson, 2005; Horwitz, 1987; Medgyes, 1992; Medgyes, 1994; Tajino & Tajino, 2000), and these differences are worthy of consideration as well.

Also important are program policies on uniformity across sections of mul-tisection courses and therefore, how much freedom coordinators or instructors have in designing their courses, lesson plans, and assessment materials. As dis-cussed in Chapter 3, many LPDs, or even institutions, insist on a degree of con-sistency across sections, both for fairness to students and ease of administration, and also to keep workloads at manageable levels for TAs and instructors whose work hours may be contractually limited. This is a delicate balancing act, and it is a policy that needs to be developed carefully and reassessed frequently.

How many courses or levels will the text serve?   The LPD should also consider the courses that may come before or after the ones for which the adoption is being considered, and adopt texts that can help ensure that learners will be prepared as they move through the sequence. Will students be prepared for future courses in terms of linguistic knowledge; skills in reading, writing, and speaking; and experience in discussing or analyzing texts of the type (lit-erary, cultural) that are the topics of those next-level-up courses? It cannot be the responsibility of an introductory course to ensure success at upper-level literature courses, but the LPD can select textbooks that work within the depart-mental courses as a whole.

Further, the importance of having a well-articulated vision that includes all levels of language instruction may not apply to all programs or LPDs. But for those who coordinate or oversee more than one level, it can be a key feature. Schultz (2005) raises a number of questions that are crucial to text selection; although she focuses on intermediate levels, the points raised are relevant to decisions at any level. For example, how should language be presented in contemporary, practical contexts? Should we focus on high ("big *C*") culture or everyday ("little *c*") culture (e.g., Brooks, 1975), and why? What skills and what degree of mastery should be expected? What amount of emphasis should be placed on literature?

Beyond basic language courses, the issue is even more complicated as we consider upper-division courses in literature, culture, or linguistics and their relationship to the language program. These are important aspects to consider as we ponder articulation across levels. Do the textbooks chosen for lower-division courses help prepare students for upper-level coursework? Are there third- and fourth-year textbooks that cater to the needs of the learners who come from the first- and second-year programs? To what extent is the LPD responsible for addressing such issues?

How does the text help students?   A related and equally important ques-tion to ask is the extent to which the textbook offers guidance and assistance to the students who use it, beyond the standard presentation and practice of material. Does the textbook cater to the needs of second language learners (e.g. Williams,

1983)? In other words, does the book offer assistance designed to help students be better learners by offering suggestions for learning strategies, self-study notes, or additional resources (e.g., web-based activities, additional practice)?

The LPD may also ask if the text caters to the needs of various types of learners, such as heritage or third language learners, or nontraditional (e.g., older, returning students, or students simultaneously working full-time) student populations. It is important to remember as well that learners differ with respect to a vast array of factors, from social and cultural to psychological and academic (e.g., Gardner, 2000; Skehan, 1991). Depending on the needs of the particular program, these issues may be more or less relevant, but a good text should ensure that students are given the tools they need to succeed.

What comes with the text?   Increasingly, a textbook is more than just the textbook, and the LPD must consider the ancillary materials that are or can be included in the program. Such packages used to mean the basic book plus audiocassettes, sample tests, and preprinted overhead transparencies. Now, however, the possibilities have expanded exponentially. Audio programs can come in various formats, ranging from audiocassettes to CDs to digital files that may be downloaded to iPods or other MP3 players. Most programs include video components (on VCR, DVD, or digitally available online) as well. We still expect testing programs to use in part, if not in their entirety. Few instructors regularly use transparencies anymore, although textbooks still tend to offer this ancillary for those who do; they also offer PowerPoint presentations and other materials in an effort to further reduce the instructor's workload. Most texts have their own websites or course management system (either stand-alone or integrated with popular systems, such as WebCT or Blackboard), which offer unique social networking opportunities to students (e.g., chatting, blogging, podcasting, wikis). In a world in which demand for hybrid and distance-learning courses continues to grow (see Chapter 6 for a discussion of the role of technology in language programs), these expanded opportunities may prove more valuable.

By considering the needs of instructors and students, the LPD can establish which ancillary components are essential, which are beneficial but not necessary, and which are unimportant or undesirable. Increasingly, these materials are being integrated with the textbook, such that they may soon cease to be considered as ancillary to the program.

Despite the number of textbooks on the market, particularly in Spanish, it is certain that no single textbook fulfills all the criteria discussed here. It is the role of the LPD, however, to prioritize the language program's needs in a textbook package and then decide which are absolutely necessary in a textbook and which are less important.

2. DIFFICULT ISSUES

Before discussing the more practical aspects of assessing a textbook, however, other issues need to be addressed. These relate to the ethics of textbook selection and how to handle difficult situations, ranging from resistance to change, to relationships and pressure from publishers, or when the LPD is an author of a textbook. These issues can come up often, and if the LPD is not equipped to handle them, they can result in uncomfortable situations.

2.1 Resistance to Change

Although the prospect of redesigning a language program or adopting a new text can be an exciting time that the LPD eagerly anticipates, there also may be other people who are resistant to the change. Multiple factors can motivate team members' resistance, ranging from loyalty to fear. Regardless of the reason, the LPD will want to assess the resistance and work to overcome it whenever possible.

Some team members may maintain a sense of loyalty to the previous text program, either out of personal connection to the materials or because of a true belief in the philosophy underlying the program. Others simply may be resistant to change out of a fear of the unknown—which in the case of textbooks can mean new technologies to learn, new philosophies to embrace, and new structures to give to their classrooms. Finally, there are issues of time commitment that a new textbook will always entail. Some instructors may be very comfortable reusing the same lesson plans and activities semester after semester, and a new text is threatening to this comfort level. In other cases, such as with adjuncts who may be working different jobs or teaching several different courses, the reluctance is based more on the sheer lack of time available to start from scratch. It cannot be denied that the process of changing textbooks is time consuming, takes energy and initiative, and requires at least a yearlong commitment to the new text; it is not for the fainthearted. However, if pedagogical and methodological concerns mandate the process, it needs to be done, even in the face of resistance.

In all these cases, however, the LPD can help ease the transition. Involving members in the evaluation and selection process will help allay many of the fears of the unknown, and the existence of a well-defined mission statement will make more evident the choice of one text over another—even one that supposes a new approach to teaching, and can help assuage discontent over new methodologies and theories. Furthermore, providing comprehensive professional development for team members will help the transition at all levels, including an introduction to the text and its ancillaries and technologies. (Chapter 5 discusses instructor development and education, an issue of great importance at all times in a language program, but especially when contemplating a change in materials.) Finally, regarding issues of time, it is important to respect the work that team members put into the courses they coordinate or teach, and to recognize that any new text will necessarily involve additional time commitments. The LPD can provide sample syllabi and lesson plans to help those with limited time during the semester. Depending on the program structure and the institution, it also may be possible to grant level coordinators a course release in recognition of the extra time they will have to put in during the first semester or year of a new textbook.

2.2 Special Interests

Other uncomfortable situations can arise with respect to interpersonal relationships and interactions. The scenarios I discuss here can be termed "special interest" cases in that they involve additional considerations beyond the text itself. Among these are when team members have relationships with authors or publishers; when the LPD is a textbook author; and the nature of the relationship between the LPD and the publisher.

2.2.1 RELATIONSHIPS WITH AUTHORS OR TEXTBOOK REPRESENTATIVES

Occasionally, the LPD or other team members will have friends or acquaintances who are on the authoring team of the books under consideration. Others may be friends with the textbook representative or have some other relationship with a publisher, independent of the language textbook situation. In and of themselves these relationships are not a problem, but they could result in team members favoring (or disfavoring) a particular text for reasons that may not directly relate to language pedagogy. The LPD needs to be aware of the potential issues in evaluating texts, and although there is no way to control such a situation, the use of a well-structured evaluation rubric (see Section 4.3) can help keep the focus on the features of the text itself.

2.2.2 LPD AS TEXTBOOK AUTHOR

A potentially problematic situation can arise when the LPD is the author of a textbook. In and of itself, of course, it is not problematic that LPDs put their expertise and experiences into practice in designing a textbook that fulfills their needs and correlates with their views on language teaching and learning. But are there ethical concerns with using your textbook in a program that you direct? From the outside one might claim that yes, there are. At the same time, though, after putting the extensive time and effort in to developing what you believe to be the best text (otherwise, why would you have done it?), why would you then turn around and choose a different text? The problems come in when considering issues of textbook evaluation and adoption, who can gain from the adoption, and any possible conflicts of interest.

In general, if LPDs write textbooks, the assumption is that their programs will use those books. But is this adoption automatic, with no further discussion of textbook selection and no evaluation process? If this is the case, and the LPD then determines the text without consultation, the reasons behind this choice should be made very clear to the rest of the team, and the LPD should be able to explain and articulate the benefits of her or his own text over the other possibilities.

In the case of a program using a book written by the LPD, there is always a potential conflict of interest, or at the very least the perception of such a conflict. Does the LPD benefit personally from adoption of his or her textbook? Of course, the answer should be no. Some institutions have policies to address conflict of interest, for example, requiring that the royalties from the author's own institution not be returned to the author but instead donated to the institution or department. But other institutions do not have such a policy. In the absence of any institutional policy, the LPD should decide to create a program-wide policy of no material benefit. Many LPD authors, for example, request that the royalties generated from their own institution adoptions be put into a fund for the graduate students in the department, to facilitate their research and travel.

Even when the LPDs have no material benefit from the adoption of their textbooks, the perception of such a conflict of interest can persist—among team members and among students using the text. For this reason, it is important for the LPD to have a clear and publicized policy to explain the reality of the situation.

Therefore, before adopting the LPD's textbook or a text written or sold by someone otherwise affiliated with the program, the LPD should check the institution's policies on authoring and conflict of interest. If there is no problem in making the adoption, then she or he will have to consider what arrangements will be necessary to ensure that students, faculty, and administrators are treated fairly and do not feel pressured. Finally, the process of ongoing evaluation and assessment is even more important when using a book that was authored locally, because the tendency is to not want to critique too much—which can result in continuing to use a text that may no longer suit the needs of the program.

2.2.3 PRESSURE FROM PUBLISHERS

Although textbook adoption decisions are based on pedagogical, methodological, and programmatic concerns, publishers may offer a variety of incentives as the LPD considers adopting their programs. Some of these incentives may be seen as beyond what is considered ethical, however, and it is the LPD's task to determine which incentives fall within professional boundaries and which do not.

For example, many textbook companies try to attract students by offering low pricing or cost-effective solutions such as renting textbooks or creating different package options. Companies may offer incentives to the adopting department, often in forms such as computers for the instructor offices or other comparable materials. Other incentives can be made directly to the instructors or even the LPD, such as offering funding to attend conferences, hiring the instructors or LPD to pilot a program, or even offering excessive payment to perform professional duties such as participating in a focus group or serving as a consultant. While low prices or cost-effective solutions would rarely be considered unethical, incentives such as computers and the like would probably be considered questionable by most LPDs. However, the situations in between fall within a gray area where it is not always so clear to determine if the incentive is professionally legitimate or if it crosses into the realm of "buying an adoption."

In these gray areas, the issue for the LPD is first and foremost to always exercise discretion and discernment in determining whether an incentive is within professional boundaries. A good rule of thumb in these cases is whether the payment or incentive goes to a program in general or to an individual; the latter cases are those that warrant closer examination. The situation is not always clear, however, and the LPD needs to be ready to seek advice whenever she or he is unsure of the ethics of a particular offer. Other LPDs are a great resource in this case, as are department chairs or deans. Finally, it is also the LPD's responsibility to decide whether offers from publishers that appear to be unethical should be dealt with in some way. Should they be reported to colleagues or other LPDs? Does the LPD have the responsibility to the profession as a whole to report this kind of behavior? I do not have an answer for this last question, but it is worth pondering.

Luckily, extreme cases of lack of ethical behavior do not seem to be very frequent. In the survey I conducted, almost every respondent indicated that they had heard of such situations, although only one had experienced it personally. This person indicated that she or he had not accepted these offers, although the other respondents replied that they had heard of cases in which the offers were accepted as well as those in which they were not. In an ideal world, such ethical considerations as these would not come into play in making our decisions. On the chance that they might, however, the LPD should be prepared to handle them in a professional and responsible manner.

3. EVALUATING

Although we know what we want in a textbook, the evaluation process can be difficult. We may find ourselves choosing a textbook based on a gut feeling, based on the reputation of a book or its authors, because we know of other LPDs and other programs that use it, because we know one of the authors, and so on. Although all are considerations to take into account, such decisions are inevitably less reliable than a systematic and rigorous criterion-based evaluation. It is for this reason that we should be sure to have a well-established and predetermined set of criteria on which to base our decisions.

3.1 Using Checklists for Evaluation

When we evaluate textbooks for adoption, we can approach the task from different perspectives. We can choose to go the impressionistic route, in which case one can pick a book based on an impression or other general criteria that are difficult to quantify or analyze. In general, according to Ansary and Babaii (2002),

> Textbook evaluation has thus far been ad hoc, with teachers trying to make decisions based on such unreliable and simplistic criteria as "appropriateness of grammar presentation" (Ur, 1996), "functional load" (Sheldon 1988), "competence of the author" (Tucker, 1975), etc. Strangely enough, some choices have been made on the basis of such simplistic criteria as "popularity." That is to say, if a book sells well, it must be doing something right, then. (p. 4)

However, assuming that we want to go about our adoption process more systematically, "it is therefore more desirable to follow established guidelines which allow for a recognition of the strengths (and deficiencies) of the text-books available, for their comparison, and eventually for the choice of the most suitable one" (Paradowski, 2010, para. 1). The next question, of course, is how to create such guidelines.

Many textbook evaluation checklists are available (e.g., Byrd, 2001; Cunningsworth, 1995; Skierso, 1991, as well as those offered at the end of this chapter). It is quite common for LPDs to create their own checklists or rubrics, usually adapted from existing ones. More likely, however, is that most "teachers believe that there is no such thing as a 'global' checklist as different learning-teaching situations warrant different approaches in evaluation" (Mukundan, 2007, p. 81). While Mukundan laments the fact that there is no "global" check-list and proposes a method by which to create one, it is also likely that there probably is not a single rubric that could meet the needs of all programs, languages, methodologies, and personnel. Ansary and Babaii (2002) agree that while there may not ever be a neat formula, we should develop and apply a "set of universal characteristics [that] will help make textbook evaluation a coherent, systematic and thoughtful activity" (p. 8).

Many programs have rubrics, checklists, or evaluation forms for assessing textbooks and other pedagogical materials. Short of those that are published (see previous references), it can be hard to find copies of such forms. Although the LPDs who responded to my online survey indicated that they used a check-list to evaluate texts (90% use these tools), none were willing to share their instruments with me. Even fewer are published online, given that LPDs would not have a reason to make them publicly available. However, as a result of reviewing various publications, searching online, and culling personal connections, the appendix at the end of the chapter includes some sample evaluation forms. Some are structured around the Standards; others are arranged more generally to reflect the primary interests or goals of the author. All contain elements that can be beneficial to the LPD looking to assess an array of texts.

3.2 Continuing Evaluation: Reflecting on the Text

After having decided on a text, the temptation is to think that the evaluation work is done. However, after the adoption is made, there is an opportunity for true ongoing evaluation. We should not forget Mukundan's (2007) recommendation, as part of his three-step, long-term text evaluation plan, to engage in reflective journaling to document the effectiveness of the newly adopted text. Reflection has become an increasingly popular technique in education in general, and particularly in teacher education (e.g., Boud, Keogh, & Walker, 1995; Brookefield, 1995; Hatton & Smith, 1995; Schon, 1987) and foreign language teacher preparation (Brandt, 2008; Hanson, 2011; Lord & Lomicka, 2007; Richards, 1990; Richards & Lockhart, 1994; among others). A reflective journal is used to document experiences in the classroom (or in this case, with the text-book) and try to understand those experiences.

The application of this type of evaluation and analysis to the textbook is a logical next step and could provide unique supplementary information to the ongoing textbook evaluation process. When using the newly adopted text, instructors should be urged to consider questions such as:

- What portions of the text work well with your students, and why?
- What portions of the text do not work well in your courses, and why?
- Do you take advantage of the resources available to you in the text?
- How do students react to vocabulary presentations, grammar explanations, exercises, and so on?
- Do students understand the underlying theoretical premise of the textbook?
- Do students take advantage of the resources available to them?
- Think of a successful class period you taught with this text. What made it work?
- Think of an unsuccessful class period you taught with this text. What made it problematic?

These kinds of responses will necessarily be personal, individual, and variable. As a sole source of information they probably would not be extremely valuable, especially when trying to consider the needs of a large program with multiple (and varied) instructors. However, when taken in conjunction with the analysis provided through checklists or rubrics, they may offer insights that can explain perceived strengths and weaknesses.

4. CONCLUSION

Choosing the right textbook for a language program is a complex but crucial process. This chapter has examined some of the key elements of the textbook evaluation process, ranging from when to evaluate to who is involved in the decisions, what features to consider, and to how to carry out an assessment. Upon deciding on a textbook, however, the LPD must remember that evaluation is an ongoing process. Textbook choice, like other administrative and programmatic decisions, should be revisited regularly.

Questions for Reflection

1. To what extent have you been involved in reviewing or assessing textbooks, either for your own use or for use in a language program? What tools and techniques have you used in text evaluations? Were they effective? Have you engaged in both predictive and retrospective evaluation? For what purposes and with what timelines did these processes occur?
2. If you were to develop your own evaluation rubric, how would you structure it? What aspects of the examples included in this chapter do you like? Are there aspects of the examples that you do not find useful or relevant?

3. Consider the textbook you currently use (either in the courses you take or in the program you coordinate). How was it chosen? By whom? By what process or procedure? Are you and your colleagues generally satisfied with the text? Why or why not?

4. What do you consider to be the role of the textbook in a basic (beginning, intermediate) language program? How can LPDs and instructors ensure that the right amount of emphasis is placed on the textbook?

Suggestions for Further Reading

Ansary, H., & Babaii, E. (2002). Universal characteristics of EFL/ESL textbooks: A step towards systematic textbook evaluation. *The Internet TESL Journal, 8*(2). Retrieved from http://iteslj.org/Articles/Ansary-Textbooks

> A summary of characteristics common to many ESL textbooks along with comparative evaluation procedures from various instructors; although related to ESL, it offers an interesting perspective on how different people approach textbook evaluation.

Blyth, C. (2009). From textbook to online materials: The changing ecology of foreign language publishing in the era of digital technology. In M. Evans (Ed.), *Foreign language learning with digital technology* (pp. 179–202). London, United Kingdom: Continuum.

> A discussion of the role of textbook programs in foreign language classrooms with an emphasis on new technologies and the changes implied in their increased adoption.

Byrd, P. (2001). Textbooks: Evaluation for selection and analysis for implementation. In M. Celce-Murcia (Ed.), *Teaching English as a second or foreign Language*, 3rd ed. (pp. 415–429). Boston, MA: Heinle Cengage.

> An overview of factors involved in textbook selection and evaluation (in ESL, but relevant to other languages as well).

http://www.denisesantos.com/research.htm

> Online bibliography of published works that consider the role of textbooks.

APPENDIX

Examples of textbook evaluation forms

EXAMPLE 1: GILLIAN LORD, UNIVERSITY OF FLORIDA

How to Assess the Textbook

- Look over the assessment form to familiarize yourself with the kind of information I'm asking you to review.
- Read the draft of the Lower Division Spanish Program (LDSP) goals and objectives.
- If you are not familiar with the *Standards for Foreign Language Learning* (also known as the five Cs), read over the short summary (attached).
- Read the introduction/preface of the textbook (usually there is a preface for the instructor as well as for the student; read both).
- Check in the preface and/or the back cover to make sure you're aware of what ancillaries come with the text (Web, CD, resources, etc.).
- Examine the scope and sequence (list of chapters and what is covered in each chapter); consider as you do this that half of the book will be used in one semester, the second half in the next semester, although students can place into any semester.
- Pick a minimum of ONE chapter in the book, not the first or last but somewhere in the middle, and read through it very carefully. (Please consult with the other person reviewing the same text as you so that you pick *different* chapters.) Consider the chapter both from your perspective as an instructor and also from the perspective of a potential student. Pay special attention to:
  - Length of chapter
  - Components of chapter; how chapter is divided
  - Grammar explanations and practice
  - What skills are taught and when (e.g., reading, listening, speaking)
  - Language used (English or Spanish)
  - Culture
  - Others

When you think you have gotten a good feel for the textbook, please fill out the form, including your numerical assessment as well as the comments and open-ended questions.

Textbook Review Form

Your name:	
Textbook:	
Publisher:	
Year of publication:	
Current edition:	

Please rate each statement on the scale of 1 to 7 indicated below, based on your assessment of the textbook. Be sure to provide detailed comments explaining your ratings, as I will consider both the number and the prose in determining finalists. (If you are completing this form by hand, circle the appropriate number; if electronically, you may simply delete all of the numbers except your rating.)

1	2	3	4	5	6	7
Unacceptable	Inadequate	Weak	Average	Good	Very strong	Excellent

Provides enough information for a two-semester course	1 2 3 4 5 6 7
Comments:	
Is appropriate for the level(s) of learners for which it will be used (for intermediate, has to accommodate students from high school, community college, our courses, etc.; for beginner, has to be suitable for true beginners as well as those with some background, for both the five-day-a-week and the three-day-a-week courses, etc.)	1 2 3 4 5 6 7
Comments:	
Has a logical division of material between chapters	1 2 3 4 5 6 7
Comments:	
Has a logical division of material within chapters	1 2 3 4 5 6 7
Comments:	
Provides clear and accurate explanations of grammatical structures	1 2 3 4 5 6 7
Comments:	
Presents useful and relevant vocabulary items in a logical manner	1 2 3 4 5 6 7
Comments:	
Encourages communicative interaction in a variety of contexts and situations	1 2 3 4 5 6 7
Comments:	
Provides complete and accurate cultural information on a variety of Spanish-speaking regions	1 2 3 4 5 6 7

Comments:							
Successfully incorporates each of the 5 Cs:							
-COMMUNICATION	1	2	3	4	5	6	7
-CULTURES	1	2	3	4	5	6	7
-CONNECTIONS	1	2	3	4	5	6	7
-COMPARISONS	1	2	3	4	5	6	7
-COMMUNITIES	1	2	3	4	5	6	7
Comments:							
Helps students take control of their own learning by presenting strategies for language acquisition and studying	1	2	3	4	5	6	7
Comments:							
Help instructors administer the most effective courses possible by providing tips, methodological information, answer keys, etc.	1	2	3	4	5	6	7
Comments:							
Provides an attractive and functional Web-based Student Activities Manual	1	2	3	4	5	6	7
Comments:							
Provides additional resources for students online	1	2	3	4	5	6	7
Comments:							
Provides a useful Instructor Resource Manual	1	2	3	4	5	6	7
Comments:							
Provides additional communicative activities for use during class time	1	2	3	4	5	6	7
Comments:							
Provides PowerPoints/lesson plans for instructors	1	2	3	4	5	6	7
Comments:							

Overall Rating:

1	2	3	4	5	6	7
Unacceptable	Inadequate	Weak	Average	Good	Very strong	Excellent

Open-Ended Questions:

What are the greatest strengths of this textbook?

What are the most problematic weaknesses of this textbook?

Would you like to teach with this textbook? Why or why not?

If there is anything you want to add about this text, please do so here.

EXAMPLE 2: GENERAL

Original source unknown, adapted and shared by Tammy Jandrey Hertel, Lynchburg College, and Gretchen Sunderman, Florida State University

Name of Textbook:
Publisher:

Using the Likert scales, evaluate the following statements (5 = strongly agree, 4 = agree, 3 = neutral, 2 = disagree, 1 = strongly disagree). Then in the space provided explain your evaluation as needed.

GRAMMAR					
Covers a range of grammatical features.	5	4	3	2	1
Sequencing of grammar coincides with the course objectives (i.e., communicative).	5	4	3	2	1
Grammatical concepts are meaningfully recycled throughout the text.	5	4	3	2	1
Explanations are clear, concise, and at an appropriate level.	5	4	3	2	1
The majority of grammar exercises/tasks are meaningful (i.e., meaningfulness is maintained even when there is a focus on form)	5	4	3	2	1
EXERCISES					
A wide range of interactional contexts are addressed (discussions, reports, interviews, playing games, conducting surveys, dialogues, role-plays, etc.)	5	4	3	2	1
Exercises represent real-life tasks.	5	4	3	2	1
Exercises are personalized and creative.	5	4	3	2	1
Tasks promote strategic competence (circumlocution, rephrasing, etc.)	5	4	3	2	1
Tasks address pronunciation and intonation.	5	4	3	2	1
Tasks address a variety of learning styles (deductive, inductive, etc.)	5	4	3	2	1
Exercises incorporate authentic cultural material.	5	4	3	2	1
Pair and group work is included appropriately.	5	4	3	2	1

READING					
Readings are related to the goals and themes of the chapters.	5	4	3	2	1
A variety of passages from various Hispanic cultures are included.	5	4	3	2	1
A variety of genres are represented (poetry, short story, newspaper article, etc.)	5	4	3	2	1
Authentic texts serve as the basis of the readings.	5	4	3	2	1
Meaningful prereading activities are included (i.e., to activate learners' schemata).	5	4	3	2	1
Meaningful postreading activities are included.	5	4	3	2	1
WRITING					
Exercises are related to the goals and themes of the chapters.	5	4	3	2	1
Meaningful prewriting activities are included (i.e., to activate learners' schemata).	5	4	3	2	1
Meaningful postwriting activities are included (i.e., synthesis activities)	5	4	3	2	1
There is a process approach to guide students' writing.	5	4	3	2	1
LISTENING					
Listening activities are related to the goals and themes of the chapters.	5	4	3	2	1
Meaningful prelistening activities are included.	5	4	3	2	1
Meaningful postlistening activities are included.	5	4	3	2	1
The provided tasks (pre-, during, and post-) require that students focus on different skills (e.g., information gathering, listening for the gist, cultural information).	5	4	3	2	1
A wide range of dialects are represented.	5	4	3	2	1
VOCABULARY					
A variety of presentational devices are included (e.g., pictures, questions, readings).	5	4	3	2	1
Meaningful practice activities are included.	5	4	3	2	1
The vocabulary chosen is level appropriate.	5	4	3	2	1

CULTURE					
Culture is a central focus throughout the textbook (i.e., not relegated to cultural snapshots)	5	4	3	2	1
Information from a wide range of Hispanic countries is included.	5	4	3	2	1
Information is presented regarding both Culture (e.g., art, literature) and culture (e.g., daily routines)	5	4	3	2	1
Activities promote sociolinguistic competence (i.e., what is appropriate in specific contexts).	5	4	3	2	1
AUDIENCE					
Chapter themes are both relevant and interesting to the target population.	5	4	3	2	1
The textbook is learner-friendly (e.g., provides strategies, explanatory tools).	5	4	3	2	1

TEACHING ISSUES					
The sequence of material in the textbook facilitates lesson planning.	5	4	3	2	1
The instructor's edition provides helpful suggestions and ideas for presenting the material.	5	4	3	2	1
Technology is soundly incorporated in both the textbook and in all ancillary materials.	5	4	3	2	1

ANCILLARY MATERIALS:

Which of the following ancillary materials are included?

For students:

_____ Workbook

_____ Laboratory manual

_____ In-class audio for instructors

_____ Tapes/CD-ROM for text

_____ Tapes/CD-ROM for workbook

_____ Supplementary activities (e.g., Internet)

_____ Others (explain)

For instructors:

_____ In-class tapes

_____ Videos

_____ Test bank

_____ Supplementary activities (e.g., Internet)

_____ Others (explain)

FINAL EVALUATION:

EXAMPLE 3: GENERAL

Paradowski, M. B. (2010). Foreign Language Textbook Evaluation Chart. Unpublished manuscript.

Textbook Evaluation Chart Course: Book:					
	1	2	3	4	5
The Structure of the Book					
Does the book have a wisely designed framework and a transparent layout? Is the content clearly organised and sequenced?					
Is the structure of the unit lucid? Is there a logical progression of activities within each unit?					
Are the units not overloaded?					

Syllabus Content					
Does the textbook meet your syllabus's requirements?					
Does it cover a balanced selection of all the language skills (listening/speaking/reading/writing/interaction/mediation) your students will need?					
Are the subsystems your syllabus aims to develop (morphosyntax, lexicon, phonetics, phonology, pragmatics) provided for?					
Does the book seem appealing and enjoyable?					
Is it the appropriate age level?					
Is the difficulty level appropriate? If need be, is it adaptable for use with a varied-level class?					
Does it link with previous and upcoming courses?					
Does the book suit the size of your group? Is it designed for group work or [autonomous learning]?					
Does the number of teaching hours it is calculated for meet your course's specifications?					
Does it suit the learners' L1 background? Is the approach to teaching grammar contrastive?					
Do you approve of the approach and teaching method implemented in the textbook?					
Are the topics and tasks varied, so that they accommodate different learner levels, learning needs, styles and strategies, interests, etc.?					
Presentation of New Grammatical Structures:					
Are the presentations systematic? Are they linked to what has been taught earlier? Are they related to the learners' L1?					
Are the rules true and reliable? Do they represent the underlying grammar rules satisfactorily?					
Are the rules clear and conceptually parsimonious (i.e., devoid of metalinguistic jargon)?					
Are they simple enough, but not at the expense of truth?					
Is grammar taught in a logical, purposeful, meaningful way? Does the book, apart from low-order rules (i.e., rules of formation) also present higher-order rules (i.e., rules of use)?					
Are there sufficient visual illustrations of grammar points (in the form of diagrams, tables, flowcharts, colours, etc.) to aid learners with preference for the visual modality?					

Language Practice and Tasks (activities, exercises):				
Does the book contain an adequate amount of activities to ensure ample practice in all the skills the students are supposed to master?				
Is there the right proportion between accuracy and fluency practice?				
Does the book present situations and tasks that are appealing, motivating, and purposeful in themselves and that are not merely mechanical language drills?				
Are they purposeful, pertinent to, and useful for your courses? Are the learners likely to perform similar tasks in real-life situations?				
Does the book include enough communicative tasks to ensure plentiful learner activity and independent language use? Does it allow moving away from the teacher-centred model?				
Simultaneously, does it allow for sufficient control, or are the tasks likely to pose classroom organization and management problems? Are these likely to overshadow the utility of the tasks?				
Are the particular activity types suitably chosen?				
Is the length of the tasks appropriate? If they are long, are they broken up into digestible chunks?				
Are the instructions unambiguous and understandable (if appropriate, in the learners' L1)?				
Is the language recycled? Are progressive revision units or regular test sections provided?				
The Teacher's Perspective				
Is your overall impression of the book favourable?				
Is it teacher-friendly? Is it easy for the teacher to use? Is it well organised, with an alphabetical index and a table of contents? Is there an instructor's annotated edition with an answer key to help you plan your activities? Does it provide adequate guidance?				
If the book does more than your syllabus requires, does it offer you more possibilities and flexibility, or is it just an additional redundant burden				
Does using the book entail arduous and time-consuming preparation?				
Is it accompanied by supplementary resources (a workbook, audio CDs, and/or video tapes/DVD, etc.)? Are these materials useful and interesting? Can the book be easily used without the extras?				
Does it help you to prepare for standardized tests if such are required by your school?				

The Students' Needs					
Do the topics reflect or relate to the students' lives and needs? Does the book present situations in which they are likely to find themselves?					
If not, is the content still likely to be genuinely interesting for the learners?					
Is the communication in the book genuine? Are the texts in the book taken from authentic sources? Is the language up to date and true to life? Do the speakers in the recording change?					
Is the book's appearance—its cover, graphic design, illustrations, and colour—appealing and attractive for your students, or does it seem unexciting and trivial in content?					
Is there enough diversity?					
Does the book facilitate autonomous self-study? Are clear language summaries provided? Can it be used by students unaided (e.g., during illness and consequent absence from classes)?					
Is the book affordable, within the means of the learners, parents, or school? Are the extra materials costly, or are they included in the price of the book?					
Does the book succeed in avoiding detrimental gender, racial, national, cultural, and religious stereotypes and prejudices?					

EXAMPLE 4: GENERAL

Provided by Lara Ducate, University of South Carolina

Criteria/Scores	0 (N/A, or not at all)	1 (Yes, but barely)	2 (Yes, to some extent)	3 (Most definitely)
1. There is an overview of the textbook at the beginning that lists the functions and structures that will be taught in each lesson.				
2. Objectives are clearly stated and are measurable.				
3. Standards are addressed in the way the tasks are designed.				
4. Tasks are communicative.				
5. Communicative tasks are contextualized.				

Criteria/Scores	0 (N/A, or not at all)	1 (Yes, but barely)	2 (Yes, to some extent)	3 (Most definitely)
6. Tasks are conducive for group/pair work.				
7. Task sequencing is logical.				
8. Integrates all three communication modes.				
9. Has good balance between meaningful and good mechanical drills.				
10. Grammar is presented in manageable chunks.				
11. Language level and cognitive demands correspond with learners' proficiency.				
12. Includes cultural aspect of L2 learning.				
13. Learners' attention is drawn to the input section of each lesson.				
14. Learners will know what is being taught/ learned in each chapter.				
15. It includes useful ancillary materials. Are they multimedia materials? Are they communicative?				
16. Cultural information is presented in a way that promotes critical thinking.				
17. Communicative tasks include a reason to listen.				
18. Reading texts have pre-, during-, and postreading tasks.				
19. Pictures and authentic materials are up-to-date and relevant.				
20. Listening texts have pre-, during-, and postlistening tasks.				

Scores:

50–60 = I would consider using this book in my FL course with no or with very few suggestions.

40–49 = I would consider using this book with a few reservations.

25–39 = I would most probably not use this book unless some important changes were made.

0–24 = I would not consider using this book in my FL course. Major improvement is needed.

CHAPTER 5

Hiring and Educating Instructors

A relatively common misperception is that teaching language is easy and that the ability to speak that language is sufficient preparation to teach it. Who has not heard comments, albeit in jest, about visiting the local Mexican restaurant to find teachers to cover sections of beginning Spanish? Leaving aside the many reasons to find such statements offensive, the truth is that those who are not directly involved in teaching or educating teachers often do not understand what goes into the creation and execution of a successful syllabus, lesson plan, or course. There are naturally gifted teachers who possess an innate talent for teaching and a presence in front of a classroom that simply cannot be taught. But for the most part, as Lee (1989) pointed out, "people are not born teachers! . . . Being a [language] major or a native speaker of [a language] does not qualify anyone to teach; there is so much more to learn and so much development to achieve" (p. 27). Luckily, it seems that many have come to realize this in recent years, and the jokes about trolling for graduate teaching assistants (TAs) at the local ethnic restaurant are diminishing. To be sure, "it is a positive sign that the profession has been putting an increased emphasis on preparing the future professoriate" (Maxim, 2005b, p. 19), as will be discussed throughout this chapter. However, Maxim also notes that a thorough investigation of the development that graduate student instructors (and by extension, all language instructors) receive is warranted. This chapter addresses the issues related to this type of professional development and the portions of it for which the language program director (LPD) is responsible. Although structures differ across institutions and the roles of LPD also vary widely, most LPDs will find themselves in charge of some aspects of hiring, educating, and evaluating instructors in their programs.

The chapter begins by discussing the process of hiring language instructors. Depending on the institution, the hiring could lie entirely with the LPD or it could be left to the committee that decides on graduate student admission. In either case, as well as in other possible scenarios, certain factors should be addressed when considering who will teach in the program. Next, the professional development that instructors receive is discussed, ranging from orientation to classes and workshops. Finally, the assessment and evaluation of instructors and their work both in and out of the classroom are addressed.

1. THE HIRING PROCESS

The importance of qualified and well-prepared instructors cannot be understated. The members of a language program are the face of the program to the students, and the members convey the implementation of the mission statement on a daily basis. Even though "one of the most important questions to ask is whether the candidate will fit the culture of the organization and conversely how well the organization will fit that candidate" White et al., 2008, p. 52), in many situations the LPD has little say in selecting the instructors in the program. In many universities the instructors are graduate students enrolled in the language program and work as instructors by virtue of their assistantships.

In institutions that rely more on adjuncts or faculty, the LPD may indeed have a larger role in hiring decisions. Even in programs whose instructors come exclusively from the graduate student body, the LPD should have some input in the selection process (see the discussion in the following sections). Regardless of who selects the language teaching staff, however, the responsibility of training these individuals rests with the LPD. What's more, if the LPD can provide "purposeful management, good internal communication, and collegiate culture," the instructors are likely to reciprocate with "commitment and loyalty" (White et al., 2008, p. 2). This "virtuous circle" (White et al., 2008, p. 2) allows a program to function well and gain success.

1.1 Criteria for Hiring

The criteria we use to select and hire instructors in our language programs depend largely on the type of program. In general, post-secondary language programs fall into two types: programs that are staffed largely by graduate students and programs that have few or no grad students and are staffed by full- or part-time faculty or adjuncts. The criteria we consider are necessarily different in these two cases.

For the first type, those staffed by graduate students, decisions on hiring those graduate students are generally made by a program or departmental admissions committee, which evaluates applicants based primarily on their suitability for graduate work. The committee may also consider language skills; but if not, then the LPD should assess the level of proficiency. Lee (1989) concurred that it is the job of the LPD to ascertain that potential graduate student instructors have the necessary language skills in both L1 and L2. (Most institutions require that international teaching assistants have achieved certain levels of English proficiency even if they will teach their native language.) This issue is not unique, of course, to foreign language, as English as a Second Language (ESL) programs often face similar problems (see Kaplan, 1997). Interestingly, Schulz (1980), in her review of language programs, noted that in their hiring criteria "not one indicated required test scores on a target-language proficiency test" among considerations for hiring TAs" (p. 2). Although there are standard measures of English proficiency, such as the TOEFL or the SPEAK test, fewer options exist for foreign languages, at least at advanced levels. In this respect, the responsibility for determining language ability generally comes down to the LPD listening to a recording or carrying out a short interview with potential instructors.

In my program, the LPD is a de facto member of the graduate studies committee, precisely to determine if the candidates are capable of teaching a beginner or intermediate language class entirely in the target language. The committee members trust my judgment, because to be successful in graduate-level coursework, candidates must possess a relatively high level of language proficiency anyway. The fact still remains, however, that our primary mission is to prepare future academics, and we often fail to connect this professional goal with the potential for success in the language classroom. I return to this issue in the final chapter of this book, since these conflicting goals can be difficult to balance for instructors, students, and administrators alike.

Either of the preceding types of program may also find itself in a situation in which insufficient numbers of graduate students are enrolled, and the LPD must look beyond the department to hire outside instructors. In these cases, the criteria used for hiring are generally language proficiency, teaching experience, and when possible, being in a cognate discipline (e.g., a graduate student in comparative literature may be better able to adapt to our class size and teaching styles than one in physics). In the case of departments that hire faculty and adjuncts from outside the university to teach elementary and intermediate language courses, the criteria often include language proficiency, an MA degree in a relevant discipline, and teaching experience. The institution may also place restrictions on these positions, ranging from a certain number of hours of relevant graduate-level coursework to other factors regarding eligibility.

Although of paramount importance in a program, the complex issue of language proficiency may often be difficult to handle. The LPD has to decide what constitutes sufficient proficiency to work in the program; this may be the ability to teach an entire course entirely in the target language, or it may be some other criterion. But even beyond that, the LPD needs to establish whether there should be a relationship between the level of instructor proficiency and the courses the individual is qualified to teach; for example, even if everyone in the program is at a particular level, are those who demonstrate stronger or more advanced language skills automatically assigned to higher-level courses? Are speaking skills more important than writing skills for some courses? One approach, which is the approach I take in my program, is to establish certain courses that provide maximum support and structure for the newest, or least experienced or least proficient instructors, such as the first-year courses. These have a master syllabus with considerable structure and prescribed day-to-day activities, all of which provide a solid framework for instructors to learn and develop. New instructors, in their first semester, observe experienced instructors at that same level and learn about lesson planning, classroom management, and the like as they sit in on those classes. In the intermediate courses, instructors are still given a common syllabus, but with a greater amount of flexibility in terms of the day-to-day delivery of instruction. At the third-year level, only the most experienced and linguistically proficient instructors are appointed, as there is freedom to develop more individual curricula.

We must also face the reality that non-native-speaking graduate students, especially those new to the MA level, may not yet demonstrate high proficiency levels. In fact, they often do not exceed those of graduating seniors, usually about an Intermediate High or Advanced Low on the American Council on the Teaching of Foreign Languages (ACTFL) proficiency scale. We hope, of course, that their proficiency will increase during their graduate studies, but it is important to be realistic. Furthermore, regardless of proficiency levels, the graduate students in a department are our responsibility, and the faculty (LPD and others) must work with them to help them to become effective teachers. That said, however, when hiring outside instructors from other departments, we can require more advanced proficiency, since we do not have the same obligation as we have to our own students.

Once the instructors are chosen, the LPD's work begins in earnest. Not only does our responsibility to our program and to our students require that we train and regularly evaluate instructors, but we also have a role in the future of the graduate students in our programs. "Job advertisements increasingly call for evidence of teaching effectiveness or an applicant's teaching philosophy" (Maxim, 2005b, p. 19), and even research institutions are focusing more on teaching philosophy and ability, documented in some cases by a teaching video to be supplied with other application materials. This is especially true in less commonly taught languages, where there may not be departmental faculty able to judge language proficiency. So it is in the LPD's best interest to establish a solid system for educating instructors, and it is ultimately in everyone's best interest that the language program prepare effective educators.

2. EDUCATION AND PROFESSIONAL DEVELOPMENT

Compared to other departments, language departments on the whole tend to train our instructors better. This is not to say that other departments do not care about their instructors, but rather that languages have recognized the importance of solid pedagogical training and have implemented concomitant programs for our instructors, more so than is evidenced in other areas. This has not always been the case:

> In fact, many of us learned to teach without formal training, with a book thrust into our hands in August and a demand to cover fifteen chapters by December. We muddled along, sometimes with the fresh enthusiasm of beginners, sometimes at the expense of our unwitting students. (Rava, 1991, p. 51)

However, we have come to realize that this is not true, and we know that "good teaching does not just happen by accident," and further that "ensuring that it does happen—and continues to do so—is one of the [LPD's] major responsibilities" (White et al., 2008). Even what we used to consider adequate preparation for our instructors may no longer be sufficient.

It is to everyone's benefit that our graduate students become well-prepared, competent language teachers. The graduate students benefit, of course, but so do the students in the language courses and the department as a whole. Although many students come to our classrooms to fulfill a requirement, we also need to remember that we may also be teaching future foreign language majors, and that a spark we ignite in a first-year course may inspire students to continue in their language studies.

Even recognizing the importance of education for language teachers, there tends to be "a great disparity in the kinds of training offered," as Waldinger (1990, p. 20) discovered more than two decades ago from a survey of PhD programs in French. Nonetheless, Waldinger did note that "almost every institution had an organized system for preparing future college teachers" (p. 20). Other data (e.g., Schulz, 1980) indicate that this has not always been the case, that not all departments have always provided education for their instructors, and that those that do, approach it in the same fashion.

2.1 How Instructor Education Happens

The respondents to my online survey, in their majority, indicated two or three primary sources of development for instructors: a preservice orientation, a teaching methods course, and occasionally, ongoing professional development opportunities and workshops. These components share the primary function of ensuring that instructors have the knowledge and skills needed to carry out their duties. These basic aspects of professional preparation are what White et al. (2008) refer to as the informational aspect: "giving your new employee all the information he or she needs to be able to do the job and successfully negotiate the first few weeks while they become accustomed to the work" (p. 58), which can range from payroll processing paperwork to information on pedagogical practices and the structure of the course syllabus. Another aspect of orienting and preparing instructors involves socialization, or "what we might call 'cultural' orientation: helping the new employee deal with and understand the culture of the [program], how things work, who is who, etc." (White et al., 2008, pp. 58–59). The latter can be accomplished through an orientation, individual meetings, printed materials such as a handbook, or a combination of these approaches.

New instructors need to know where to find resources on how and when their work will be evaluated and assessed. It is also wise to spell out the consequences of a less-than-satisfactory observation report to alleviate some of the pressure and fear. With instructors who are graduate students in the department, teaching assistantships are rarely revoked for poor teaching; on the contrary, it is our responsibility as LPDs to work with instructors to help them improve their pedagogical skills. Only on very rare occasions are TAships rescinded, and these cases have to do with egregious breaches of program or institutional policies (e.g., cancelling classes repeatedly, failing to administer exams according to the planned timeline, inappropriate relationships with students) rather than pedagogical issues. The following sections of this chapter deal with instructor orientation and professional development, as well as the evaluation process. I conclude with the rationale for and approaches to ongoing education and development.

2.2 Orientation

As mentioned earlier, all of the survey respondents indicated that the instructors in their language programs participate in some kind of orientation prior to beginning their teaching duties. In most cases these orientation sessions occur the week before the start of the semester, and they range from one to several days; the most common pattern is two to three days. In many institutions, department- or program-specific orientations must be coordinated with institution-wide orientations for incoming graduate students. A sample orientation agenda can be found at the end of this chapter.

It is common to divide the orientation session into two parts, one for new TAs and the other for returning graduate student instructors as well. Programs whose teaching staff includes adjuncts, lecturers, and other non-tenure-track faculty may have a different structure, given that these individuals may not be contractually obligated to attend such sessions. The financial saving to the institution for not having to compensate contingent faculty for professional development time is offset, unfortunately, by the lost opportunity to inform these instructors about the program structure, policies, and its teaching goals and methodologies. Furthermore, getting everyone involved in these orientations helps create collegiality and collaboration and promotes the creation of a productive team that can work together during the semester.

The fall orientation serves many purposes. In the most basic sense, it "provide[s] access to information about the program (including its mission, faculty, students, curriculum, resources, student services, and extracurricular activates), job expectations, and performance standards" (Soppelsa, 1997, p. 137) so that the instructors have a clear overview of how the program functions and what is expected of them within that function. Another key element of the orientation are the interpersonal relationships that are initiated: "The intense nature of the hours or days spent together helps create a positive work environment by fostering cooperation and collaboration, and helps everyone get acquainted" (Lee, 1989). From the LPD perspective, a collaborative environment is crucial because it creates the conditions for LPDs to become acquainted with their instructors. For the instructors, it is perhaps even more important, because it is the beginning of the process of imagining themselves as a close-knit working group. LPDs will agree that the best instructors, not just in terms of talent in the classroom but also for what they bring to the program, are those who connect with the group, feel themselves to be part of a team, and are happy to work together. This sense of collaboration and community takes root during these first few days of getting to know each other and working together.

The other essential component of these orientations is, of course, the introduction to language teaching in the program. In this respect, the orientation serves the "very immediate need" of preparing these instructors to "walk into a classroom and become a functioning member of a language program not of their own design. Since they are part of a larger whole, they need to know how to function in that light" (Lee, 1989, p. 21). Many new instructors have no prior teaching experience or, if they do have some experience, it is often in different settings (e.g., K–12). Other instructors may have a couple of years of post-secondary language teaching experience from a previous graduate program that may or may not share the methodological and curricular goals and objectives of the new program. So although some come to the presemester orientation as blank slates ready to adopt the specifics of their current language program, others may arrive with the belief that there is only one correct way to teach a language. The goal of the LPD in these cases is to widen the horizons of these individuals and over time, lead them to understand that all programs have their distinct methodological signature that when implemented coherently and with effective teaching practices, will lead to student learning.

As an example, the general format of the three-day orientation in Spanish at the University of Florida is presented in Table 1 and is described further. (A more detailed sample schedule is provided in the appendix.) From the survey responses, it appears that many of these elements are common to most programs. Elements included in other programs but not in this one are also described.

The orientation session begins with introductions. Some of the incoming instructors are familiar with the university and may know some of the experienced instructors; others know nobody and may feel quite overwhelmed. I usually introduce myself and describe my experience in teaching languages and directing the program, followed by the other members of the program team. We then ask the instructors to introduce themselves, explain where they are from, and give a bit of information on their teaching experience and what

TABLE 1 Components of the three-day orientation

Day 1	Welcome and introductions
	Introduction to program and policies
	Basic teaching principles
	Teaching examples
Day 2	Lesson planning and teaching with textbook X
	Sample activities for classroom use
	Breakout sessions with lead instructors and coordinators
Day 3	Microteaching
	University and departmental policies
	Course management system setup and use

they are studying. The goals of this simple activity are to encourage people to interact with each other and to set an upbeat tone and put everyone at ease. Refreshments (e.g., coffee and bagels, often provided by the sales representatives of the publishing company whose textbooks we use) on this first morning help establish an informal, friendly atmosphere. Because the information load of the orientation is so heavy, setting a positive, pleasant tone will increase the effectiveness of the session.

The next portion of the orientation focuses on administrative issues, starting with the policies and regulations that are explained in the handbook. We also talk about institutional requirements, such as those concerning the number and location of office hours required (e.g., in a university-assigned office, not in the library or a coffee shop). Although it can be tedious to present a great deal of administrative information, it is important that instructors learn about all such institutional policies and expectations at the outset to prevent confusion or complications later. It is also crucial that the instructors, especially those who have not taught before or who come from instructional settings where they had complete autonomy over their courses, understand that they represent the program, the department, and the institution and are contractually obliged to comply with the policies and philosophy of the language program. This is particularly important if instructors teach in multisection courses, where such things as instructional practices and grading policies and standards must be standardized across all sections of the course. It is helpful to lay out for the instructors the areas in which they exercise their professional autonomy and the areas in which they must adhere to established policies and norms. This topic is a complex one whose details shift over time, so LPDs will find themselves revisiting it throughout the semester.

How LPDs position themselves with respect to their programs is crucial to program functioning. If the instructors see the LPD as involved in and concerned about the program, observing classes and in daily contact with the coordinators, then they are likely to feel like a valuable part of a well-functioning team. If the LPDs position themselves as distant overseers of their programs with more of an evaluative role than a developmental one, instructors are likely to align themselves with their sections and their students, rather than see themselves as members of an integrated program.

Besides the administrative issues, the task of the first day is to introduce the instructors to the basic tenets of communicative language teaching. Although many programs offer a semester-long course on teaching methodology for new teaching assistants, the introduction to language teaching during the orientation gives new instructors a working understanding of what they need to know for the first weeks of class. I present a summary of the National Standards (the five Cs) and give some examples of how they could be incorporated into class activities. At our orientation we have instructors of beginning and intermediate language, so I make this session general and use examples from textbooks and curricula at both levels. My orientation is for instructors of only one language, but in a multilanguage environment examples can be given in various languages or even in English to illustrate the points in ways that everyone can understand.

The last essential element of the first day is to talk about target language use in the classroom. While LPDs hold different positions and establish different policies on this topic, most programs do have a language policy. I am a firm believer in the value of using the target language (almost) exclusively at all levels, even from the very beginning. Recently, ACTFL issued an official position statement advocating at least 90% target language use in the classroom at all levels (ACTFL, 2010). I give this statement to my instructors, and we read it together and discuss it. Novice instructors should be encouraged to aim for at least 90% target language use, although LPDs know that the reality will be a lower percentage. With experience and instruction in teaching methods, instructors find it easier over time to achieve near-100% use of the target language in class by both instructors and students. We also discuss ways to stay in the target language. The tips come from a variety of sources, including my own personal experience, but Curtain (n.d.) also provides an excellent overview of the reasons for advocating target language use as well as useful tips for encouraging instructors to stay in the target language.

The morning of the second day of orientation consists of a textbook walk-through. I want instructors to understand the philosophy behind our textbook, the layout of material in each chapter, and the scope and sequence, particularly with respect to the chapters they will cover in the first semester. An often-overlooked resource is the preface (to instructors and to students) of the textbook, which explains the book's philosophy and describes its components. I remember mentioning to a TA who had been with us for several years something about the second of two grammar presentations in each chapter, and she looked at me in surprise and said, "Oh, I didn't realize there were two in each chapter." Although this instructor was an effective teacher who always got positive evaluations from both the coordinators and her students, her effectiveness could have been enhanced if she had been aware of the underlying organization of the textbook. I have the instructors read the preface of their respective books and also map out the components of a single chapter to get a feel for the organization of the components and the sequence of activities in each chapter.

We discuss the philosophy that underlies the textbook, and we also compare everyone's chapter map (with the inevitable conclusion that all chapters share the same structure). I then walk though a sample chapter and point out features (additional resources, teacher notes, answer keys) and pedagogical aspects of the layout (e.g., pictures for vocabulary, if English is used for grammar explanation or in instructions, pair and group work, exercises). We also talk about how many class days are usually assigned to each chapter and share ideas about what to cover on each day. I encourage the instructors to change the order of sections if they feel it meets their needs better—move culture from day two to day one, postpone the reading to day three, and the like—as long as it does not affect the timing of a course-wide assessment or students' ability to complete online homework assignments (these are assigned at the course level rather than at the section level, which means that the deadlines cannot be changed).

Another crucial component of our orientation involves teaching the instructors how to use the online course management system that accompanies our textbook. In the more commonly taught languages, nearly all textbooks come with online ancillaries, now ranging from student activities manuals to video conferencing and social networking capabilities. The less commonly taught languages have fewer options, although publishers are beginning to make some of these resources available for textbooks in these languages as well. During orientation we show the instructors how the system works, how to create an account and set up their section(s), and how to accomplish such basic tasks as making assignments, grading assignments, and interacting with students via messages, announcements, or chat. We also make sure they know where to find additional resources for themselves (instructor resource manual, additional activities, technological support) and their students (additional machine-scored activities that provide feedback to the student without the instructor's involvement). I often ask a representative of our textbook company to give a presentation on the online resources associated with our textbook. It is important to limit this session to the basics, saving the rich array of advanced options of the online platforms for future semesters. Anyone who wants to learn more or experiment with other tools is more than welcome to do so, but at this initial session the goal must be to familiarize the instructors with what they need to master for the first days of class.

The remainder of the orientation sessions is used for instructors to meet in small groups with their level coordinator, lead instructors, or both. At these small sessions they go over the syllabus for the course they will be teaching, discuss the process for materials creation, and generally learn more about the specifics of that course. This is also the time the instructors ask questions and get a better idea of what their teaching experience will be like.

At times in the past I have incorporated other elements into the orientations as well, and based on my survey findings, there are some standard ones that LPDs like to include. One of the most common of these is a language learning session, often referred to as a *shock language* session, in which new instructors are taught a lesson in a language that nobody knows (e.g., Hungarian, Greek). The goal of such a session is to remind the instructors what it feels like to be beginning language students. Discussions after the mini-lesson usually revolve around the affective factors involved in the experience—anxiety, intimidation, shyness, fear of making mistakes—as well as what it takes for learners to make use of the input they receive and how they process new linguistic information. I remind my instructors that they are all above-average language learners, and they cannot expect their students to have the same level of skill or language learning experience. So this reminder of what not being able to speak the target language feels like adds to the preparation and perspective the instructors receive before entering the classroom.

Other orientation sessions involve teaching demonstrations, which may take different forms. One option is to invite experienced instructors to demonstrate a lesson using the techniques and textbook we have discussed. In many ways this session is the most useful of the three days, since it allows new teachers to see what everything looks like when put into practice. Experienced instructors benefit from seeing how the specific textbook works, while novice teachers benefit from seeing how the classroom interaction works. When I do these sessions, I usually ask someone to show what she or he does on the first day of class, as well as sample lessons with each of the components of instruction, such as presenting vocabulary, practicing a grammar point, or teaching reading. Many LPDs also incorporate microteaching sessions by the new instructors, in order to allow them to start to develop that teaching persona in a safe environment that offers constructive feedback. Microteaching has come to be recognized as a valuable tool for learners to reflect and share on the professional development process (e.g., Cripwell & Geddes, 1982; Geddes, 1979; Kasambira, 1984; Ogeyik, 2009). Some LPDs find that microteaching is more effective in the teaching methodology course, rather than trying to fit it into the packed schedule of the orientation. However, many LPDs indicated that it is a valuable component of their orientation sessions because it allows them to make sure everyone understands what is expected of them. Some LPDs find that it is also builds rapport in the group, because it encourages mutual support.

Finally, depending on the institution, there may be opportunities to collaborate with other language teaching groups for a joint section on a topic of interest to all, such as testing, technology, or target language use. These sessions will be particularly useful if an expert can be invited to run a half-day workshop on the topic. The other great advantage is the camaraderie achieved by bringing together instructors of various languages. So often the issues we face are the same, but we do not talk about them beyond the limited scope of our own languages. We can learn a great deal from colleagues in other languages, and beginning this bond of sharing and working together benefits new instructors as they embark on their careers.

In sum, the orientation provides instructors with a wealth of information. Time is always a concern, so the specific elements have to be chosen carefully. If the program has adopted a new textbook or a new approach, the orientation sessions will devote time to those changes, so the content may not be exactly the same each year. But whatever the elements, it is important to remember that this orientation is the instructors' first experience in the language program. The tone the LPD sets will likely define the instructors' impressions of the program. It is important to establish a productive and respectful working relationship with all members of the program, and it begins during these three days. Lee (1989) concurs:

> I cannot sufficiently underscore how important I consider orientation to be regardless of the role of the participant. From the perspective of the Director of Basic Language Instruction orientation introduces and explains the fundamental expectation of TAs as instructors. From the perspective of the new TA it is an invaluable learning experience. From the perspective of the students enrolling in our courses it is a kind of quality control. From the perspective of the Department it is all of the above and the beginning of a good working relationship among the TAs themselves and between them and the Director of Basic Language Instruction. (p. 44)

The orientation is then often followed up by a semester-long teaching methodology course, which is discussed in the next section.

2.3 The Methodology Course

The methodology course is an essential component of the training process. This section discusses the nature of the course, its design, and the materials and assignments incorporated. Some institutions require this course of all new instructors, regardless of previous experience (e.g., Lee, 1989); others require it only of those without previous experience teaching language at the college level. Because the orientation serves only as a brief introduction to teaching in a program, a semester-long (or occasionally full-year) methods course is vitally important to the education the instructors receive.

Interestingly, the methods course has not always been viewed as the integral component of professional development that we recognize today. Schulz (1980), who carried out a survey to assess the type of training language instructors received, found that 69% of departments required a formal preservice orientation, but only 38% required a methods course. Her data were compared to a previous study of a decade earlier in which it was found that only 38% offered orientations and only 25% required the methods course. In the more than three decades that have passed since her study, emphasis on professional development seems to have grown; in the survey I carried out, all of the respondents reported having both a preservice orientation and a methodology course. Based on these numbers as well as on anecdotal knowledge, I am confident that more than one-third of programs currently offer a teaching methods course for their instructors. In general terms, this course provides instructors the opportunity to combine the practical training they get in the classroom with more theoretical education to supplement and enhance that classroom experience (Maxim, 2005b, p. 16), although programs vary in the degree of historical and theoretical background they give to their instructors in this course.

The course allows greater analysis of pedagogical approaches, administrative tips, and even the issues related to working as part of a team. Even if the instructors who come to teach in our programs are brilliant intellectuals and gifted language learners themselves, there is no guarantee that they are aware of research in language acquisition and teaching or that they necessarily understand what is required to be a successful language teacher (Waldinger, 1990, p. 21). In more extreme cases they may not view language teaching as among their priorities; without a well-designed methodology course, there is a danger that they will not dedicate the time or energy necessary. Therefore, the design of the course is of paramount importance.

For someone unfamiliar with research on language teaching and language learning, designing this course can be a daunting task. Even for those who have a background in second language acquisition, the connection between our theoretical or empirical knowledge and best practices for language classrooms is not always easy to see. The preparation of the methodology course, from activities to textbook to calendar, requires time, knowledge, and expertise on subjects that can change over time. As Waldinger noted in 1990, "an enormous amount of research has been done in the last ten years and the number and quality of publications on language acquisition and pedagogy have increased tremendously" (p. 20). That statement is even more applicable in the decade and a half that have passed since her article.

The LPD's best recourse is to select a textbook that can provide a solid background and framework, and then supplement it with other articles or readings according to our own interests. We also must be sure to design appropriate activities to allow new instructors to apply the theoretical aspects of the course to their classrooms. A variety of textbooks are published for us in this kind of course, so searching online or asking publishers' representatives to provide sample copies of new or popular methods textbooks is a good way to start the selection process. In my experience and from the survey responses, the textbooks presented in Table 2 are among the most widely used in foreign language methodology courses.

As many of these texts were published more than a decade ago, another option is to supplement an older book with portions of a more recent one or with articles. Such an approach would allow instructors to provide an interesting complement to traditional methodology textbooks by offering different points of view or strategies. Decisions regarding these materials depend in large part on the audience and the nature of the course. For example, at my institution the course was, until recently, offered as a two-credit course that was graded on a pass/fail basis, which limited the scope of the syllabus and the workload. Offering the course on a graded basis for three credits allows for more readings, projects, and other assignments.

After choosing a text, the next step is to design the course around the text and the various supplemental activities and readings.[1] In general, the methods course should include readings dealing with both theory and practice, which can be accomplished through the texts indicated in Table 2. Ideally, these readings will be supplemented by activities to help new teachers, such as observation, analysis and reflection, and materials creation.

I usually have the instructors in the methods course carry out a number of class observations of their peers, as well as of themselves (video recorded). When carrying out these observations (self or of others), they note general aspects of the class, or I have them focus on a particular element of the class that is related to our ongoing discussion in the methods course. For example, for one observation they might focus on target language use; for another they could be asked to pay attention to time management and transitions between activities. Each observation is followed by a report in which they reflect on the strengths and weaknesses of the lesson and apply it to their own experiences

---

[1]The Foreign Language Teaching Forum (http://www.FLTeach.org), referenced in the appendix to Chapter 1, compiles a list of methods class syllabi and lesson plans. FLTeach is currently unfunded, so the materials may not be entirely up to date, but there is a valuable collection of resources that can serve as inspiration and guidance.

Table 2 Some commonly used textbooks for foreign language teaching methods courses (see References for complete bibliographic information)

Author	Title	Publisher	Date of publication (most recent edition)
Blyth, C. (Ed.)	*Foreign Language Teaching Methods* online modules http://www .coerll.utexas.edu/methods	COERLL, University of Texas, Austin	2010
Brandl, K.	*Communicative Language Teaching in Action: Putting Principles to Work*	Prentice Hall/ Pearson	2007
Brown, H. D.	*Principles of Language Learning and Teaching*	Prentice Hall/ Pearson	2007
Brumfit, C. J., & Johnson, K.	*The Communicative Approach to Language Teaching*	Oxford	1979
Cook, V.	*Second Language Learning and Language Teaching*	Oxford	2008
Kumaravadivelu, B.	*Beyond Methods: Macrostrategies for Language Teaching*	Yale University Press	2002
Lee, J., & VanPatten, B.	*Making Communicative Language Teaching Happen*	McGraw-Hill	2003
Lightbown, P. M., & Spada, N.	*How Languages Are Learned*	Oxford	2008
Omaggio Hadley, A.	*Language Teaching in Context*	Heinle Cengage	2001
Richards, J. C., & Rogers, T., R.	*Approaches and Methods in Language Teaching*	Cambridge	2001
Shrum, J., & Glisan, E.	*Teacher's Handbook*	Heinle Cengage	2010

and their ongoing development as educators. In Waldinger's (1990) experience with the methodology course, she found the process of self-observation accompanied by critical reflection to be valuable. It made them "*think* about teaching" and "raised their consciousness about an aspect of their future careers to which they had given very little thought" (p. 21; emphasis in the original). Lee (1989) also advocated the use of a reflective journal to help teachers consider their abilities, as well as a tool to communicate with the LPD regarding their teaching experiences (p. 22). Other research confirms the value of reflection (Arnold, Ducate, Lomicka, & Lord, 2005; Lomicka & Lord, 2007; Lord & Lomicka, 2007, 2008) in developing skilled language teachers. These reflections can be graded or assessed on a complete/not complete basis, and can even be carried out in teams rather than individually. In fact, the previously cited research found that reflection is more meaningful and more engaging when done collaboratively. Finally, an extension of these observation and reflection activities can be mock teaching carried out in the methods course. Many LPDs incorporate this activity to help novice instructors hone their teaching skills as well as to practice critical reflection.

One other element of many methodology courses is the creation of a teaching portfolio. The contents of the portfolio may vary depending on the needs and makeup of the instructors in the class, but standard elements include teaching activities, lesson plans, and a statement of teaching philosophy. Although crafting a teaching philosophy is a challenge for first-year instructors, I have found it to be a useful exercise, especially when revisited over the course of the semester. Even gifted instructors need to be encouraged to be deliberate and intentional in their teaching approach, and putting their instincts into words is not always as easy as they think it will be. Given that the majority of job openings in higher education now require a teaching philosophy statement in the application dossier, it will benefit graduate student instructors to begin work on this document early. Most important, instructors should be encouraged to view the methods course as the beginning, not the end, of their professional development. None of us ever finish learning, and we always benefit from opportunities to reflect on our teaching and revisit our beliefs and how we implement them in class. As suggested by Whitney (2011), such ongoing reflection can be as easy as using sticky-notes to jot down what worked and what did not in any given lesson, and then to go back and revise as needed if teaching the material again. The same sense of constant reflection and continual development should be the spirit that motivates our classroom observations.

3. INSTRUCTOR EVALUATION

Instructor evaluation and assessment are essential to professional development. Although evaluation and assessment are two different concepts—the first connoting a judgment based on data, the second referring to the process of making improvements and decisions based on data—they often can be carried out simultaneously. The process of assessing an instructor's strengths and weaknesses generally leads to an evaluation of the individual's skills in the classroom, and both have as an end goal the improvement of teaching and learning. According to Geddes and Marks (1997), evaluation procedures should provide the basis for feedback on instruction, but it also allows the LPD to diagnose and solve instructional problems that may be evident, to assist teachers in developing strategies for more effective instruction, and to help them develop a positive attitude toward professional development. Such assessment comes from multiple sources, as will be discussed in the following subsections: classroom observations, student evaluations, and holistically rated student achievement results.

3.1 Classroom Observations

Classroom observations, usually by supervisors but also by peers, form the backbone of instructor evaluation and assessment. Regular observations of teaching, pre- and post-observation conferences, and suggestions for improvement are among the LPD's most well-known and most time-consuming duties. These visits provide valuable information to the instructor in the form of a performance assessment, and also to the LPD and the department in the form of the instructor's performance record. Additionally, although we often lose sight of this perspective, our instructors are essentially learning on the job:

> It is well recognized by other professions that none of their members are fully competent when they first enter practice: full competence is achieved (if ever) only after extensive experience in actual practice. Most of what a professional needs to know can only be learned on the job—that is why we say that she or he *practices* a profession. (Medley, Coker, & Soar, 1984, p. 18)

In that light, the LPD's regular visits to the classroom are an important tool in the instructors' development. They also enable LPDs to engage with their instructors and to get a sense of the kind of teaching that is going on in classrooms.

Three decades ago, Schulz (1980) found that 13% of the LPDs who responded to her survey conducted no direct classroom observations of TAs during the TAs' first term of teaching (p. 3). Similar to other topics addressed in this chapter, it seems that this practice has changed, as all of the respondents in my survey indicated that first-year instructors were in fact observed with some degree of regularity. (Beyond the first semester, however, it is unclear whether these observations continue.) Oddly enough, although these visits should be welcomed, most instructors tend to dread the day when the supervisor comes to their classroom. Instructors tend to think the purpose of these observations is to judge and criticize, when in reality the intention is to assess what is working and what could use improvement and, crucially, offer guidance in that respect: "In theory, teacher observations ought, first and foremost, to be developmental. In practice, they are often perceived as being judgmental" (White et al., 2008, p. 69). Defusing the fear of these evaluations is one of the jobs of the LPD, who needs to make sure instructors realize that the observations are intended to help them, not punish them.

All classroom observation procedures will share some common goals and characteristics (e.g., Medley et al., 1984; White et al., 2008). The following steps come from various literature as well as my own experience and survey responses:

Defining the scope of the observation. This refers to the lesson plan to be administered, the learning objectives for the class sessions, and so on. We tend to assume that both the instructor and LPD are in agreement on what makes a good class and what factors the observation will encompass. It is true, however, that one of the biggest problems with evaluating teaching, especially when there are many instructors, is that the standards are not clear to the instructors or the evaluators. Schulz (1980) also noted the need for "better or more objective evaluation instruments to assess TAs' teaching effectiveness" (p. 7). In reality, the observation should note the whole of the period—from teaching approach and activities to interaction with students and time management, and anything else that comes up— but the instructors need to know this beforehand.

Establishing a quantifiable record of how this task is performed. White et al. (2008) note that one of the first steps to take in planning classroom observations is "establishing standards of performance, which are guidelines set up as a basis for measurement, including tolerance of deviation from performance standards" (p. 10). Based on my experience and the nearly unanimous responses to my survey, the most common tool is a rating sheet (see the appendix for a sample). This sheet includes a space for the observer to note the behavior and at the same time place a value on that behavior according to the degree that it measures up to the preestablished standard.

In many cases, such sheets can conclude with a total score or an average score, to provide a numerical "grade" to the class, although it is not required. Having such a quantifiable score is especially convenient in cases of any conflict between the LPD and the instructor, or in a worst-case scenario, if the need arises to document failure to perform job duties satisfactorily. We must note, however, that the numbers cannot tell the whole story, and a cumulative score can indeed be misleading or obscure important information about what was done extremely well or extremely poorly.

Comparing the score to the predetermined accepted standard. The last element of the observation process is to establish how the class—and by extension the instructor's overall performance—measures up to the established standard of what is expected. Often this ultimate evaluation step becomes evident through the quantifiable score. The comparison does not have to be purely numerical, however, and it can often be more valuable to evaluate a class qualitatively. Most LPDs meet with the observed instructor shortly after the class to discuss it and to go over the LPD's comments. This meeting is the ideal time to make these comparisons. It is important to remember, however, that these assessments should provide both positive and negative feedback. The former is crucial for motivating and encouraging instructors. The latter, in the form of constructive criticism, can be difficult to deliver, but if it is done "in such a way as to limit defensiveness and promote growth" (White et al., 2008, p. 65), it too is of great value in the instructor's ongoing development.

We also need to remember that our observation process, no matter how we design and implement it, is based on only snapshots of teaching performance:

> Performance evaluation is designed to evaluate the teacher on the basis of the quality of the teaching she provides in a specific setting—with a particular class, in a particular school, in a particular community. It is, of course, process based . . . . (Medley et al., 1984, p. 19)

That specific setting—the class period, the classroom, the students—come together to produce what may or may not be a representative sample of that instructor's capabilities. We cannot base an entire annual evaluation on one hour of observed teaching out of an annual load of something close to 1,000 hours, particularly when that hour, by its very nature, has a significant difference from all of the others—that of the presence of the observer. (White et al., 2008, pp. 69–70)

Although this may be the case, the more frequent the observations, the more normal a practice it becomes and the more likely that an observed period will resemble the norm for that instructor. Such observations are time-consuming, however, and the LPD needs to find the balance that allows for representative information to be gathered about all instructors without spending an impossible amount of time carrying out observations. We need to also remember the other types of feedback available to the LPD and to instructors.

3.2 Other Sources of Feedback

Other forms of feedback are available, although they vary in their reliability. For example, student evaluations can provide additional information on the success of a class, but it is important to interpret them cautiously. Some institutions mandate uniformity in the evaluation forms across departments; in these cases, not all of the questions will be relevant to lower-level language courses.

The Association of Departments of Foreign Languages (ADFL) issued a *Statement of Good Practice* (2001), which notes that evaluations of teaching should derive from multiple assessment measures, beyond the standard class observation:

> Teaching can be more effectively evaluated by using multiple measures. Departments need to create environments where teaching is a subject of ongoing formal and informal discussions. The review of teaching should be approached with the same care and conscientiousness used to evaluate scholarly work. (para. 5)

It is largely the LPD's responsibility to ensure that other measures of effectiveness are employed, because essentially the LPD is responsible for evaluating instructor effectiveness. The ADFL suggests various possible methods of evaluating teaching, ranging from portfolio creation to materials evaluation, and they note, in support of the position taken in this chapter, the importance of ongoing training and professional development at all levels. Further, a recent article (Wood, Harms, & Vazire, 2010) noted that the evaluations we perform tend to reflect our own philosophy and style of teaching, rather than those of the person we are evaluating. For example, if an LPD has worked hard in his or her teaching on such areas as time management and transitions between activities, these will be the areas, according to Wood et al., that this LPD will focus on in observations of teaching and in the teaching methods course.

In my program, I strive to incorporate other forms of assessment to supplement my observations and student evaluations. A common and valuable practice is to have an informal midsemester evaluation procedure for instructors to administer to their students. At approximately the 5th and 15th weeks of the semester, the instructors give their students a form that asks them to list the aspects of the course that are contributing to their learning and that they want to see more of, as well as what things they are finding unhelpful and would like to see changed (related to the teaching only, not to infrastructure items like the syllabus or test content). The instructors are asked to carry this process out in their classes but do not have to share any of the results with the LPD or their coordinators. Instead, the goal is to provide timely and relevant feedback directly to the instructor. Such immediate and unofficial reactions from the students in a class can help instructors refine their teaching style and also learn to recognize the different needs each particular class will have.

I also meet yearly with coordinators to assess the instructors' teaching skills as well as their contributions to our program. A number of years ago I created the "Award for Cooperative Leadership in Teaching" to recognize team members who have made valuable contributions not just in the classroom, but to the well-being of the program as a whole. (There are other places for us to recognize pure teaching talent, such as university-sponsored teaching awards.) Assignments to upper-level teaching or to the coveted content courses are based on not just performance as instructors, but also on collegiality. It is my hope that the instructors in my program will see their classroom performance as one of many elements of their job, and that their performance is judged on a variety of factors, all of which contribute to the program. At the end of the day, it is the LPD's responsibility to "oversee and assess objectively the job performance of each employee in a manner that will promote personal and program growth" (Geddes & Marks, 1997, p. 206).

3.3 Putting it into Practice

There are many factors to consider when designing and planning classroom observations. A structured, well-planned approach to the classroom visits, followed throughout the program, controls for a significant number of variables and reduces instructor uncertainty about the nature and purposes of the observations. To use my program as an example, all instructors are observed at least once a year. Although visits are unannounced, instructors are informed of a two-week period in which their classes will be visited. This announcement allows them to put their best foot forward without artificially overpreparing one particular class session. The instructors fill out a pre-observation form when this two-week period is announced (see the appendix for this and other observation materials) in which they describe their approach to teaching and what they hope to accomplish in the courses they teach. They may also indicate features of the class they want the observer to pay special attention to or on which they would like feedback.

Instructors are provided with the observation form we use, so they know what elements of their classes will be observed and evaluated. I include the form in the appendix, although it undergoes frequent modification. In addition to noting the main components and times of the lesson, the form includes specific aspects of the class, such as target language use, types of activities, incorporation of the five Cs, and classroom environment. It is important to remember that not everyone has the same teaching style, even in a program whose LPD advocates a particular approach (e.g., communicative). For example, my classes tend to be fairly relaxed, and although I am clearly the authority in the classroom, I use humor to interact and connect with my students. Other instructors prefer a more overtly structured, formal relationship between students and instructor. We cannot evaluate everyone based on our own personality traits, so I try to evaluate performance in terms of the parameters of the observation form without comparing an instructor's style to my own.

Following the observation, instructors receive a post-observation form to facilitate reflection on the class before receiving my feedback. The questions on this form ask what their goals were, if they were accomplished, what worked best, and what did not work as well as they had intended (and why). Even the best lesson plans can fail for reasons beyond our control, so the instructor can address these issues on the form as well. I make sure everyone is aware that an instructor's performance on any one given day may or may not be representative of that instructor's normal class, and for that reason this dialogue between instructor and observer is crucial, in addition to encouraging ongoing reflection.

After this form has been completed, the instructor receives the report and meets with the observer. My observation form has a place for both observer and instructor to sign, indicating that they have both read and discussed the relevant documents. Again, the signature is simply a way of requiring a meeting and hopefully, a dialogue on the teaching process.

All of these components of the observation work together to foster a reflective attitude toward teaching and to encourage instructors to view this process as a crucial part of their professional development. It is, however, only one part. "A good evaluation system should . . . not only list the desired effects . . . and how these will be observed and confirmed, but also describe the actions that will be taken to adjust" (White et al., 2008, p. 267) if adjustments are warranted. In other words, the LPD needs to ensure that opportunities are provided for instructors to continue reflecting, learning, and growing as instructors.

4. ONGOING PROFESSIONAL DEVELOPMENT

Given the pressures of administrative and teaching tasks, it is a challenge for the LPD to offer ongoing development opportunities. So much of our energy and focus are taken up with preparing the new instructors that it is possible to overlook the needs of the experienced instructors. Workshops, courses, and other professional development opportunities are an integral part of teaching organizations (White et al., 2008, p. 70). The methods course is an introduction; we need to remember "that teacher development is a constant process and that we have only sensitized our students and made them aware of some of the resources available to them" (Waldinger, 1990, p. 23), and we need to provide these resources. We all need to remember, as well, that everyone, from the LPD to the coordinators to the instructors, is involved in this continuing process (White et al., 2008, p. 43).

In my program, to build a culture of ongoing professional development we offer a series of teaching workshops that, although designed for the lower-division instructors, are often relevant to instructors at all course levels. These are in-house events: the coordinators or advanced instructors lead sessions on practical topics such as grading written work or assessing oral performance, or on less tangible topics, such as working with disruptive students. Topics vary from year to year according to the needs and interests of the instructors.

Depending on the institution and the interests of the graduate students, another option for ongoing professional development is to offer a graduate seminar on language program administration (e.g., Mason, 1992; Stepp-Greany, 2008). Although most graduate students in a language program will not end up as LPDs, many will continue to teach language and perhaps be responsible for some aspects of program coordination, so this kind of course could prove useful to them. Even if they do not ultimately have faculty positions with supervisory responsibilities, the awareness of how a language program works and is run could be a valuable asset to their lives as teachers and, crucially, as members of a language program. Another option is to establish a mentoring system that allows newer instructors to be guided by those with more experience (e.g., Silva, Macián, & Mejía-Gómez, 2006). Such a system not only alleviates some of the burden on the LPD but also encourages experienced instructors to continue reflecting on and refining their skills.

Another source of ongoing development for teachers is provided by textbook publishers, who host seminars or increasingly webinars on topics related to language teaching and curricula. Although some such seminars have as their unspoken goal to market the materials of that publisher, the content is valuable to instructors regardless of the materials used. Further, they provide an opportunity for instructors to connect with others, share experiences, exchange suggestions, and develop a working community. Finally, the best source of continuing development and awareness of teaching comes in the form of regular observations by supervisors, coordinators, and directors. It is worth noting that all of these sources of evaluation and development are generally free to the program and the institution and so without additional costs can provide essential feedback to instructors.

Finally, LPDs can consider other systematic ways to promote ongoing development among both new and experienced instructors. For example, the model of a "master section" can be used in multisection programs. The model entails one section taught by an experienced instructor who is known to be an excellent teacher, whose syllabus is set one day ahead of the others. The new instructors, and anyone else looking for guidance or inspiration, observe that class several times per week, and essentially see the next day's class in action. The master instructor shares lesson plans and provides mentoring to the other instructors, and often receives a course release or a supplement to the stipend in compensation. While such an approach would not work in every program, it could be a valuable outlet for ongoing professional development in many settings.

5. CONCLUSION

The LPD has the responsibility to ensure professional working conditions and a stable, effective language program. Much of this is accomplished by straightforward tasks such as textbook selection and syllabus design, but instructor development and preparation, as well as continual assessment, are integral parts of a successful language program. We should do our best to ensure that our instructors are encouraged to be creative and flexible while simultaneously demonstrating their commitment to the program (Barsi & Kaebnick, 1989, cited in Stoller, 1997), and administrators must do the same. White et al. (2008) note that "the individuals who make up the [program] must also be constantly learning and developing their own personal goals" (p. 43). It requires constant evaluation, reflection, and modification, as well as communication among all members of the program. An unexpected compliment came my way recently that is worth repeating here. The recently retired office manager in my department commented that she never heard complaints from undergraduate students about their (largely graduate student) instructors. This surprised her, given the instructors' varied backgrounds, teaching experience, English proficiency, and knowledge of U.S. culture. She said that the methodology course, the orientation, the mentoring, the assessments we provide, and in general, the whole network of support we offer them seemed to be really helping the instructors know what they need to do and how to do it. She did not know that I was working on this book, so it was a timely comment that made me proud.

Questions for Reflection

1. What education have you received to prepare for teaching a language at the college level? What aspects of professional development seem most beneficial? In what ways did these elements help prepare you for your role? What areas (if any) were lacking in the education you received prior to beginning to teach? How were these areas

insufficient? When did you notice these deficiencies, and what made you notice them? (If you are not currently a teacher, consider the styles and approaches that your language teachers have used in class.)

2. What models of development for instructors are most appropriate and most effective for new language teachers? Consider issues related to pre-service orientations, ongoing training throughout the teaching career, and other opportunities for professional development.

3. What are the advantages and disadvantages of a rating sheet evaluation and a systematic evaluation approach? What other methods of classroom observation could we consider using, and why?

4. Consider how both instructor evaluation and assessment come into play in professional development and classroom observations. Are both aspects equally important? Is one easier to carry out than the other? Does one shed more light than the other on an instructor's skills and effectiveness?

Suggestions for Further Reading

Kumaravadivelu, B. (2002). *Beyond methods: Macrostrategies for language teaching*. New Haven, CT: Yale University Press.
> Explores language pedagogy in a post-pedagogy era and offers strategies and advice for language teaching, applicable at any level and with any language.

Mason, K. (1992). Beyond the methods course: Designing a graduate seminar in foreign language program direction. In J. C. Waltz (Ed.), *Development and supervision of teaching assistants in foreign languages* (pp. 113–133). Boston, MA: Heinle Cengage.
> Advice for designing a graduate seminar on language program direction. Offers a valuable perspective on the design of language programs, even for those who may not plan to offer such a seminar.

Reagan, T. G., & Osborn, T. A. (2001). *The foreign language educator in society: Toward a critical pedagogy*. New York, NY: Routledge.
> Links foreign language teaching with critical pedagogy to provide an overview of what current and future language teachers should know and understand about language, including ideas on language attitudes, practices, rights, policy, and other related issues. Also provides pedagogical advice for applying the practices to one's own situation.

APPENDIX

Sample Orientation and Training Materials

1. LOWER-DIVISION SPANISH (LDSP) PROGRAM: SAMPLE ORIENTATION SCHEDULE

(The Graduate School holds a two-day general orientation program for all new graduate students. My orientation is always scheduled for the three following days.)

Wednesday, August 17th	Who	
9:00 AM–9:30 AM	Welcome and introductions	All NEW instructors
9:30 AM–10:30 AM	Introduction to LDSP program and policies	
10:30 AM–11:30 AM	Some basic teaching principles	
11:30 AM–1:00 PM	(Lunch break)	
1:00 PM–2:00 PM	Hybrid classes	All new instructors to 1000-level (others welcome)
2:00 PM–3:30 PM	Teaching examples (teaching grammar, encouraging pair work, staying in the target language, what to do on the first day)	
3:30 PM	Pick up textbook (if needed)	ALL instructors
4:00 PM–7:00 PM	GRADUATE STUDENT MEETING/RECEPTION —introductions, advising, registration —refreshments and socializing	All (SPS) grad students and faculty
Thursday, August 18th	**Who**	
9:00 AM–12:00 PM	Teaching with textbook X	All new instructors
12:00 PM–2:00 PM	Lunch break	Any interested
2:00 PM–4:00 PM	Breakout sessions with lead instructors and coordinators	All 1130 1131 1134 2200 2201
Friday, August 19th	**Who**	
9:00 AM–12:00 PM	Course management system setup and use	Room 1: 1130 1131 1134 2200 2201 Room 2: 2240
12:00 PM–1:00 PM	(Lunch break)	
1:15 PM–2:15 PM	Discussion on professional behavior Dean of Students office representatives	All graduate students and faculty

Observation Forms

Lower-Division Spanish Program:
Pre-Observation Information

Instructor:

Course:

1. Please tell me about your approach to second language teaching.

2. What do you see as the strengths of your class (including students, interactions, your strengths as an instructor, etc.)?

3. What are the typical patterns of interaction and class participation?

4. Would you like specific feedback on any particular aspect of your class?

5. Is there anything else you would like me to know before my visit?

Please email this completed form to the program director.

Lower-Division Spanish Program:
Class Observation Form

Name of Instructor:

Date:

Course/Section:

Room:

Number of students:

Observed by:

Description of Class Organization / Activities

Time	Activity

Class Evaluation
(RATING SCALE: 5 = excellent; 4 = very good; 3 = good; 2 = adequate; 1 = needs improvement)

Aspect of Class	Rating	Comments
• Evidence of lesson plan		
• Clearly identifiable goals and objectives for period		
• Warm-up activity		
• Language of interaction		
• Effective use of class time		
• Contextualization of activities		
• Relation and transition between activities		
• Variety of activities		
• Student/teacher interaction patterns (instructor to student; student to student; groups; etc.)		
• Clarity of explanations and examples		
• Use of visuals or other multisensory learning tools		

Aspect of Class	Rating	Comments
• Error correction		
• Evidence of five Cs: (communication, cultures, communities, connections, comparisons)		
• Overall Classroom Environment		
• Overall Class Rating		
• Overall Instructor Rating		

Other Comments?

_____ _____ _____ _____
Instructor   Date   LPD   Date

Lower-Division Spanish Program:
Post-Observation Questionnaire

Name of Instructor:

Course/Section:

Date observed:

Observed by:

1. What were the main goals of your lesson?

2. What do you think the learners learned in the lesson?

3. What did you expect of your students for today's class hour?

4. What teaching procedures did you use?

5. What problems did you encounter, and how did you deal with them?

6. What were the most effective parts of the lesson?

7. What were the least effective parts?

8. Would you do anything differently if you taught this lesson again?

Please print out and return this form to the program director.

CHAPTER 6

Incorporating Technology

A friend's recent status update on Facebook read: "What I used to do in 15 minutes, now takes me hours in my online classes! AHHHH!" Anyone with experience using technology to teach, enhance, or otherwise administer language courses can relate to my friend's lament. It is easy to look back on our Luddite ways with fondness for the simplicity of class preparation that involved only a textbook and perhaps a piece of chalk. This situation raises the question of the role that technology has—and should have—in our language programs. It is safe to assume that we have all felt pressure to incorporate or at least investigate new pedagogical tools in our language classes, but are we convinced? Should we be? Are we even asking the right questions?

In the last 20 years or more, and particularly in the last decade, research into computer-assisted language learning (CALL) has flourished. Levy (1997) defines *CALL* as "the search for and study of applications of the computer in language teaching and learning" (p. 1), and Beatty (2003) claims that "a definition of CALL that accommodates its changing nature is any process in which a learner uses a computer and, as a result, improves his or her language" (p. 7). However, it is worth noting that many other phrases and acronyms have been used. Levy and Hubbard (2005) question the legitimacy of the *CALL* acronym, and they raise a number of valid points. For example, the very name has become somewhat outdated in that the technologies we use in our lives today go far beyond what we think of when we mention "computers." Similarly, "language learning" is too vague a term—do we consider language acquisition or just learning? Explicit instruction in a classroom? What type of classroom? Self-directed learning? Computer as tutor, tool, or something else? Levy and Hubbard (2005) further note that other disciplines, such as music or history, make extensive use of various technologies in connection with their fields, but we do not have a "computer-assisted history" subfield, nor do we talk about "book-assisted language learning." In other words, the very name itself raises the question of why we have to have a name in the first place. As I said, these are valid points. In spite of these complications, however, I adopt the term *CALL* for the same reasons as Levy and Hubbard: The term is recognized and is understood as encompassing the whole array of technological tools employed to enhance experiences related to language teaching and learning.

Numerous studies have shown that online and technology-enhanced learning can be beneficial and at least as effective as traditional methods that are not supplemented with technological tools. Therefore, the inclusion of a chapter on technology and language programs seems warranted. Whole books have been written on this topic, so the goal of this chapter is not to lay out all of the research relevant to CALL, but rather to address the issue of technology incorporation from the perspective of the language program director (LPD). Specifically, this chapter examines the questions the LPD must confront when contemplating adopting new tools or adapting our programs to technological methodologies.

1. WHY USE TECHNOLOGY?

The first, and admittedly most obvious, question to address is whether and why we should use technology in our courses. To be clear, although *technology* at one point did refer to audiocassettes, overhead transparencies, online workbooks, and DVDs, this chapter will not deal with those tools that are largely becoming obsolete in our classrooms. Nor is the term intended to refer to the many tools that commercial publishers often provide with their textbook programs, especially for the more commonly taught languages. These include websites, electronic activities manuals, flashcards, and grade books, and their use is recommended whenever possible.

As used in this chapter, the term *technology* moves from the broad issue of CALL to the more specific domain of tools that fall under the rubric of web 2.0; they can be considered as an addition to the standard curriculum of our courses. The term *web 2.0* is difficult to define, but it is usually understood as the array of tools, devices, platforms, and websites that encourage participation, sharing, and collaboration among users. In the words of Tim O'Reilly (of O'Reilly Media, who has been credited with coining the phrase *web 2.0* in 2003), web 2.0 tools "have embraced the power of the web to harness collective intelligence" (O'Reilly, 2005, n.p.). The Wikipedia entry on *web 2.0* presents a tag cloud (a visual representation of terms used, where font size is positively correlated to popularity) for the phrase *web 2.0* and paints an interesting picture of the concepts and tools subsumed therein.

Having operationalized the term *technology* for the purposes of this chapter, we must consider why instructors and, crucially, LPDs should consider using technology. Most instructors today experience a certain pressure, spoken or unspoken, to be on the cutting edge of new tools, to be aware of their development and use, and to be familiar enough with the correct terminology to engage in conversations on their advantages and disadvantages. Why is this? This pressure has different sources, some more valid than others.

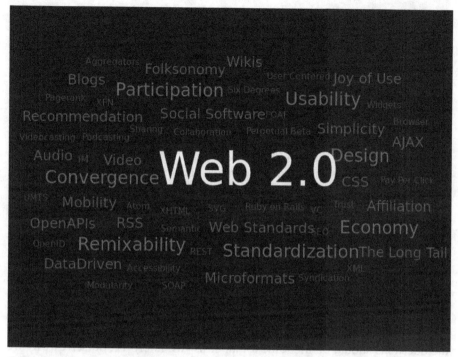

FIGURE 1   Web 2.0 Tag Cloud
Source: http://en.wikipedia.org/wiki/Web_2.0

1.1 Sources of Pressure for Including Technology

Perhaps the greatest impetus for adopting new technology tools is that it seems like everyone else is doing it. This peer pressure can come from high-level administrators. For example, Bernhardt, Valdés, and Miano (2009) note that their institution, Stanford University, underwent major curricular reform driven by the University Senate's concern that "campus-wide internationalization could not come about without a serious commitment to language teaching and learning," one component of which was the use of "significant" technology in their classes (p. 54). More recently, a survey of college and university presidents revealed that "just over half . . . believe that online courses offer a value to students that equals a traditional classroom's" (Young, 2011, para. 2). Interestingly, this same survey conducted among adult Americans not in academia revealed that only 29% of that population believed that online education could be comparable in quality to face-to-face classes.

The cynical will wonder to what extent financial and logistical considerations lie behind the push for increased technology use. Young (2011) interprets the university presidents' support of online learning methods to these very concerns: "colleges trying to cut costs and serve students who want more convenient options are embracing [online] teaching" (para. 4). Even in the late 1980s, LPDs had already recognized the importance of staying up-to-date with technology:

"The compleat administrator of a forward-looking foreign language program cannot sidestep the emerging technologies. Nor can that administrator's dean long afford to dismiss these developments as too costly" (Otto & Pusack, 1988, p. 18).

In addition to the push for technology that comes from above is a corresponding lateral push. As our coworkers become proficient in new skills, LPDs feel obliged to gain this knowledge as well. What's more, it is becoming necessary that we all have a working knowledge of different media to evaluate colleagues' work. As Beyer (2001) pointed out, "more colleagues are spending time acquiring the skills and using computers for classes and for research. We are now expected to appreciate, evaluate, and guide that work" (p. 119). Nor can we forget that our students are a rapidly changing demographic, having never known a time when computers were not widely available and widely used for everything from word-processing to making friends. "Our students today are all 'native speakers' of the digital language of computers, video games and the Internet" (Prensky, 2001, cited in Oxford & Oxford, 2009, p. 1; also see Tapscott's, 1999, coinage of the term "Net Generation"). If we want to reach them, we should probably consider meeting them on their terms and with their tools.

Given these pressures, it is not surprising that we tend to embrace new tools without carefully considering first our learning objectives or teaching styles. Many of us do. On the other end of the spectrum are those who are intimidated by technological innovations and are reluctant to make changes. But the questions should be the same for all of us. We rarely ask ourselves why we adopt certain approaches or embrace particular tools, at least from a pedagogical perspective. Yet as Terry (1998) noted with respect to any authentic materials we choose for a course,

> there should be a purpose—not simply to decorate the page or to fill
> (or kill) time but to introduce learners to specific cultural concepts,
> to illustrate something that has just been taught (or that is going to
> be taught), to serve as a stimulus for an activity. (p. 282)

As educators in general and as LPDs in particular, we have the responsibility to ensure that any changes we implement in our programs are based on research, investigation, and consideration of the tool's applicability to the issue at hand.

1.2 Challenges to Incorporating Technology

Before jumping on the technology bandwagon, whether we have justified pedagogical motivations or not, we must recognize that there are challenges as well as benefits to incorporating new tools in our programs and courses. These challenges range from personal preferences to skill levels to the time needed for implementation.

Perhaps the most apparent challenge in adapting our teaching and learning methods to incorporate new tools is the time it takes, as evidenced by my friend's Facebook post. Any new course design, whether to use a new textbook, incorporate new projects, or embrace a new delivery system, entails a great deal of preparation time and in the case of technology, training. What is more, creating pedagogically sound, useful tasks through technological tools may take more time than it would to design them in a more traditional way, at least at first. Given how overworked language teachers are already, it might seem unreasonable to ask them to redesign lessons using constantly changing tools and websites. The endeavor is worthwhile, but the learning and development curve is steep; therefore, care must be taken in deciding when, how, and why it is undertaken.

Although technological tools have the advantage of bridging space and time, another apparent negative is the blurring of the lines between work and nonwork hours that comes with it. "Ironically, the very tools expected to save time now occupy increasing uses of our time. For many, both in the office and at home, we are now technically available 24/7," notes Beyer (2001, p. 119). Furthermore,

> departments and faculty members have web pages that must be created, updated, and maintained. We can reach out to our students in Irkutsk or Yaroslavl or Moscow, and they can reach back to us—and they expect reasonably prompt replies. (p. 119)

In many cases, in addition to the time factor is the knowledge factor. Instructors often find themselves reluctant to adopt new tools or practices, not so much because of the time it may take but because of the skill set it will require. Although our students often feel very comfortable in online forums, "without training, few teachers will have the knowledge, understanding, and confidence to incorporate the new technology into their teaching effectively" (White et al., 2008, p. 252). This point is an important one, as it relates directly to the education of language instructors, a topic discussed in the previous chapter. "With training, familiarity, and practice, teachers will be in a position to extend and finally transform their teaching using the new technology" (p. 252), although this is, of course, easier said than done. Such training requires that we the LPDs be knowledgeable about the tools available to us so we can use them with ease. Furthermore, we must include hands-on training as well as discussions of how and why to incorporate certain tools into our methodology seminars and orientations. Given the challenges of limited time and extensive material, this additional topic may seem overwhelming to some LPDs.

Finally, we must be aware of our population; that is, the students whom we teach. Although the vast majority of our students come from the so-called Net Generation, "caution must be exercised to avoid overestimating the actual skills of digital natives" (Bennett, Maton, & Kevin, 2008, n.p.). Although almost every undergraduate student I know has a Facebook account and spends a considerable amount of time on the site, most of my projects involving podcasts, blogs, or wikis have required extensive training for most of them. They may be digital natives, but they have explored only small corners of that digital land. I have also encountered resistance among my students when adopting these popular tools, like Facebook or Twitter, because they do not want this overlap between their academic and social lives. From the student perspective, those tools are for fun, for nonacademic socializing, and for playing, and not for connecting with teachers or classmates, as some studies have confirmed (e.g., Parry & Young, 2010). There are ways to get around this problem; for example, by creating a Facebook group, students and instructor can interact in ways that are completely separate from students' personal Facebook pages. In addition, more recent surveys indicate that students may be becoming less resistant to mixing school and social networking:

> Although 90% of college students indicate that they use Facebook for social purposes, 58% say they feel comfortable using it to connect with other students to discuss homework assignments and exams. One out of four students even went so far as to say they think Facebook is "valuable" or "extremely valuable" to their academic success. (Rice, 2011, para. 2)

Thus we need to consider student attitudes toward these tools as well as their role in academics.

1.3 Advantages to Using Technology

With all that said, however, incorporating emerging technologies into our classes and programs has obvious advantages, which can be summarized as follows (Sayers, 1993):

- *Experiential learning:*   Students learn by doing and thus become creators in addition to receivers of knowledge.
- *Motivation:*   Computers are usually associated with games and fun activities, which makes the learning process more enjoyable and helps students feel more independent.
- *Enhanced student achievement:*   Technology can help students learn better strategies, take responsibility for their own learning, and increase self-confidence.
- *Authentic materials:*   The internet has made authentic target language materials—audio, visual, and so on—abundantly available for study.
- *Increased interaction:*   Computer-mediated communication (e.g., e-mail, text, chat, blogs) puts students in greater contact with each other and their instructor.
- *Individualization:*   All students can become equally engaged in student-centered collaborative learning.
- *Independence from a single source of information:*   Students are offered the chance to explore multiple information sources and thus increase interdisciplinary and multicultural learning.
- *Global understanding:*   Multicultural communication can be practiced on a comprehensive level.

Interestingly, when Sayers proposed these advantages, the tools we now consider for our classes had not even been imagined. What is more, much of what Sayers noted in the early 1990s is even more important today, given our current teaching approaches and the tools currently available to us.

Possibly of greatest relevance to us as LPDs, and in consideration of the general mission of beginning and intermediate language programs, is how increased interaction seems to be an essential component of CALL. This is not to say that the benefits of technology are limited to lower-division courses; on the contrary, the possibilities for successful inclusion of technological tools in upper-level content courses are endless. However, given that the LPD's role deals primarily with lower-division language courses, I focus on this aspect here. Readers are encouraged to consult the References section for further information on integrating such tools at the upper levels. Although in the past computers were viewed as tutors, and learners interacted with the computer solely to drill certain forms (e.g., Bax, 2003), today we see computers and media as a way to connect learners to each other and to other target language users. Thus the very nature of communicative language teaching—collaborating and sharing—is also at the heart of web 2.0. Researchers working in CALL have noted this recent move from interaction with a computer to interaction with people as a central component of today's technology use:

> Instead of self-contained, autodidactic computer applications designed specifically for language learning, networked technologies give learners access to existing discourse communities, and they make it possible for learners to create new ones via CMC [computer-mediated communication], hypertext, and various forms of social networking applications. (van Compernolle & Williams, 2009, p. 11)

Web 2.0 tools mesh successfully with social and cognitive perspectives on language learning. As Kern and Warschauer (2000) observed, "sociocognitive approaches to CALL shift the dynamic from learners' interaction with computers to interaction with other humans via the computer" (p. 11). Any tools that encourage students to talk to each other, share ideas and thoughts, communicate messages, and work together to achieve a goal are logically poised to benefit their language learning process:

> CALL . . . focuses not on using the computer to replace the teacher, but using the computer to enhance language teaching within the broader context of the collaborative classroom by expanding the opportunities students have to communicate with other people. (van Compernolle & Williams, 2009, p. 11)

This does not mean, however, that class time should be sacrificed in favor of technology-based interaction: These collaborative communication tools can be used to supplement and enhance the opportunities available to students beyond the classroom.

Another related tenet of the communicative approach is that the instructor is no longer the central figure responsible for imparting knowledge; rather, students become responsible for their learning through interaction with others. Many have noted that in computer-mediated environments, it becomes easier for the instructor, who no longer is "the authoritative figure and sole distributor of knowledge, but [rather] is an open-minded facilitator of learning who guides and supports learners in the process of knowledge construction" (Oskoz, 2009, p. 109). By engaging in out-of-class collaborative or communicative activities, Oskoz notes, learners "take responsibility for their own learning as they take part in the collaborative construction of knowledge" (p. 109).

We tend to think of speaking and listening skills when we talk about this type of interaction—and with today's audiovisual tools, it is very easy for learners to engage in oral and aural practice via technology. Research has shown that "computer-mediated communication has aided in improving the development of listening and speaking abilities" (Niño, 2009, p. 23). Nonetheless, we cannot forget that reading and writing are essential components of computer-mediated communication as well, because students can work in text-based chat rooms, blogs, and wikis. Indeed, research has shown that the increased and improved interactional possibilities available through technology do have potential benefits to all skills (e.g., Arnold, Ducate, & Kost, 2009; Beauvois, 1992; Ducate & Lomicka, 2008; Lee, 2001, 2002, 2010a, 2010b; van Compernolle & Williams, 2009; among others). "In addition to its place in fostering intercultural communication and the development of sociolinguistic and sociopragmatic competence, [computer-mediated communication] can be used to promote linguistic accuracy as well" (van Compernolle & Williams, 2009, p. 14). Van Compernolle and Williams note that Long's focus-on-form (e.g., Long & Robinson, 1998) pedagogical approach, which aims to draw learners' attention to their own language use and accuracy, fits well with CALL, given the various media involved. If designed well, technology-based tasks can help "develop learners' autonomy, as well as aid the development of the learner's capacity for a more active, reflective, and self-directed approach to learning" (Oskoz, 2009, p. 109).

Finally, if we think of language learning in terms of the *Standards*, technology tools also allow students to explore other content areas, share knowledge on a variety of topics, and connect to other users in the target language communities. As Oskoz (2009) succinctly puts it, "technology—particularly the web-based applications—is ideally suited to provide an environment that supports" the integration of the *Standards* (p. 106). Forums such as blogs or discussion boards, "where anyone can read others' messages, write responses, raise questions, and expect answers, have provided an ideal environment for students to share knowledge and cultural perspectives" (p. 106).

Given that our students are indeed digital natives, "to reach and teach these individuals, traditional pedagogical techniques need to be revisited and new techniques developed and/or perfected using media that they understand" (Oxford & Oxford, 2009, p. 1). At the same time, however, we must keep in mind the caveats addressed in the previous section of this chapter. For example, Walsh (2010) discusses how Facebook can be used essentially as a learning management system. Additionally, tools such as Facebook have the advantage that "many students are already familiar and comfortable with it; it is a 'known entity' to them" (Walsh, 2010, n.p.). Essentially, educators need to realize that "an interactive, technology-based approach is a necessary adjustment to the new genre of students, in a sense reaching them by speaking their language" (Moyer & Gonglewski, 1998, p. 57).

What's more, the plethora of resources available via technological tools now enables us to address different learning styles and preferences, as Sayers (1993) alluded to. According to Lively (1997), different technologies can provide new ways to address the differing needs of our students and can help the language be more relevant and more accessible to them (p. 35). Research has shown that shyer or more introverted students tend to participate more in online activities than in classroom activities (e.g., Beauvois, 1992; Chun, 1994; Kern, 1995; Warschauer, 1996a). Learners with different learning preferences can also benefit from different presentation modes (e.g., audio, visual), and students who work can take advantage of the flexibility offered by chats or videoconferences outside of class time. Increased motivation has also been observed as a positive outcome related to the incorporation of technology in language learning (e.g., Warschauer, 1996b).

In light of these benefits, it is not surprising that considerable research on second language acquisition (SLA) and CALL confirms that technology can play an important role in the language learning process. Numerous books and articles, as well as several journals themselves, are devoted to this topic. The following section presents some of the basic tenets of CALL and its effectiveness, insofar as these issues are relevant to the LPD.

2. TECHNOLOGY AND THE LPD

"We [LPDs] design or oversee the development of all course syllabi and examinations; we are actively involved in programmatic planning (i.e., selection of textbooks, materials) and the establishment of methodologies for classroom language teaching" (Harris-Schenz, 1993, pp. 45–50). Therefore, it is also our responsibility to ensure that our delivery methods and the various media chosen to carry out our goals are relevant, practical, and well suited to our mission. We do not adopt new tools because of the bells and whistles they offer, just as we would not adopt a new textbook or use a different colored pen just because it was flashy and caught our eye. In this light, it is crucial that we remember that technology is not "a means for language learning in and of itself, but rather another pedagogical tool whose value is determined by its use for specific pedagogical objective in the classroom" (van Compernolle & Williams, 2009, p. 15). In this respect, I concur with these authors that technology is only "one part of a larger, cohesive, multifaceted approach to world-language teaching and learning" (p. 15). It should not be afforded a particularly special place in our curricula or in our mission, and it should be considered only for how it can enhance our language teaching and learning experiences. I do, however, view technology as at least a secondary mission to prepare our students for global citizenship, which includes not only linguistic and cultural knowledge, but also multiple literacies in the tools they will need in this world.

2.1 Current Technology Use

Technology has a significant presence in many language programs, and LPDs most likely are already aware of its benefits and drawbacks. To gauge the extent of technology's reach in our programs, my online survey asked LPDs about their current and projected use of technology in the programs they direct. All of the respondents (100%) agreed with the statement that technology is important in language programs, but there was less unanimity about which tools are used and how.

PowerPoint was the most commonly used tool (of a list provided), with 63% of the LPDs responding that PowerPoint had a role in their programs. The same percentage also indicated that students in their language classes carry out projects using various technology tools, demonstrating the current view of technology not as only a presentational aid but also a communicative or interactional opportunity. Close behind, 60% of respondents reported using video clips from YouTube, TeacherTube, or similar sites. (However, respondents were not asked how they used those video clips; it could have been as passive as having a video playing while students entered the classroom or as engaging as a fully designed task with previewing, viewing, and postviewing activities to accompany the video.) About half of the respondents reported having students in their language classes engage in web-based activities: 54% indicating that these activities are provided by the textbook and 49% saying that they and their colleagues create the web-based activities. Collaborative web 2.0 tools, however, have yet to gain the same popularity as the standard tools just discussed: PowerPoint, video, and the web. Only 20% of the respondents said they used blogging, wikis, or podcasting, and only 11% said they had used Twitter in their language programs. These numbers show that although we may recognize the value of incorporating emerging technologies in our programs, and we might be familiar with the SLA and CALL research that supports it, we have not yet embraced these newer tools. The reasons for the slow adoption of these tools were not explored in the survey. By anecdotal experience, however, I suspect this delay is due to many of the aforementioned reasons: limited time to learn about new tools, lack of knowledge regarding how to implement them, reluctance to modify our teaching styles to best accommodate various technologies, and so on. At the same time and as was previously discussed, we need to remember that many students—and instructors—might prefer to reserve some of these more social tools (e.g., Twitter) for personal, non-academic use, which could explain these lower percentages as well.

A small number of LPDs who took part in the survey reported using other projects and tools. Some programs have students video-record their projects or skits for class and then either play them during class time or upload them to a class site or public site for viewing and commenting. Others use audio-recording software and voice boards (e.g., Wimba) to expand learners' opportunities for oral interaction or to work on pronunciation. One mentioned having classes engage in peer editing of writing assignments in a computer lab; although this activity does not use any new tools, it does use long-established word-processing tools in a collaborative way. Finally, one LPD mentioned using webcams to host virtual guest speakers in their classes.

When LPDs were asked how well integrated they felt technology was in their programs, on a scale of 1–10 (1 = not at all integrated, 10 = fully integrated), the average response was 7. It should be noted, however, that the term *integration* was not defined. I hoped to ascertain the extent to which technology tools were an integral part of language classes and programs, versus their use as add-ons to the curriculum (i.e., not essential but interesting additions). Viewing the results, I cannot be certain that all the respondents interpreted *integration* in the same way.

The responses did indicate interesting plans for the future and for continuing to explore the role of new technologies in their programs. One respondent mentioned the goal of developing enough technology-based activities to avoid using a commercial textbook—a practice that is becoming more and more common in higher education institutions (see, e.g., *Acceso,* the open-access University of Kansas Collaborative Digital Spanish Project for intermediate Spanish, http://www2.ku.edu/~spanish/acceso). Others reported eagerness to explore activities and tasks in collaborative writing and publishing, including digital storytelling. Several respondents said they would like to explore the potential of mobile devices in language learning, and many also said that virtual worlds, immersive environments, and gaming (e.g., Second Life, World of Warcraft) were areas to explore in the future. Finally, more than 75% of those who responded to this question indicated an interest in learning more about blogs, wikis, and podcasting.

The next sections examine possible models for integrating technology into our programs, followed by project ideas and a brief review of relevant CALL research. The goal of the remainder of this chapter is to help LPDs decide the role of technology in their programs and then explore some possible outlets for that technology.

2.2 Models for Using Technology

Incorporating technology into language programs may take a variety of formats, and the extent to which instructors in a program will embrace various tools and uses is determined largely by factors external to the technology itself. For example, how available are the tools in the rooms where language classes are taught? To what extent do students have easy access to technologies that could be used outside of class? What online resources are provided by the publisher of the language textbook, and what resources must be supplemented? How supportive is the administration, at all levels, of incorporating technology into the language program? There is, in addition, one internal question that should be central to all pedagogical and technological decisions: How can tool X help me achieve my goal of Y? The goal must come first. If technology does not enable language teachers to achieve their goals better, more efficiently, and more naturally, then the tool's use is not warranted. The primacy of sound pedagogical design and practice must be maintained even in the face of exciting new tools. Advocates for exploring and incorporating new technologies into language programs must also advise caution, whether considering the incorporation of short activities or a whole new approach to delivering material.

2.2.1 ENHANCING CURRENT CURRICULA

We can enhance our current offerings by taking advantage of learning management systems (LMSs) that help teachers organize materials and make them available to students, incorporate external media, and create easy-to-navigate websites for courses or programs. Many universities have a platform they already use (e.g., Blackboard, Sakai, Moodle), while textbook publishers are increasingly creating more sophisticated LMSs suited just for language learning (e.g., Cengage's iLearn, McGraw-Hill's Connect, or Pearson's MyLanguageLabs).

We may also view technology as an opportunity to enhance our current curricula by offering otherwise unavailable resources or experiences. Tasks or activities may be designed with a specific technology tool or resource in mind to achieve short-term goals, such as listening practice or cultural awareness. As with any other resource, the activities should be designed in phases: activate background knowledge with a preactivity, actively engage learners during the activity, and after checking comprehension, require learners to do something new with the information they have gained from the activity or tool. In Salaberry's (2001) words, "the success of a technology-driven activity will likely depend as much or more, on the successful accomplishment of pre- and post-activities than on the technology activity itself" (p. 51). Thorne's (2010) perspective is also relevant here: He asserts that the incorporation of any tool will effectively change the interaction and learning associated with that tool. In spite of the potential for circularity in this argument, the case should still be that the goal, not the technology, drives the pedagogy.

Finally, as we become more comfortable with the options available for incorporating technology-based activities into our teaching, we can also consider extensive tasks that can run through the course of the semester. For example, a semester-long language course could focus on the theme of a cybertrip, and each assignment and assessment could relate to that theme: writing letters home, giving directions to attractions, interviewing people in the community, and so forth (e.g., Lomicka, Lord, & Manzer, 2003).

2.2.2 HYBRID DELIVERY

The notion of hybrid, or blended, learning is rapidly gaining popularity in higher education as administrators are asked to reduce the costs associated with language instruction. Although the term *hybrid* can have different meanings, its most basic interpretation is "blended learning . . . that is facilitated by the effective combination of different modes of delivery, models of teaching and styles of learning, and is based on transparent communication amongst all parties involved with a course" (Heinze & Proctor, 2004, pp. 8–9).[1] A hybrid approach to language instruction generally assumes a learning space where instruction takes

---

[1]See Goertler (2011, p. 472) for a comprehensive definition of various related terms, such as *face-to-face, technology-enhanced, blended,* and *open/online learning.*

place in a traditional classroom setting and is enhanced or supplemented by computer-based or online activities. The hybrid approach to language instruction assumes that students interact with the instructor, other students, or both, in person as well as virtually. The online activities often replace classroom seat time, the feature that makes the approach so attractive to administrators concerned with classroom space, instructor budgets, and class size.

A common approach to hybrid language programs is to reduce the number of weekly contact hours, usually from four or five meetings a week to two or three, with the remaining hours replaced by online work. Other patterns are possible too, such as lecture-type meetings and small group tutor sessions in conjunction with the online materials. Regardless of the approach, Rosen (2009) points out that in addition to increased computer time and reduced seat time, the other defining characteristic of hybrid learning is that "an attempt has been made to combine the best elements of traditional face-to-face instruction with the best aspects of distance education" (p. 66).

2.2.3 ONLINE AND DISTANCE COURSES

In more extreme cases of technology integration, we find language programs that are entirely online. However, just as the definition of hybrid learning is somewhat slippery, so is that of distance learning. As Blake (2009) notes, distance learning "comes in a great many flavors, as evidenced by the following collection of terms: *online learning, e-learning, open learning, distributed learning, teleconference* or *videoconference learning, blended* or *hybrid learning, life-long learning,* or *independent study*" (p. 824). The tools available for these delivery formats range from print, audio, and video components, to computer-based or internet-based materials. Students and instructors interact virtually in synchronous or asynchronous modes, but the primary defining factor is that something separates the instructor from the students (i.e., time, space, or both).

Given the near-universal belief that communication and interaction are essential to language development, distance learning in language programs has been slower to take off than in other fields. Nonetheless, the number of language courses offered online or at a distance is slowly growing, evidenced by the offerings listed in venues such as California's Virtual Campus (http://www .cvc.edu), Florida's Distance Learning Consortium (http://www.distancelearn .org), or even in brick-and-mortar campus catalogs. The increasing popularity of this delivery mode is most likely due to the same diminishing resources (and in some cases, increasing demand) discussed earlier as those that lead us to adopt blended or hybrid approaches. Recent research has also shown that the outcomes of these online courses are comparable to traditional face-to-face environments, and in some cases, they may even be better linguistically or in terms of other skills developed, such as citizenship or technological literacy (see Blake, 2009, and Goertler, 2011, for overviews). Goertler points out that there are reasons to embrace emerging technologies in the service of language learning, given the relative ease with which the ACTFL Standards (five Cs) "can be addressed through the vast access to target culture and language materials, resources, and speakers in technology-enhanced, blended and online learning environments" (p. 479).

Language programs housed online, in part or wholly, will need to address issues beyond the pedagogical aspects. For example, the LPD will need to consider costs to the university and the students, technology literacy and preparation, attrition and retention, tech support, and assignment of duties (e.g., equitable distribution of work across online and face-to-face classes). The challenges are evident, but given the motivations for online delivery, it is clear that distance learning "will continue to figure into the L2 curriculum in some significant fashion in the coming years," in spite of the controversies surrounding it (Blake, 2009, p. 824). As Goertler (2011) so succinctly puts it, "blended and online learning are here to stay" (p. 474). Therefore, it is in the LPD's best interest to consider potential benefits and drawbacks to these delivery modes proactively, rather than wait for a particular course delivery format to be imposed from above.

2.2.4 OTHER CONSIDERATIONS

The primary factors when considering technology's integration into our curricula are pedagogical and logistical, although these are not the only ones. Bernhardt et al., (2009) discuss the adoption of various technologies in their program and note that the use of a website to publicize documents offered "a vehicle for accountability" (p. 59); others note the commercial value of increased visibility: "Social network sites such as Facebook, MySpace, and Bebo offer opportunities for marketing, advertising, recruitment, staff induction and communication" (White, et al., 2008, p. 4). It is necessary to underscore, however, that technology in and of itself is not a pedagogical or methodological approach to language teaching or learning, but simply a tool (or set of tools) to help us achieve our goals: "Any technology-enhanced task—as any other task—must be theoretically grounded and pedagogically motivated. Therefore, teachers cannot simply use technology for technology's sake, but they must take advantage of these relatively modern tools to accomplish specific pedagogical objectives" (van Compernolle & Williams, 2009, pp. 16–17). Nor can instructors or LPDs undertake the implementation of technology-based activities quickly or without forethought: "Technology integration must be thoughtfully planned out based on curricular goals and instructional models—implying the use of new teaching strategies that actively engage students and rely on collaboration among teachers" (Oxford & Oxford, 2009, p. 2). It is with these caveats in mind that the next section discusses possible incorporation of some of the most common and popular tools of today. These ideas are just that—ideas—and not blueprints, plans of action, or anything concrete; rather they are suggestions based on research and experience. They should serve as inspiration to the LPD who is considering such activities, but every program is unique and every activity must be tailored to the needs of its students.

3. IDEAS FOR USING TECHNOLOGY IN A LANGUAGE PROGRAM

As discussed previously, the interactional and collaborative nature of web 2.0 tools is ideally suited to the creation of communities, which in turn can foster language acquisition and use. Many of the projects described in this chapter depend on the development of a sense of community or collaborative effort among learners. Outside of academe, these communities exist for real reasons and to accomplish real purposes, so simply "sending learners off into cyberspace for so-called 'language practice' may not necessarily be beneficial given the expectation of many online communities to communicate in accordance with established criteria (e.g., topic of discussion, participation framework)" (van Compernolle & Williams, 2009, pp. 9–10). In other words, we must be careful and intentional in designing the tasks we give students and prepare them well for the norms of the media in which they will be working. Students enjoy the opportunities to interact with native speakers (e.g., Kinginger, 1998; van Compernolle & Williams, 2009), and doing so in controlled, safe, and appropriate ways is likely to lead to successful outcomes. The sheer number of options available to communicate with web 2.0 tools precludes a discussion of each one. The sections that follow showcase some well-designed pedagogical projects that maximize the benefits of each tool employed and thus provide good models for future task elaboration.

3.1 Blogs

A blog (a blend of the *web* and *log*) is essentially an online journal, usually hosted on a website but occasionally on its own site. The content depends on the author, or *blogger*, but usually contains commentaries, descriptions, and reactions, as well as links and other media, such as audio, photos, or video. Entries in the blog are displayed in reverse chronological order so that the most recent addition appears first; this is one of the features of blogs that sets them apart from traditional web pages. Another feature is the ability for blog readers to leave comments and feedback for the author, which allows for interaction that static web pages cannot provide. Blogs can serve various purposes in education, ranging from an informational website (e.g., Lazo-Wilson and Espejo, 2009) maintained by the instructor to reflective journals maintained by students (Niño, 2009, p. 23). Between these two extremes are blogs that native speakers of the students' L2 create and maintain for their personal, nonacademic purposes, which offer real-language examples in context and usually offer cultural insights as well. Ducate and Lomicka (2008), for example, report on a multisemester project in which language students progressed from reading target language blogs to creating their own blogs in the L2. Students who took part in this project enjoyed it and believed that it helped their reading skills as well as their vocabulary knowledge, in addition to their learning more about the target culture. Interestingly, the authors had anticipated that the blogs would afford students an "authentic window into the target culture" (p. 21), but they found instead that students learned more about the bloggers they followed than any general cultural facts. Nonetheless, these connections resulted in "students learn[ing] to focus on similarities that the two cultures share" (p. 21), a valuable lesson in and of itself. Crucially, the authors took away this lesson for the future:

> As the blogosphere continues to grow and teachers search for the most pedagogically sound applications of blogs, the results of this study suggest that they should be used as they are outside of the classroom: a forum for expressing oneself and one's opinions, similar to a diary, where the topics are mostly self-selected. (p. 24)

We also have to remember, as Niño (2009) points out, that maintenance of a blog "can be time consuming and may require incentives for participation" (p. 23). With appropriately designed tasks, blogs can offer students the opportunity to engage in written communication and explore aspects of the target culture.

3.2 Wikis

Similar to blogs, wikis offer opportunities for both reading and writing in the target language. In its most well-known sense, wikis are collaborative web pages that have multiple authors. Wikis use simple editors so that no text programming knowledge is required, and while some are open to editing from anyone (think Wikipedia), others can be restricted to members only and thus be more secure. There are wikis for many different purposes, ranging from private businesses use to personal use, but they are especially well suited for any endeavor where more than one person's knowledge or opinion is important. As such, wikis are ideal tools for collaborative projects and writing assignments.

In the teaching methods course I taught several years ago, I collaborated with three colleagues who were teaching similar courses at their respective institutions. The students worked together in cross-institutional teams to create a wiki, which was designed as a resource to foreign language teachers (see Levy, (1997); Arnold, Ducate, Lomicka, and Lord, (2009). Although not currently maintained, the wiki can be viewed at http://flteaching.wikispaces.com. While interesting tendencies emerged with respect to leadership roles and cooperation styles, the end product was a collaborative effort of students in four different courses at three different institutions, working together across space and time.

Other wiki projects that focus on language learning have had similar success, and ideas range from creating encyclopedia-like entries to authoring branching stories (like the Choose Your Own Adventure book series that many of us grew up with, http://www.cyoa.com, although more technologically advanced). Arnold, Ducate, and Kost, (2009) report on a study that compared two different class projects whose goal was to collaboratively create wikis relevant to their courses. They examined the writing and creation process, revisions, learner perceptions, and instructor roles using quantitative and qualitative analytical tools. For revision, they found that students replaced or revised about 35 of every 100 words, primarily to correct meaning or to fix grammatical mistakes;

stylistic changes were less frequent. Interestingly, more than 75% of the formal (linguistic or grammatical) revisions resulted in a correct form, which tells us that even at lower levels learners are capable of making successful revisions. Also worth noting is that student feedback was overall positive and they tended to enjoy the project. There were different opinions regarding the role of the instructor in the wikis, but generally speaking, students favored the instructors playing an active role. Finally, a word of caution to those who would undertake wiki projects: It is difficult to ensure equal and fair participation, an aspect that instructors must consider, plan for, and monitor carefully.

3.3 Audio and Video Tools

The broad category of audio and video tools encompasses everything from podcasts to digital internet video and videoconferencing, among others. The following discussion is limited to these three tools, given that they are the most popular and commonly available.

3.3.1 PODCASTS

Podcasts consist of a series of digital media files, usually audio but more frequently video as well, that are released periodically in episodes and to which users can subscribe through any syndication service (RSS feed aggregators, of which iTunes is perhaps the most well-known for podcasts). Although many people use the term to refer to any audio that is available online, its essence involves the syndication and delivery of periodic episodes, and it is in that light that podcasts are discussed here.

There are three primary options for incorporating podcasts into education: (1) using previously created or professional podcasts, (2) using podcast materials created by the instructor for the class; and having students create their own podcasts (e.g., Lomicka & Lord, 2011). The first category has numerous target language podcasts on almost any topic available from iTunes or other repository sites, including iTunes U. Within this category are also podcasts created by native speakers for an audience of language learners. For example, Niño (2009) notes that the Notes in Spanish site http://www.notesin-spanish.com provides podcast files of authentic conversations in Spanish about real-life topics (p. 23).

Using authentic material involves risks: The level may be too high, the content may be inappropriate, or the focus of the material may not match the instructor's purpose. In these cases, instructors can create their own podcasts using a free hosting site. For example, Bird-Soto and Rengel (2009) noted an "absence of relevant listening materials, especially for language learners at the intermediate level," and they adopted easy-to-produce podcasts to help address this problem (p. 101). They created interviews and conversations with artists, authors, and other well-known individuals, which were then archived and syndicated and made available to students; subsequent class assignments incorporated these podcasts for culture and instruction.

Finally, given that it is generally free and easy to create podcasts, many instructors have begun assigning their students language podcast creation activities to promote speaking, comprehension, or other skills, such as pronunciation. I have used collaborative podcasts in my Spanish phonetics courses, for example, in which students record themselves and analyze their pronunciation and that of their group mates (see Lord, 2008). Students not only enjoy the community aspect of these projects, but also improve their pronunciation skills as well as their attitudes toward pronunciation. Ducate and Lomicka (2009) engaged in a similar project and also found that their students enjoyed it and were able to pay more attention to their oral skills.

3.3.2 YOUTUBE, TEACHERTUBE, AND SO ON

The primary advantages of sites such as YouTube (http://www.youtube.com) and TeacherTube (http://www.teachertube.com) are that they are "fun and visual and [show] authentic culture-related materials such as trailers, TV ads, films, show extracts, news, music, documentaries, and cartoons" (Niño, 2009, p. 23). TeacherTube is similar to YouTube but is designed for educators to post teaching and teaching-related materials. Because it has more pedagogical content than open sites like YouTube, many school districts do not block it, which makes it an ideal tool for those who work in educational contexts with restricted internet access.

Using these resources in language courses is nothing new, although the availability of media has increased dramatically, thanks to video-sharing sites such as those described here. Instructors can find authentic language input and design tasks for their students to "practice listening, reading, pronunciation, [or] intonation skills" and also enjoy the benefits of pausing and repeating video clips at their leisure (Niño, 2009, p. 23). Instructors should remember the advice previously offered by van Compernolle and Williams (2009) and Salaberry (2001), however, of the primacy of pedagogical considerations (i.e., task design, preparation for activity, follow-up activity), regardless of the tool used to carry out the task.

3.3.3 REAL-TIME COMMUNICATION

The growing array of tools available to language teachers to connect learners with native speakers of the target language has changed the way we view communication. Gone are the days of pen pals and even key pals. With the ability to text chat, voice chat, and videoconference with anyone, anywhere, at no cost, students have an unlimited supply of native speakers with whom they can interact in real-time communication.

Chatting can take place through a variety of clients, from AOL Instant Messenger to GoogleTalk or Wimba Voice tools, among others. Many textbook publishers have developed tools within their course management systems that allow users to interact with each other as well. Chats can take place via text, which offers good writing practice to students, or via voice chat, which allows for oral communication. Crucially, the implementation of chat-based tasks "provides students with opportunities to speak outside of class, thus increasing the amount of time that they are communicating interpersonally in the target language" (Rosen, 2009, p. 71), which is one of our primary goals. Most text chats can be archived and retrieved by instructors for evaluation or feedback, and some clients offer this possibility with voice chat as well.

In addition to chatting, videoconferencing has emerged as an alternative, thanks in large part to Skype, Facebook chat, and other (often free) programs that allows users to make voice and video calls over the internet. The advantage to videoconferencing over written or oral chatting is that it provides learners with the visual and nonlinguistic or extralinguistic cues (e.g., facial expressions, gestures) characteristic of authentic, real-world interactions, which also support learners' comprehension.

Although many instructors use Skype to engage their students on their own or with native speakers, other possibilities are developing as well. For example, Soziety (http://www.soziety.com) is:

> a language-exchange social network based on Skype. For language learning, it is useful for instant free conversational practice with distant users or for class-to-class exchanges, although because it concentrates mostly on oral skills, it is more suited to one-to-one sessions. (Niño, 2009, p. 23)

Just last week I observed a class in which the instructor set up a Facebook chat with a Guatemalan friend of his, allowing the student to ask the friend questions in Spanish related to the content of their current chapter. Tools such as these are being developed every day and offer learners an ideal space for practicing their emerging language skills.

3.3.4 TWITTER

A somewhat newer tool for interaction is microblogging, similar to traditional blogs in content but in a much smaller format. The most popular microblogging service is undoubtedly Twitter, although there are others such as EdModo (for education), or Identi.ca. Microblogs have limited post length, usually 140 characters, so they allow bloggers to exchange very short snippets of information, or often links to images, videos, or other content. In principle, these microblogs are appealing to language learners precisely because of the limited amount of language needed and can thus offer attractive possibilities to instructors and LPDs.

Technologies such as these have been referred to as "disruptive" technologies (e.g., Godwin-Jones, 2005) because of their potential to not only distract students and instructors but also potentially change the way we perceive the educational environment. Thus the question when dealing with such tools (e.g., Twitter) is, What role, if any, can they or should they have in our courses? As discussed earlier, privacy issues may come into play when using these primarily social tools for academic purposes. Another question is whether students are willing to engage in academic endeavors in spaces that are otherwise reserved for personal and social interactions. I was an early adopter of the Twitter application for my personal use, in spite of my doubts about its possible success (clearly, I was wrong!). Shortly, I came to see the benefits of Twitter for connecting to colleagues as well as to news outlets, professional organizations, and the like. However, it took longer to embrace Twitter as an educational tool for use with my students.

A number of articles tout Twitter's potential as an educational tool, suggesting idyllic scenarios in which Twitter can enhance our classrooms and connect and engage students. Not surprisingly though, as is the case with many emerging tools, empirical studies documenting such processes are still scarce. Two empirical studies on the effectiveness of Twitter in language-learning scenarios can be found, Antenos-Conforti (2009) and Lomicka and Lord (2012), which are discussed later.

Twitter can be used with students to have them engage with each other and with other users (tweeters) outside of class time. For example, in a language class, students have to tweet in the L2 three times a week, and they also have to respond to a classmate's tweet. Both Antenos-Conforti (2009) and Lomicka and Lord (2012) have found that this kind of connection between students and between students and their instructor helps create a stronger connection both within and beyond the class, and may contribute to relationship building during the semester. Another plus is that native speakers of the target language can also join the conversation and make the tweet interactions more realistic and more meaningful for the learners.

I have also used Twitter in the teaching methods course for new language teaching assistants (TAs). I connected my instructors to more than 100 other new language instructors in the United States and Canada, all of whom tweeted weekly about their experiences in the classroom (see Lomicka & Lord, 2010). These tweeters shared experiences, reflected on their development as teachers, and engaged in professional interactions not only with their local peers, but also with people they would otherwise not have had the chance to meet or speak with. We created a community for that semester that never would have existed without the Twittersphere.

Another option, for the braver among us, is to use Twitter during class time. Rather than ask students to turn off their electronics or pretend that they do not have them turned on, why not use them to our advantage? Here are some ideas for using a live Twitter feed (or back channel) that you can project on your screen during class time:

- At the beginning of the semester, rather than ask students to introduce themselves face-to-face, students could tweet a greeting and brief autobiographical information to the class. It takes less time and may be less intimidating. It also gives the instructor a record of what everyone said.
- Encourage questions on your class presentations via Twitter. This is a less obtrusive method than students raising their hands to ask a question, and the more timid students may feel comfortable tweeting their questions.

- Have students tweet what they understand to be the main point of your lecture or presentation, conveniently under 140 characters, throughout the class. This is a good way to assess their understanding and comprehension, and it can help keep the rest of the class on track as well.
- Encourage the class to add their reactions to what you are discussing, while you are discussing it. While this may sound distracting, it has the effect of increasing student interest and involving a larger percentage of the students.
- Get input and feedback from students on any aspect of the class. It is quick and efficient to poll the class, and you have a written record of students' responses.

3.3.5 VIRTUAL WORLDS

The last set of tools discussed here are those that offer students virtual realities or worlds. The most popular of these are sites like Second Life (http://www .secondlife.com) or World of Warcraft (http://www.worldofwarcraft.com), but others appear constantly, some with learning goals underlying their design. Educators are often reluctant to send their students to these unknown places, but researchers have begun to show that such activities can be valuable in the language acquisition process.

Cooke-Plagwitz (2009) suggests that sites like Second Life are valuable in education because they offer "several of the learning elements that [students] crave. Second Life is at once entertaining, visual, hands-on, immediate, and online" (p. 174). Language teachers have used virtual worlds like Second Life to engage students in communication (which can be text or audio based), to offer cultural perspectives, and to hold a scheduled meeting for virtual or online classes. Further, institutions and organizations have created spaces, or islands, to help educators. For example, the island created in Second Life by the Cervantes Institute (http://secondlife.cervantes.es) offers activities "for the promotion of the language and culture of Spanish-speaking countries" (Niño, 2009, p. 23).

In Kuriscak and Luke's (2009) investigation of student attitudes toward Second Life, they found that overall students enjoyed interacting there, particularly when they could engage with native speakers rather than only among themselves. In addition, they found that students were considerably self-aware of their linguistic production and often engaged in both self-correction and corrections of their peers. Cooke-Plagwitz's (2009) study went a step further to claim that interacting in a virtual world can be correlated with improved student communication: "Many educators who use Second Life for instruction have indicated that communication among their virtual students is livelier and more engaged than their face-to-face classes" (p. 175).

Researchers have also noted that in addition to improving communication skills, these virtual worlds have the potential to help learners improve their pragmatic abilities, an area that is all too often neglected in L2 classrooms. Kuriscak and Luke (2009) gathered some preliminary data to investigate leave-taking strategies used among learners in Second Life. Although their results were somewhat inconclusive, it is worth noting this feature of language use and others can be studied in a virtual setting. Sykes and her colleagues (e.g., Sykes, 2009; Sykes & Holden, 2011; Sykes, Oskoz, & Thorne, 2008; Thorne, Black, & Sykes, 2009) have investigated pragmatic awareness and performance in virtual worlds, which they call immersive environments, as well as through online games. Thorne has also extensively investigated the gaming and virtual world environments (e.g., 2012), examining various literacies associated with participation in such sites. In all, these researchers have found that immersive environments and online games that are designed for language learners not only increase motivation and interest in the language learning process, but also promote linguistic gains. LPDs may consider adopting some of these practices into their programs, especially as they continue to become more readily available and our students become increasingly comfortable in this kind of setting.

3.3.6 DIGITAL PORTFOLIOS AND MORE

The ideas and projects discussed here are a few of the many that incorporate a variety of new and emerging technologies. LPDs who want to incorporate more technologies and tools into their programs may wish to begin with them, but they will soon discover that the possibilities are endless. Educators will want to consider their comfort level, their students' abilities and access to technology, and their learning goals in making decisions in this area.

It is worth noting that many educators have created technology-based projects by combining different tools on their own, rather than using off-the-shelf applications. One such example is the revival of the portfolio as a graded component of a language course (e.g., Woody, 2005) in an electronic, rather than paper, delivery mode. The new e-portfolios use electronic media to house, organize, and present the components, which are also electronically based. Godwin-Jones (2008) lists tools available for this kind of project, and Ambrose (n.d.) has created a new term, *Googlio,* for portfolios that make use of tools available through Google. According to Ambrose, a Googlio is:

> a hybrid next-generation e-portfolio that utilizes emerging open, social, web 2.0, and Google applications such as blogs, wikis, social networks and software to create a student created and controlled personal learning environment and lifelong content management system that can be shared and viewed from different perspectives, within various contexts, and for multiple purposes. (n.p.)

These projects, which combine multiple tools, multiple skills, and multiple assessments, may serve LPDs when integrating technologies into language classes.

4. CONCLUSION

A great deal of work investigating CALL has responded to vague and somewhat inappropriate questions such as "Does technology work?" and "Is X better with technology?" As Blake (2009) has noted, these are the wrong questions to ask. In many ways, the question of whether educators, program directors, administrators, or learners are in favor of using technology in language courses has become moot, because technology is here to stay and it will continue to evolve. We no longer have the luxury of asking ourselves if we should incorporate technological tools into our curricula. We now have to ask how to do so, where such implementation can be most beneficial, and why.

To a great degree, the success of any technological implementation depends first and foremost on the LPD, not just for creating solid tasks and activities for language classes, but also for ensuring that technology be an integral part of our programs and that instructors be competent and confident in its use. Crucially, van Compernolle and Williams (2009) aptly note that "the full integration of technology into the world-language curriculum is difficult to envision as long as technology and teaching methods remain independent from one another" (p. 18). As LPDs, we must refrain from talking about technology as one of the components of a program, a class, or a methodology course. Instead, we must consider it an essential element that permeates everything we do.

The methodology course should prepare instructors in the use of various tools, along with the theoretical and pedagogical motivations for doing so. But we must not do so as an add-on unit. Instead, we should use these very tools, such as wikis, blogs, and Twitter, in the course to model and teach simultaneously. Other programs offer a whole course on technology in language teaching (e.g., Lord & Lomicka, 2004; Parry & Young, 2010), which can also provide invaluable support for teachers. The ongoing professional development we offer in our programs must also consider these aspects of technology integration as a continual theme and a constant source of ongoing education.

Questions for Reflection

1. When you took language courses, what technology tools were considered especially new and exciting? How were they used in class? How were they used out of class? Were they effective? Explain.

2. Of the tools described in this chapter, with which ones are you most familiar? How have you used them in your personal life? Professional life? Teaching duties? Administrative duties? Are they effective? If so, how? And if not, why not?

3. Brainstorm a list of ideas for incorporating new technologies into individual language classes and lesson plans as well as into a language program as a whole. What advantages are there to these additions? What difficulties can you foresee in such implementation?

Suggestions for Further Reading

Blake, R. J. (2008). *Brave new digital classroom: Technology and foreign language learning.* Washington, DC: Georgetown University Press.

> Combines anecdotal experience with data-based empirical research to discuss the best ways to incorporate technology into language classrooms. Focuses on effective use and critical competencies associated with newer technologies (i.e., web 2.0).

Lord, G. & Lomicka, L. (2010). "Into the Twittersphere: Using microblogging technology to build community." *Paper presented at the American Council on the Teaching of Foreign Languages Annual Meeting and Exposition*, Boston, MA.

> However, if it's too late to add that to the references, we can simply remove the reference entirely here, since it was my own work.

Lively, M. (1997). The changing demographics of the traditional student: Making our classrooms relevant for the new generation. *ADFL Bulletin, 28*(3), pp. 32–36.

> Discusses the changing population of students with respect to technologies in language classrooms. Although somewhat dated, the overview is a valuable one for assessing the importance of technologies in today's world, academic and otherwise.

O'Reilly, T. (2005, September 30). What is Web 2.0? *O'Reilly Network.* Available at http://oreilly.com/web2/archive/what-is-web-20.html

> A useful overview of the notion of web 2.0, along with the corresponding assumptions that underlie these tools. Not specific to education, but a good source for engaging in critical discussion on the best use of technologies.

CHAPTER 7

Looking to the Future

Perhaps the most daunting, yet simultaneously rewarding, aspect of being a language program director (LPD) is that the job is never done. Chapter 1 discussed the multifaceted nature of the job and the feeling LPDs share that there is never a break, because they are constantly preparing for the next semester, writing the next syllabus, or working on the next textbook implementation. In addition to these day-to-day tasks, LPDs deal with the larger issue of the need to be thinking outside the box, anticipating the next new tool, approach, or textbook that promises to enhance teaching and learning languages. This chapter examines the LPD's role as innovator and discusses issues relevant to conceiving and implementing change in the program. This topic then serves as a springboard for a discussion of the future of the LPD—our role, what it can and should be, and where we should see ourselves in the coming years.

1. THE LPD AND INNOVATION

It is not the LPD's task to foster dialogue and innovation for an entire department, but it is within our job description to assess and update our programs on a regular basis. Often these changes imply modifications well beyond the elementary and intermediate language courses. At the risk of exaggerating our importance, I believe we have a significant responsibility to our departments and institutions in setting future. As with all change, "we must . . . be able to recognize the need for change. We need to know when it is time to think about renewal, when it is time to formulate a new strategy, and when it is time for stability and continuance" (Mintzberg, 1987, p. 75). Although Mintzberg was referring to innovation in the business world, LPDs have expressed similar sentiments.

Moyer and Gonglewski (1998), for example, maintain that the responsibility for implementing change must come from the LPD: "The LPD must project a strong image as the source from which innovation and ultimate responsibility emanate" (p. 54). Crucially, they note that such a role requires a solid understanding and discussion of our purpose beyond the language department, that is, not just beyond our language classes and the language program, but beyond our department as well, looking toward the college, university, or profession as we make our choices. As Stoller (1997) also asserts, "although rarely listed in our job descriptions, one of our most important responsibilities as language program administrators is to serve as catalysts for change and innovation" (p. 33). She maintains that the LPD can accomplish this role through "strong leadership and involvement in programmatic change and innovation" and in so doing, we can reap the benefits of "greater job satisfaction among faculty and staff, better learning conditions for students, improved reputations for our programs, and more effective management of program resources" (p. 33). Most LPDs did not sign on for all this when taking over a language program, but with time and experience, they can in fact be catalysts for change, as they are responsible, directly or indirectly, for larger issues in their departments.

The job of today's LPD may seem even more intimidating than it did at the outset of this book. Nevertheless, a well-informed LPD is naturally positioned to lead the program, and even the department, toward change. By necessity, language programs deal with issues that affect our larger organizations, and we have experience handling them: student engagement and retention, teacher training, technological innovations, and so forth. Thus when it comes to assessing the LPDs' role in their departments, institutions, and the language profession, they emerge as leaders. The guidelines laid out in the previous chapters can help LPDs get to the point where innovation becomes the next logical step.

1.1 What is Innovation?

According to Baldridge and Deal (1983), innovation is a fundamental element of any thriving educational program. It is difficult to define what innovation encompasses, and it is equally challenging to determine the best way to put our efforts into that end goal of innovation, especially in academic settings (e.g., Kirschner, 2012). For example, in contrast to innovation, change is predictable and inevitable, but may not result in improvement. Innovation, on the other hand, is the end product of consistent and conscious efforts to bring about improvements. A change could be replacing faculty, for example, but innovation comes from designing new courses, adopting new textbooks, or articulating old and new courses. Although change is inevitable, innovating change may not be, and innovative change is what we need because it "is the key to raising standards in that it facilitates self-renewal, promotes a sense of well-being, enhances teachers' careers, prevents burnout, improves instruction, and allows programs to be responsive to changes that are likely to impact them" (Stoller, 1997, p. 34).

The nature of innovation implies movement away from the norm, and that generally entails controversy because some may fear it, not understand it, or be generally resistant to all change. Thus programmatic innovation may lead to anxiety, insecurity, and discomfort, especially because innovations tend to entail, at least in the short term, increased workloads to learn new approaches, train personnel, and adjust to different systems.

So why would anyone want to undertake such a potentially traumatic experience? Innovation brings with it short- and long-term benefits to the organization, and "the exhilaration that comes from such exploration can invigorate a program and lead to improved teaching and learning" (Stoller, 1997, p. 33). With these benefits in mind, we must consider when the time is right to undertake programmatic innovations.

1.2 When Innovation Happens

Research has shown that the most frequent cause for undertaking innovative projects is dissatisfaction with the status quo, be it in terms of curriculum, personnel, recruitment, evaluation, or the like (e.g., Stoller, 1992, 1995a, 1995b). Stoller's work with intensive English programs investigated precisely these kinds of incentives for programmatic innovation, based on LPDs' input. In her survey, she noted that LPDs also indicated that innovation can come about as a perceived need for more professionalism, redefined responsibilities, or further training. Other common incentives for innovation come from students or faculty, redundancy usually in the form of requests or proposals.

That mandates from administrators should spark innovative change more frequently than requests from students and faculty colleagues may appear contradictory to the goals of LPDs. The explanation may lie in the increased workload that innovative projects entail. Why, for example, contemplate a programmatic change such as new delivery systems or new course alignments, when the status quo is, more or less, functioning? Contemplating the hours of work and effort that go into such a large undertaking is daunting, and since innovation is not generally necessitated by an abrupt shift in circumstances, it is by nature optional. In my case, the message I received when I took on the role of LPD of an intermediate language program was that the program was working well and little hands-on direction would be needed. To some extent that was true; on the surface, the program appeared to be functioning well. It took only a few weeks of observing the program, however, to realize that it could be much better. We needed to rethink our course sequence and our placement policies, as well as our delivery of classes, which will be discussed more in the coming sections. These modifications would take time, patience, and some dedication, not to mention convincing a group of people who were satisfied with the status quo that they should not be satisfied.

1.3 Encouraging Innovation

One challenge for the LPD is to identify when and where innovation is needed, but a greater challenge is getting buy-in from the other members of the language program. Even as the LPD recognizes the impetus for innovations, others may be equally resistant. Thus LPDs must temper their enthusiasm for innovation with a realistic approach to what is possible:

> There is clearly a good case for sitting down with all your staff . . . to ask them what it is they like about their jobs, what they would like to change, and how their work life could be made more satisfying— but without raising their expectation that you will be able to wave a magic wand to bring about instant improvements. (White et al., 2008, p. 243)

An LPD who aims to create a program that is open to and ready for innovation is justified and properly motivated, because it is within this type of program culture that cutting-edge projects are most likely to be successful.

Research has shown that there are common characteristics among programs that tend to stimulate or encourage innovative modifications (e.g., Stoller, 1997). Primary among these are the faculty members themselves, who need to be committed to the program, able to collaborate successfully, and feel that they are valued in a stable organization. Faculty who feel that they are members of a committed, professional organization are more likely to contribute to the overall potential of that program. So as LPDs we "need to nurture stability, professional working conditions, and a sense of belonging or permanence, whenever possible" (Stoller, 1997, p. 37), and we need to "ensure that faculty and other team members are confident that their commitment to the program will be appreciated and even rewarded" (Barsi & Kaebnick, 1989). Tied to this point is another aspect of programs that enables innovation: leadership (Stoller, 1997), usually in the person of the LPD. The program leader needs the vision to foresee the need for innovations, and he or she needs to have the leadership skills to implement innovative projects. That same leader also needs a certain degree of dynamism to encourage buy-in and engage collaborators. Furthermore, there is great value in a leader who is not only strong and dynamic, but also flexible and interested in listening to and collaborating with others. The strongest teams rely on the abilities of all of their members, and the strongest leaders are those who recognize that this is the case.

The structure that the LPD establishes in the program is crucial to the success of any innovations:

> We play an instrumental role in shaping the organizational and philosophical framework of our programs. We must structure our programs so that the possibility for innovation is built into them, and we must share the responsibility for innovation with our faculty so that innovation has the potential to spread. (Stoller, 1997, p. 38)

On a related note, members of a program need to perceive a transparency in governance procedures; if members do not understand how the system is run and how decisions are made, they are not going to feel the commitment or investment needed to spur innovation.

1.4 How to Implement Changes

The process of making proposed innovations become reality can be complicated. Stoller (1997) suggests that the LPD present innovative proposals so that the program participants can see that the advantages outweigh the disadvantages. Furthermore, we need to justify these modifications by explaining why they are desirable. Have they emerged in response to faculty, staff, or student dissatisfaction? Do they result from requests by college-level administrators? Are they proposed as a result of student learning outcomes (e.g., Barr & Tagg, 1995)? Finally, the LPD should establish a clear outline of the feasibility and practicality of the proposed innovation so it is seen as a challenge, but a surmountable one. We need to be conscious of what we are proposing and to be enthusiastic but reasonable. We need to ensure that our innovations are seen as different enough from the status quo to solve problems, but not so different as to create too much fear of the unknown: "Implementing such an organizational innovation will require consultation, analysis of work, grouping of jobs which most appropriately go together, communicating the changes to all affected staff, monitoring the effect of the staff changes and making adjustments if necessary" (White et al., 2008, p. 245). Clearly, programmatic innovation should not be undertaken lightly or without plenty of planning and considerable time for implementation.

It is also important to weigh the advantages and disadvantages of gradual change. In some cases moving slowly is necessary: "Complex problems, such as setting up a new course or introducing or changing coursebooks, cannot be dealt with quickly" (White et al., 2008, p. 243). For example, for adopting a new textbook, as described in Chapter 3, I used a meticulous and gradual process that involved months of reviewing and discussing, and then multiple semesters of phasing in the change. This approach helped both the instructors and the students. The former had time to become accustomed to the idea of switching from the comfortable book they knew and loved, and were slowly drawn into the excitement of new resources; they also had time to adapt their current practices and materials to the new system. Students, on the other hand, have different considerations that may be related, for example, to purchasing new textbooks. The LPD should consider phasing in new books over semesters to maintain the sequence and not require two different texts for a two-semester sequence. Financially, the students appreciate not having to buy a new textbook, and they also benefit from not having to learn a new textbook layout or online system midyear.

Conversely, other innovations can be approached in a less-measured (but still meticulously planned) way. One example is my program's recent switch to hybrid delivery for our first-year courses. Many programs study and pilot their hybrid platform for several semesters before implementing it full-scale. I respect and admire their decisions, and I am sure they learned valuable lessons along the way. It is likely that the full-scale implementation had its glitches nonetheless. Based on my knowledge of our program and student body, however, I chose to implement the hybrid approach in a single semester for all courses at that level. Although perhaps drastic, this implementation allowed me to train all instructors and coordinators at one time, to prepare all materials at one time, and to sell the changes to the students all at once. We had glitches and concerns, of course, but for the most part we solved them in the first semester. If we had slowly piloted and phased in the platform, my hunch is that we would have been dealing with these glitches in each new semester. Of course, this kind of decision depends entirely on the population of students and instructors, and the resources available. The important point, however, is that sometimes a quicker approach can work too. Prior to this all-at-once change, I worked for about eight months to educate myself and others to advise and prepare everyone for what was coming.

After the implementation of change, the LPD has to follow through: "Managers responsible for introducing . . . transformational change have to be prepared to find ways of rewarding and remotivating staff in order to sustain effort and commitment" (White et al., 2008, p. 240). Some innovations will be embraced immediately upon adoption, but instructors, students, or both may take more time to adjust to others: "Change is a learning process (and therefore needs to be regarded as such). Change is a journey, not a blueprint . . . Problems arise from the change process; these are natural and expected and must be identified and solved" (White et al., 2008, p. 243).

Any innovation is likely to be viewed differently by those who advocate the change and those who are asked to take responsibility for implementing it. To that end, it is important that the advocator, often the LPD, take into account the various viewpoints of the other team members (White, Martin, Stimson, & Hodge, 1991). When we adopted the hybrid platform in my program, some of the instructors, who were used to the 5-day-a-week format, were not entirely convinced by the new approach. I expected this reluctance and preempted it to some extent with my training sessions, workshops, and frequent communications. Those who remained skeptical, however, needed longer to adapt. From my perspective in this situation, it was crucial to let them voice their doubts, allowing the dialogue with me, but simultaneously ensuring that they were following the program requirements. This approach relates to what was stated earlier about the importance of a leader who can relate to and work with a team. I noticed in my classroom observations that semester that some subtle (or occasionally overt) messages were creeping into the instructors' presentations in class, in which they communicated to the students their disagreement with the approach, implying that they were sorry that students were having to learn a language this way. If these were the messages they were conveying in my presence, surely the messages were stronger when I was not there. This situation was difficult to handle, because it required striking a balance between listening to and respecting dissenting voices, while also ensuring the overall consistency of a program decision. In this case, one-on-one meetings with those instructors were convened to explain again the motivations for our decision, and to recognize both the advantages and disadvantages of the new system. The members of the LPD team were reminded of the importance of unity among the members to preserve the integrity of the program. An organization can be jeopardized from the bottom up as well as from the top down. Those one-on-one meetings may not have changed anyone's opinions—only time and experience can accomplish that—but they were effective in substantially reducing the negative messages these instructors sent to their students.

In the case of our change to a hybrid format, I was at a slight disadvantage because the innovation was not entirely internally motivated. We need to be aware and accepting of the fact that some decisions that will have a direct impact on the language program may come from outside the program. Such a scenario does not reflect negatively on the members of the language program or on their abilities, but instead is a reality of the fact that "constraints are often imposed by the institution" (Henry, 1997, p. 81). External mandates may be a disadvantage, because the LPD is put in the situation of arguing enthusiastically for innovations on the basis of pedagogical or empirical information that may be weak or nonexistent. It is not necessary for LPDs to pretend to believe fully in something they are asked to do, but it is important that LPDs support the decisions once they have been made, explain why innovations are happening, and reiterate the importance of team cooperation and follow-through. It is also the LPD's job to find ways to make such innovations work well. In the case of our hybrid transition, for example, the instructors were required to do far less grading with our new system, and they received a great deal of prepared (optional) materials to help with the transition. Likewise, when adopting a new textbook, I ensure that instructors have access to a few chapters' worth of lesson plans, complete with PowerPoint presentations and activities to help them learn to use the new resources. As LPDs we must pick our battles carefully and wisely, and then be prepared to fight the ones we have chosen (Henry, 1997). Then we do our best to make the transition as smooth as possible.

2. THE BIGGER PICTURE

Envisioning and implementing our vision for our programs is exciting and rewarding. LPDs have opportunities to engage in essential questions involved in language teaching, and also in questions relevant to the larger programs to which we belong—curricular, departmental, institutional, and professional. Moyer and Gonglewski (1998), recognize that our job goes beyond the day-to-day tasks of syllabus design and text selection: "It is the LPD's job, as much as possible, to unify the teaching staff toward building an integrated, coherent curriculum that reaches through all levels, with obvious objectives at each stage for developing skills, fluency, and knowledge" (p. 56). As such, our role as program directors is a crucial one, and we must ensure that our position is understood as one that serves to contribute to departmental, college, and even institutional initiatives.

As has been discussed, not everyone comprehends what the LPD does: "A language program director frequently faces a job that has been ill-defined, that may be controversial in its implication of upcoming change or systematization, and that requires a component of gradual enlightenment in order to gain collegial support" (Moyer & Gonglewski, 1998, p. 53). This predicament is an interesting one, however, given the potential for the LPD to help shape departmental vision and policy. Historically speaking, the LPD has not always been viewed as an integral part of institutional governance.

Not all LPDs come to their positions after graduate work in applied linguistics or other related fields. In Schulz's (1980) survey of language programs and their directors, she found that 87% of LPDs held doctorates, which was up from the 64% Hagiwara had found in his earlier (1970b) study, but that "academic preparation of TA supervisors appears to have changed little" (p. 2), since only 17%–19% claimed any kind of background or specialty in language teaching. Additionally, the LPD position is often not a tenure-track line. In a study on the role of the LPD in German programs, Maxim (2005b) discovered that "according to MLA statistics during the five-year period from 1993 to 1998, 64% of the PhDs granted in German were from institutions that do not have a tenure-track position for their TA supervisor" (p. 16). Lacking the status of a ranked faculty position, LPDs are often relegated to lower status in the department, which implies reduced resources for professional development or limited influence in departmental governance.

Even though LPDs may still struggle for the recognition they deserve, language departments continue to need LPDs. An examination of the jobs advertised in the MLA Job Information List in recent years reveals a consistent number of LPD positions, often as tenure-track lines, in a variety of academic settings (see the example in Chapter 1). It remains, therefore, in our best interest to continue to educate our colleagues and our students about our roles and to insist on respect and representation in our departments and institutions. This ongoing education becomes even more important when considering that LPDs who are in tenure-track positions must maintain an active program of research and publication, as well as teach and carry out their administrative duties. By default (and perhaps through well-intentioned ignorance), many department chairs assume incorrectly that graduate degrees in second language acquisition or formal linguistics entail expertise in pedagogy and language program direction, and they advertise their positions and choose their new LPDs accordingly. Many LPDs quickly learn the administrative and mentoring aspects of the position and embrace the opportunity to develop a research agenda that complements their LPD work. Although not necessary, this approach helps LPDs reconcile their dual roles as scholars and administrators.

2.1 What Does the Future Hold?

As more language departments recognize the need for directors to shape their language programs, the number of LPDs will continue to grow and the role of the LPD in the profession will evolve as well. As we look to the future, we can contemplate what the position will be, what innovations lie ahead, and what we will need to do to offer the best direction to our programs. The following sections address some of these areas, with a view toward making the most of our role as LPDs.

2.1.1 STRUCTURAL MODIFICATIONS

In Schulz's (1980) survey, she offered suggestions to LPDs from a practical, day-to-day perspective (pp. 7–8). One suggestion for programs that depend on graduate student instructors was not to assign them to teach during their first semester, letting them take the teaching methodology course, observe, and get acclimated first. This is an ideal scenario, but not common: All of the respondents in my survey more than 30 years later indicated that their TAs teach during their first semester as graduate students. In general, only a few private universities have the luxury of paying stipends for training, not teaching.

There may be ways to help new graduate students adapt quickly to their roles as TAs, such as pairing them with experienced TAs or instructors for their first semester in a sort of team-teaching approach (e.g., Silva et al., 2006). This approach is also viable for all new instructors, not necessarily graduate students. The experienced instructors could receive a course release (e.g., teach one instead of two sections) for their work with new instructors, and they would be responsible for helping the novice TAs with their lesson plans. They would attend and teach classes with the new instructor at first, gradually shifting to total independence for the new instructor. Alternately, the master section could be implemented, as discussed in Chapter 5. If a course release is not feasible compensation due to institutional limitations, perhaps the LPD could offer a graduate course, a type of advanced teaching practicum, in which experienced TAs would earn credit for serving in this mentor role. It is the LPD's responsibility to ensure the highest quality of instruction in the language courses while also providing as much support and mentorship as possible for the instructors.

Schulz (1980) also recommended that instructors be rewarded for their efforts through teaching awards or other recognition. Many universities have awards to recognize excellence in teaching, but LPDs may be able to establish program-level awards as well. These awards may recognize teaching excellence, collegiality, commitment to the program, or some combination of these and other qualities that are important to specific programs. The monetary award may not be nearly as important as the recognition of and gratitude for outstanding contributions to the language program. Program-level awards can help cement and promote program cohesion and functionality.

Schulz (1980) also recommended that LPDs and course-level coordinators be given released time. According to my survey and anecdotal reports, most LPDs do get some kind of course release, although often not enough to compensate for the time they spend preparing courses, writing syllabi, producing tests, observing classes, and other tasks, all of which require careful management. The issue of program size comes into play in this issue too: LPDs of small programs may get less released time due to the smaller number of people to supervise, but they often have to work with the same number of courses and even contend with fewer resources and ancillaries, at least in the case of less commonly taught languages. To ensure proper compensation, LPDs must have the support of their chairs, if not the departmental faculty as a whole, and all members need to understand the scope of the LPD's tasks. Gaining this support from administrators or colleagues who do not understand the complexity of the LPD job depends on the LPD to provide information and updates on the accomplishments of the language program.

Finally, Schulz (1980) asserted that LPDs should have special training in applied linguistics, pedagogy, psycholinguistics, educational research, curriculum building, and supervisory techniques. The reality is that few LPDs come into the position fully equipped for the task and often with little training to prepare them. Although a background in applied linguistics or language acquisition is undoubtedly a plus when it comes to directing language programs, the position demands more than academic preparation. As I have argued, successful LPDs must, of course, be experts in language pedagogy, but the job requires other types of expertise as well. Interpersonal skills, management abilities, and organizational talents are all required, but are rarely taught. Because many LPDs did not as graduate students know that they would accept LPD positions later on, the best approach is to work with our graduate student instructors as though they might someday work in a supervisory role in a language program. This approach includes, but is not limited to, making transparent not only our policies but also the reasons for them, articulating program goals frequently, and offering graduate student instructors opportunities to collaborate in program administration work under the LPD's direction.

2.1.2 INNOVATION IN (AND BEYOND) THE CLASSROOM

The Association of Departments of Foreign Languages' Statement of Good Practice (ADFL, 2001) maintains that "good teaching begins with imaginative, conscientious course design and ongoing efforts to maintain and develop subject-area and methodological expertise" (para. 4). To a great degree this responsibility falls on the shoulders of the LPD: We design courses, we train instructors, we are the vision of the program. So it is also part of our duty to stay informed about innovations in areas of language pedagogy, education, and teacher training.

Today, the most common loci of innovation and modification are generally those that revolve to some extent around technology. Not only do new tools become available to us at a dizzying rate, but our students are changing as well, thanks in part to these tools. We must consider innovations in the way we present material, the way students complete assignments, and even the media through which students interact with us and with each other. Even something as relatively simple and presumably traditional as the syllabus is now subject to change; Jones (2011) notes modifications in layout, presentation, and delivery of the traditional syllabus content to reach our diverse and technologically savvy student populations. LPDs must keep up with the rapid technological changes to be well equipped to decide what role new tools, if any, have in our curricula. Thanks to organizations that educate and support language teachers (see the appendix in Chapter 1 for the complete list), we have resources available to us. But as these changes continue, LPDs will need to consciously set aside time for our own ongoing professional development in these areas.

2.1.3 SCHOLARSHIP AND THE ACADEMY

Although a great majority of the LPD's time is spent on issues specific to our departments, programs, and instructors, we do need to remember the larger issues as well. As we consider what the future holds for LPDs and our role in our departments, our institutions, and the profession, these issues must be addressed. Both the ADFL (2001) and the MLA (2007) recognize that the continuing dichotomies between teaching and research, as well as between language and literature, need to be addressed so that departments recognize both as equally valuable contributions to the profession. The ADFL statement stresses that striking the right balance depends on all parties involved:

> A department should develop rewards and assessment procedures for teaching and scholarship that fit its institution's history, mission, students, and resources. Departments and institutions can benefit from encouraging faculty members whose interests shift among teaching, scholarship, and administration or service over the course of their careers. (ADFL, 2001, para. 2)

Even though many LPDs do not study specifically to take on this role, it is understandable that their interests, the more time they spend working on curricular and pedagogical issues, may shift away from their original areas of scholarship and tend more toward areas where they spend their administrative and pedagogical time.

In addressing the issue of where LPDs stand in language departments or institutions, ADFL suggests that "scholarship on teaching—its methods, assessment procedures, and ways to improve it—should be valued on a par with traditional forms of scholarship" (para. 10). In other words, researching language teacher training, exploring connections between language acquisition theories and classroom pedagogies, writing textbooks, and other work done in relation to language program direction should be considered legitimate scholarship with equal value to other scholarly endeavors in terms of its contribution to the profession, to the creation of new knowledge, and toward tenure and promotion.

The MLA (2007) report also recognizes that language departments need to reconsider the relative importance given to language studies and upper-level (usually literature-focused) courses:

> Foreign language departments, if they are to be meaningful play-
> ers in higher education—or, indeed, if they are to thrive as
> autonomous units—must transform their programs and structure. . . .
> [F]oreign language faculty members have been working in creative
> ways to cross disciplinary boundaries, incorporate the study of all
> kinds of material in addition to the strictly literary, and promote wide
> cultural understanding through research and teaching. It is time for
> all language programs in all institutions to reflect this transformation.
> (para. 8)

This important recommendation strives to remedy the inequality between the work of LPDs and that of other faculty members. This task is ongoing, but the acknowledgment of the problem by the MLA and its recommendation are a step in the right direction.

Finally, LPDs cannot exist in a vacuum. Often they are the only linguists in a language department, and in small institutions they may be the only LPD. Given these facts and the nature of the position, LPDs often work in isolation, without the benefit of mentoring from a more experienced colleague. With this potential risk of isolation in mind, LPDs must actively seek mentors and colleagues: "It is critical to connect with colleagues with similar . . . interests in order to strengthen one's own identity as a scholar and to seek opportunities for feedback and collaborative work" (Moyer & Gonglewski, 1998, p. 54.). Organizations like the American Association of University Supervisors and Coordinators (AAUSC) are invaluable in this respect: They connect LPDs across institutions, and they offer a wealth of resources on their website and through conference presentations and yearly volumes (see the appendix in Chapter 1). Collaboration in research projects and publications is another way to learn from other LPDs. Membership in a community of LPDs contributes greatly to make this challenging job more manageable and considerably more enjoyable.

3. CONCLUSION

The impetus that pushed me to write this book was the knowledge that information was available to help LPDs, but it was scattered across many resources and not easily accessible as an integrated whole. I set out to accumulate these resources for my reference and learning. Numerous articles published over the past decades have addressed issues related to language program direction and all that it entails, and I have referenced several throughout these pages. Also, some useful practical guides for LPDs have been written by experienced LPDs with a great deal of advice to offer, and I have made considerable use of them in this work. What I sought, however, was the combination of the theoretical with the practical, a guiding resource that offered the philosophies along with advice for enacting them.

The more I read and learned, the more I found myself saying, "I wish there were some way to have all of this kind of thing in one place." So that is what I have aimed to do with this volume. I have focused on the articles and books that provide background and insight, reflection and interpretation, and application and practice most relevant to my role as a director in a language program. I believe that the combination of these perspectives can offer LPDs the needed resources to understand our responsibilities, carry out our day-to-day tasks, and engage with our profession on a meaningful level.

Questions for Reflection

1. Considering the difference between change and innovation discussed in this chapter, reflect on the modifications your language program has undergone in recent years. How would you classify them? What were the motivations and justifications for their implementation?
2. What innovation have you been responsible for? Are you satisfied with your approach to it, and its outcome? Explain. What innovations would you like to see in the language program you work in? How would you propose, justify, and implement such innovations?
3. What do you think the role of the LPD will be like in 10 years? In 25 years? Why? What do you think the LPD's role should be in the future?
4. What crucial issues are facing language programs that LPDs will need to address in the near future? How should they be addressed?

Suggestions for Further Reading

Association of Departments of Foreign Languages. (2001). *Statement of good practice: Teaching, evaluation, and scholarship.* Retrieved from http://www.adfl.org/resources/resources_practice.htm
> Although now somewhat dated, the ADFL statement offers LPDs a blueprint for balancing their multiple roles and a vision for LPD incorporation in language departments.

Kirschner, A. (2012, April 8). Innovations in higher education? Hah! *Chronicle of Higher Education.* Retrieved from http://chronicle.com/article/Innovations-in-Higher/131424/
> Frank discussion of the need for college leaders to move beyond talking about transformation and suggestions for making innovations happen.

Modern Language Association. (2007). *Foreign languages and higher education: New structures for a changed world.* Retrieved from http://www.mla.org/flreport

> Challenges the traditional two-tiered system of language departments, arguing for a more seamless and prominent role of language instruction that includes other upper-level content. Valuable perspective for LPDs functioning within the larger structure of the language department.

Stoller, F. L. (1997). The catalyst for change and innovation. In M. A. Christison & F. L. Stoller (Eds.), *A handbook for language program administrators* (pp. 33–48). Burlingame, CA: Alta Book Center.

> Perspectives on change and innovation in language programs. Offers useful advice to LPDs seeking to implement change.

White, R., Hockley, A., van der Horst Jansen, J., & Laughner, M. (2008). *From teacher to manager: Managing language teaching organizations.* New York: Cambridge University Press.

> Overall a good reference for LPDs, but also relevant to the current chapter's themes of innovation and future directions.

REFERENCES

Afros, E., & Schryer, C. F. (2009). The genre of syllabus in higher education. *Journal of English for Academic Purposes, 8,* 224–233.

Allen, H. W., & Maxim, H. (Eds.). (2011). *Educating the future foreign language professoriate for the 21st century.* Boston, MA: Heinle Cengage.

Allen, L. Q. (2002). Teachers' pedagogical beliefs and the *Standards* for foreign language learning. *Foreign Language Annals, 35,* 518–529.

Allwright, R. L. (1981). What do we want teaching materials for? *ELT Journal, 36,* 5–18.

Ambrose, A. (n.d.). *What is a Googlio?* Retrieved from http://sites.google.com/site/googlioproject/home/what-is-a-googlio

American Association of University Professors. (1993). *The status of non-tenure-track faculty.* Retrieved from http://www.aaup.org/AAUP/comm/rep/nontenuretrack.htm

American Council on the Teaching of Foreign Languages. (1999). *ACTFL proficiency guidelines: Speaking.* Retrieved from http://www.actfl.org/i4a/pages/index.cfm?pageid=4236

American Council on the Teaching of Foreign Languages. (2001). *ACTFL proficiency guidelines: Writing.* Retrieved from http://www.actfl.org/i4a/pages/index.cfm?pageid=4236

American Council on the Teaching of Foreign Languages. (2006). *Standards for foreign language learning in the 21st century.* Yonkers, NY: ACTFL.

American Council on the Teaching of Foreign Languages. (2010). *Position statement on the use of the target language in the classroom.* Retrieved from http://www.actfl.org/i4a/pages/index.cfm?pageid=5151

Anderson, R. (1997). Educating the dean: Who are we and what do we do? *ADFL Bulletin, 29*(1), 20–23.

Ansary, H., & Babaii, E. (2002). Universal characteristics of EFL/ESL textbooks: A step towards systematic textbook evaluation. *The Internet TESL Journal, 8*(2). Retrieved from http://iteslj.org/Articles/Ansary-Textbooks/

Antenos-Conforti, E. (2009). Microblogging on Twitter: Social networking in intermediate Italian classes. In L. Lomicka & G. Lord (Eds.), *The next generation: Social networking and online collaboration in foreign language learning* (pp. 59–90). San Marcos, TX: CALICO.

Arens, K. (2009). Teaching culture: The *Standards* as an optic on curriculum development. In V. M. Scott (Ed.), *Principles and practices of the* Standards *in college foreign language education* (pp. 160–180). Boston, MA: Heinle Cengage.

Arnold, N., Ducate, L., & Kost, C. (2009). Collaborative writing in wikis: Insights from culture projects in German classes. In L. Lomicka & G. Lord (Eds.), *The next generation: Social networking and online collaboration in foreign language learning* (pp. 115–144). San Marcos, TX: CALICO.

Arnold, N., Ducate, L., Lomicka, L., & Lord, G. (2005). Using computer-mediated communication to establish social and supportive environments in teacher education. *CALICO Journal, 22,* 537–566.

Arnold, N., Ducate, L., Lomicka, L., & Lord, G. (2009). Assessing online collaboration among language teachers: A cross-institutional wiki case study. *Journal of Technology and Teacher Education, 8,* 121–139.

Aski, J. M. (2003). Foreign language textbook activities: Keeping pace with second language acquisition research. *Foreign Language Annals, 36,* 57–65.

Association of Departments of Foreign Languages. (2001). *Statement of good practice: Teaching, evaluation, and scholarship.* Retrieved from http://www.adfl.org/resources/resources_practice.htm

Bailey, K. M., Curtis, A., & Nunan, D. (2001). *Pursuing professional development: The self as source.* Boston, MA: Heinle Cengage.

Baldridge, J. V., & Deal, T. E. (Eds.). (1983). *The dynamics of organizational change in education.* Berkeley, CA: McCutchan Publishing.

Barr, R. B., & Tagg, J. (1995). From teaching to learning: A new paradigm for undergraduate education. *Change, 27*(6), 12–25.

Barrette, C., & Paesani, K. (Eds.). (2005). *Language program articulation: Developing a theoretical foundation.* Boston, MA: Heinle Cengage.

Barsi, L. M., & Kaebnick, G. W. (1989). Innovative universities. *AAHE Bulletin, 41*(6), 10–13.

Bax, S. (2003). CALL—Past, present and future. *System, 31,* 13–28.

Bean, W. C. (Ed.). (1993). *Strategic planning that makes things happen: Getting from where you are to where you want to be.* Amherst, MA: Human Resources Development Press.

Beatty, K. (2003). *Teaching and researching computer assisted language learning.* New York: Longman.

Beauvois, M. H. (1992). Computer-assisted classroom discussion in the foreign language classroom: Conversation in slow motion. *Foreign Language Annals, 25,* 455–464.

Bell, R. (1983). *An introduction to applied linguistics.* London, United Kingdom: Batsford.

Belz, J. A., & Thorne, S. L. (Eds.). (2006). *Internet-mediated intercultural foreign language education.* Boston, MA: Heinle Cengage.

Bennett, S., Maton, K., & Kervin, L. (2008). The "digital natives" debate: A critical review of the evidence. *British Journal of Educational Technology, 39,* 775–786.

Benseler, D. (Ed.). (1993). *The dynamics of language program direction.* Boston, MA: Heinle Cengage.

Bernhardt, E., Valdés, G., & Miano, A. (2009). A chronicle of *Standards*-based curricular reform in a research university. In V. M. Scott (Ed.), *Principles and practices of the* Standards *in college foreign language education* (pp. 54–85). Boston, MA: Heinle Cengage.

Beyer, T. R. (2000). What standards? *Standards*—so what? *ADFL Bulletin, 31*(2), 59–60.

Beyer, T. R. (2001). The foreign language department in a liberal arts college. *ADFL Bulletin, 32*(3), 118–119.

Bird-Soto, N., & Rengel, P. (2009). Podcasting and the intermediate-level Spanish classroom. In R. Oxford & J. Oxford (Eds.), *Second language teaching and learning in the Net Generation* (pp. 101–110). Honolulu, HI: University of Hawai'i, National Foreign Language Resource Center.

Blake, R. J. (2008). *Brave new digital classroom: Technology and foreign language learning*. Washington, DC: Georgetown University Press.

Blake, R. J. (2009). The use of technology for second language distance learning. *The Modern Language Journal, 93*, 822–835.

Blyth, C. (Ed.). (2003). *The sociolinguistics of foreign language classrooms: Contributions of the native, the near-native and the non-native speaker*. Boston, MA: Heinle Cengage.

Blyth, C. (2009). From textbook to online materials: The changing ecology of foreign language publishing in the era of digital technology. In M. Evans (Ed.), *Foreign language learning with digital technology* (pp. 179–202). London, United Kingdom: Continuum.

Blyth, C. (Ed.) (2010). *Foreign language teaching methods*. Texas Language Technology Center, University of Texas at Austin. Retrieved from http://coerll.utexas.edu/methods

Boud, D., Keogh, R., & Walker, D. (1995). *Reflection: Turning experience into learning*. London, United Kingdom: Kogan Page.

Bragger, J. D., & Rice, D. B. (2000). Foreign language materials: Yesterday, today, and tomorrow. In R. Terry (Ed.), *Agents of change in a changing age* (pp. 107–140). Lincolnwood, IL: National Textbook Company.

Brandl, K. (2007). *Communicative language teaching in action: Putting principles to work*. Upper Saddle River, NJ: Prentice Hall.

Brandt, C. (2008). Integrating feedback and reflection in teacher preparation. *ELT Journal, 62*(1), 37–46.

Breen, M. (1984). Process syllabuses for the language classroom. In C. Brumfit (Ed.), *General English syllabus design* (ELT documents No. 118). Oxford, United Kingdom: The British Council/Pergamon Press.

Breen, M. (2002). Syllabus design. In R. Carter & D. Nunan (Eds.), *The Cambridge guide to teaching English to speakers of other languages*. Cambridge, United Kingdom: Cambridge University Press.

Breen, M., & Candlin, C. N. (1980). The essentials of a communicative curriculum in language teaching. *Applied Linguistics, 1*(2), 89–112.

Brookefield, S. D. (1995). *On becoming a critically reflective teacher*. San Francisco: Jossey Bass.

Brooks, N. (1975). The analysis of foreign and familiar cultures. In R. Lafayette (Ed.), *The culture revolution in foreign language teaching* (pp. 19–31). Skokie, IL: National Textbook Company.

Brown, H. D. (2007). *Principles of language learning and teaching.* New York: Pearson Longman.

Bruce, I. (2005). Syllabus design for general EAP writing courses: A cognitive approach. *Journal of English for Academic Purposes, 4,* 239–256.

Brumfit, C., & Johnson, K. (1979). *The communicative approach to language teaching.* New York: Oxford University Press.

Byrd, P. (2001). Textbooks: Evaluation for selection and analysis for implementation. In M. Celce-Murcia (Ed.), *Teaching English as a second or foreign language* (3rd ed.) (pp. 415–429). Boston, MA: Heinle Cengage.

Byrnes, H. (1990). Foreign language program articulation from high school to the university. *ERIC Digest,* ED 321586. Retrieved from http://www.eric.ed.gov:80/PDFS/ED321586.pdf

Byrnes, H. (1998). Constructing curricula in collegiate foreign language departments. In H. Byrnes (Ed.), *Learning foreign and second languages: Perspectives in research and scholarship* (pp. 262–295). New York: Modern Language Association of America.

Byrnes, H. (2001). Articulating foreign language programs: The need for new, curricular bases. In C. G. Lally (Ed.), *Foreign language program articulation: Current practice and future prospects* (pp. 157–180). Westport, CT: Bergin & Garvey.

Byrnes, H., & Maxim, H. (Eds.). (2004). *Advanced foreign-language instruction.* Boston, MA: Heinle Cengage.

Canagarajah, A. S. (1999). On EFL teachers, awareness, and agency. *ELT Journal, 53,* 207–214.

Carkin, S. (1997). Language program leadership as intercultural management. In M. Christison & F. Stoller (Eds.), *A handbook for language program administrators* (pp. 49–60). Burlingame, CA: Alta Book Center.

Chaffee, J. (1992). Teaching critical thinking across the curriculum. In C. A. Barnes (Ed.), *Critical thinking: Educational imperative* (pp. 25–35). San Francisco: Jossey-Bass.

Chambers, F. (1997). Seeking consensus in coursebook evaluation. *ELT Journal, 51,* 29–35.

Christison, M., & Stoller, F. (Eds.). (1997). *A handbook for language program administrators.* Burlingame, CA: Alta Book Center.

Chun, D. (1994). Using computer networking to facilitate the acquisition of interactive competence. *System, 22,* 17–31.

Coady, S. (1990). Hiring faculty: A system for making good decisions. *CUPA Journal, 41*(3), 5–8.

Collins, J. C., & Lazier, W. C. (1992). *Into the academic mainstream: Guidelines for teaching language minority students.* Alexandria, VA: TESOL.

Cook, V. (2008). *Second language learning and language teaching.* New York: Oxford University Press.

Cooke-Plagwitz, J. (2009). A new language for the Net Generation: Why Second Life works for the Net Generation. In R. Oxford & J. Oxford (Eds.), *Second language teaching and learning in the net generation* (pp. 173–180). Honolulu, HI: University of Hawai'i, National Foreign Language Resource Center.

Cowan, R. (2008). *The teacher's grammar of English: A course book and reference guide*. New York: Cambridge University Press.

Crawford, J. (2002). The role of materials in the language classroom: Finding the balance. In J. Richards & W. Renandya (Eds.), *Methodology in language teaching: An anthology on current practice* (pp. 80–91). New York: Cambridge University Press.

Cripwell, K., & Geddes, M. (1982). The development of organizational skills through micro-teaching. *ELT Journal, 36*(4), 232–236.

Cunningsworth, A. (1995). *Choosing your course book*. Oxford, United Kingdom: Heinemann.

Curtain, H. (n.d.). Teaching in the target language. *National Capital Language Resource Center*. Retrieved from http://www.nclrc.org/about_teaching/topics/PDFs/FeatureCurtain-TeachingintheTargetLanguageFINAL.pdf

Dalby, T. (2009). Adapting your course book: Becoming skilled in the art of manipulation. *TESOL Review, 1,* 145–166. Retrieved from http://tesolreview.org/down/7.%20Tim%20Dalby.pdf

Davidson, J., & Tesh, J. (1997). Theory and practice in language program organization and design. In M. Christison & F. Stoller (Eds.), *A handbook for language program administrators* (pp. 177–198). Burlingame, CA: Alta Book Center.

Davies, N. F. (1980). Putting receptive skills first. *Canadian Modern Language Review, 36,* 461–467.

Diffey, N. (1992). Second-language curriculum models and program design: Recent trends in North America. *Canadian Journal of Education, 17*(2), 208–219.

Dubin, F., & Olshtain, E. (1986). Course design: Developing programs and materials for language learning. New York: Cambridge University Press.

Ducate, L., & Lomicka, L. (2008). Adventures in the blogosphere: From blog readers to blog writers. *Computer Assisted Language Learning, 21*(1), 9–28.

Ducate, L., & Lomicka, L. (2009). Podcasting: An effective tool for honing language students' pronunciation? *Language Learning & Technology, 13*(3), 66–86.

Ellis, R. (1993). The structural syllabus and second language acquisition. *TESOL Quarterly, 27,* 91–113.

Ellis, R. (1997). *SLA research and language teaching*. New York, NY: Oxford University Press.

Ferguson, A. (2005). Student beliefs about their foreign language instructors: A look at the native-speaker/non-native-speaker issue (Unpublished doctoral dissertation). University of Arizona, Tucson, AZ. UMI #3164576.

Fernandez, C. (2011). Approaches to grammar instruction in teaching materials: A study in current L2 beginning-level Spanish textbooks. *Hispania, 94*(1), 155–170.

Field, H. S., & Gatewood, R. D. (1989). Development of a selection interview: A job content strategy. In R. W. Eder & G. R. Ferris (Eds.), *The employment interview: Theory, research, and practice* (pp. 143–157). Newbury Park, CA: Sage.

Finocchiaro, M., & Brumfit, C. (1983). *The functional–notional approach: From theory to practice*. New York: Oxford.

Firth, A., & Wagner, J. (1997). On discourse, communication, and (some) fundamental concepts in SLA research. *The Modern Language Journal, 81,* 285–300.

Gardner, R. C. (2000). Correlation, causation, motivation, and second language acquisition. *Canadian Psychology, 41,* 10–24.

Geddes, J., & Marks, D. (1997). Personnel matters. In M. Christison & F. Stoller (Eds.), *A handbook for language program administrators* (pp. 199–218). Burlingame, CA: Alta Book Center.

Geddes, M. (1979). Microteaching and foreign language teacher training. In K. Cripwell & M. Geddes (Eds.), *Microteaching and EFL teacher training: A report of a workshop*. Washington, DC: ERIC Clearinghouse.

Godwin-Jones, R. (2005). Skype and podcasting: Disruptive technologies for language learning. *Language Learning and Technology, 9*(3), 9–12. Retrieved from http://llt.msu.edu/vol9num3/emerging/default.html

Godwin-Jones, R. (2008). Web-writing 2.0: Enabling, documenting, and assessing writing online. *Language Learning and Technology, 12*(2), 7–13. Retrieved from http://llt.msu.edu/vol12num2/emerging/

Goertler, S. (2011). Blended and open/online learning: Adapting to a changing world of language teaching. In N. Arnold & L. Ducate (Eds.), *Present and future promises of CALL: From theory and research to new directions in language teaching* (pp. 471–501). San Marcos, TX: CALICO.

Goethals, M. S., Howard, R. A., & Sanders, M. M. (2004). *Student teaching: A process approach to reflective practice* (2nd ed.). Columbus, OH: Merrill Prentice Hall.

Guntermann, G., & Phillips, J. K. (1981). Communicative course design: Developing functional ability in all four skills. *Canadian Modern Language Review, 37,* 329–343.

Guthrie, E. (2001). The language program director and the curriculum: Setting the stage for effective programs. *ADFL Bulletin, 32*(3), 41–47.

Hagiwara, M. P. (1970a). *Leadership in foreign-language education: Trends in training and supervision of graduate assistants*. New York: MLA–ERIC.

Hagiwara, M. P. (1970b). The T.A. system: Two wrongs do not make a right. *ADFL Bulletin, 8*(3), 26–28.

Hanson, J. (2011). Teacher reflection and identity—teaching a language from within an L2 cultural identity, or teaching from within L1 culture about L2. *The Journal of Language Teaching and Learning, 1*(1), 1–38.

Harris-Schenz, B. (1993). Between a rock and a hard place: The position of the language program coordinator. *ADFL Bulletin, 24*(2), 45–50.

Hatton, N., & Smith, D. (1995). Reflection in teacher education: Towards definition and implementation. *Teaching and Teacher Education, 11*(1), 33–49.

Heilenman, L. K. (Ed.). (1999). *Research issues and language program direction.* Boston, MA: Heinle Cengage.

Heinze, A., & Procter, C. (2004). Reflections on the use of blended learning. *Education in a changing environment.* University of Salford, Education Development Unit. Retrieved from http://www.ece.salford.ac.uk/proceedings/papers/ah_04.rtf

Henry, A. R. (1997). The decision maker and negotiator. In M. Christison & F. Stoller (Eds.), *A handbook for language program administrators* (pp. 77–90). Burlingame, CA: Alta Book Center.

Horwitz, E. (1987). Surveying student beliefs about language learning. In A. Wenden & J. Rubin (Eds.), *Learner strategies in language learning* (pp. 119–129). Cambridge, MA: Prentice Hall.

Johnson, K. (1996). *Language teaching and skill learning.* Oxford, United Kingdom: Blackwell.

Jones, J. B. (2011, August 26). Creative approaches to the syllabus. *The Chronicle of Higher Education.* Retrieved from http://chronicle.com/blogs/profhacker/creative-approaches-to-the-syllabus/35621

Jurasek, R. (1996). Intermediate-level foreign language curricula: An assessment and a new agenda. *ADFL Bulletin, 27*(2), 18–27.

Kaplan, R. B. (1997). An IEP (Intensive English Program) is a many-splendored thing. In M. Christison & F. Stoller (Eds.), *A handbook for language program administrators* (pp. 3–19). Burlingame, CA: Alta Book Center.

Kasambira, K. (1984). *Microteaching handbook: Skills, planning, and critiquing.* Washington, DC: ERIC Clearinghouse.

Katz, S., & Watzinger-Tharp, J. (2005). Toward an understanding of the role of applied linguists in foreign language departments. *The Modern Language Journal, 89,* 490–502.

Katz, S., & Watzinger-Tharp, J. (Eds.). (2008). *Conceptions of L2 grammar: Theoretical approaches and their application in the L2 classroom.* Boston, MA: Heinle Cengage.

Kern, R. (1995). Restructuring classroom interaction with network computers: Effects on quantity and characteristics of language production. *The Modern Language Journal, 79,* 457–476.

Kern, R., & Warschauer, M. (2000). Theory and practice of network-based language teaching. In M. Warschauer & R. Kern (Eds.), *Network-based language teaching: Concepts and practice* (pp. 1–19). New York: Cambridge University Press.

Kinginger, C. (1998). Videoconferencing as access to spoken French. *The Modern Language Journal, 82,* 502–513.

Kirschner, A. (2012, April 8). Innovations in higher education? Hah! *Chronicle of Higher Education.* Retrieved from http://chronicle.com/article/Innovations-in-Higher/131424/

Klee, C. (Ed.). (1994). *Faces in a crowd: The individual learner in multisection courses.* Boston, MA: Heinle Cengage.

Klinghammer, S. (1997). The strategic planner. In M. Christison & F. Stoller (Eds.), *A handbook for language program administrators* (pp. 61–76). Burlingame, CA: Alta Book Center.

Krahnke, K. (1987). *Approaches to syllabus design for foreign language teaching.* Englewood Cliffs, NJ: Prentice Hall.

Kramsch, C. (1995). Embracing conflict versus achieving consensus in foreign language education. *ADFL Bulletin, 26*(3), 6–12.

Kramsch, C. (Ed.). (1995). *Redefining the boundaries of language study.* Boston, MA: Heinle Cengage.

Kramsch, C. (1998). Constructing second language acquisition research in foreign language departments. In H. Byrnes (Ed.), *Learning foreign and second languages: Perspectives in research and scholarship* (pp. 23–38). New York: Modern Language Association.

Kramsch, C. (2000). Second language acquisition, applied linguistics, and the teaching of foreign languages. *The Modern Language Journal, 84,* 311–326.

Kramsch, C. (2006). From communicative competence to symbolic competence. *The Modern Language Journal, 90,* 249–252.

Krashen, S. D., & Terrell, T. D. (1983). *The natural approach: Language acquisition in the classroom.* Hayward, CA: Alemany Press.

Kumaravadivelu, B. (2002). *Beyond methods: Macrostrategies for language teaching.* New Haven, CT: Yale University Press.

Kuriscak, L., & Luke, C. (2009). Language learner attitudes toward virtual worlds: An investigation of Second Life. In L. Lomicka & G. Lord (Eds.), *The next generation: Social networking and online collaboration in foreign language learning* (pp. 173–198). San Marcos, TX: CALICO.

Lalande, J. F. (1991). Redefinition of the TA supervisor-language program coordinator position into the lecturer series: A sensible idea? *ADFL Bulletin, 22*(2), 15–18.

Lally, C. G. (2001). Foreign language articulation: Using the *National Standards* as a guide for local articulation efforts. In C. G. Lally (Ed.), *Foreign language program articulation: Current practice and future prospects* (pp. 17–28). Westport, CT: Bergin & Garvey.

Lange, D. L. (1982). The problem of articulation. In T. V. Higgs (Ed.), *Curriculum, competence, and the foreign language teacher* (pp. 113–137). Lincolnwood, IL: National Textbook Company.

Lange, D. L. (1994). The curricular crisis in foreign language learning. *ADFL Bulletin, 25*(2), 12–16.

Larsen-Freeman, D. (2003). *Techniques and principles in language teaching.* New York: Oxford University Press.

Lazo-Wilson, V., & Lozano Espejo, C. I. (2009). The coalescence of Spanish language and culture through blogs and films. In R. Oxford & J. Oxford (Eds.), *Second language teaching and learning in the Net Generation* (pp. 127–140). Honolulu, HI: University of Hawai'i, National Foreign Language Resource Center.

Leaver, B. L., & Oxford, R. (2000). Mentoring in style: Using style information to enhance mentoring of foreign language teachers. In B. Rifkin (Ed.), *Mentoring foreign language teaching assistants, lecturers, and adjunct faculty* (pp. 55–88). Boston, MA: Heinle Cengage.

Lee, J. (1987). Toward a professional model of language program direction. *ADFL Bulletin, 19*(1), 22–25.

Lee, J. (1989). *A manual and practical guide to directing foreign language programs and training graduate teaching assistants.* Boston, MA: McGraw-Hill.

Lee, J. (1999). What is second language acquisition and what is it doing in this department? *ADFL Bulletin, 30*(3), 49–53.

Lee, J., & Valdman, A. (Eds.). (2000). *Form and meaning: Multiple perspectives.* Boston, MA: Heinle Cengage.

Lee, J., & VanPatten, B. (1991). The question of language program direction is academic. In S. S. Magnan (Ed.), *Challenges in the 1990s for college foreign language programs* (pp. 113–128). Boston, MA: Heinle Cengage.

Lee, J., & VanPatten, B. (2003). *Making communicative language teaching happen.* Boston, MA: McGraw-Hill.

Lee, J., Binkowski, D., & Binkowski, A. (1993). Issues and perspectives on when TAs supervise TAs. In D. Benseler (Ed.), *The dynamics of language program direction* (pp. 223–239). Boston, MA: Heinle Cengage.

Lee, L. (2001). Online interaction: negotiation of meaning and strategies used among learners of Spanish. *ReCALL, 13*(1), 232–244.

Lee, L. (2002). Enhancing learners' communication skills through synchronous electronic interaction and task-based instruction. *Foreign Language Annals, 35*(1), 16–23.

Lee, L. (2010a). Exploring wiki-mediated collaborative writing: A case study in an elementary Spanish course. *CALICO Journal, 27*(2), 260–276.

Lee, L. (2010b). Fostering reflective writing and interactive exchange through blogging in an advanced language course. *ReCALL, 22*(2), 212–227.

Levine, G. S., & Phipps, A. (Eds.). (2010). *Critical and intercultural theory and language pedagogy.* Boston, MA: Heinle Cengage.

Levy, M. (1997). *CALL: Context and conceptualization.* New York: Oxford University Press.

Levy, M., & Hubbard, P. (2005). Why call CALL "CALL"? *Computer Assisted Language Learning, 18*(3), 143–149.

Lightbown, P., & Spada, N. (2008). *How languages are learned.* New York: Oxford University Press.

Likert, R. (1967). *The human organization: Its management and value.* Boston, MA: McGraw-Hill.

Liskin-Gasparro, J. (Ed.). (1996). *Patterns and policies: The changing demographics of foreign language instruction.* Boston, MA: Heinle Cengage.

Lively, M. (1997). The changing demographics of the traditional student: Making our classrooms relevant for the new generation.*ADFL Bulletin, 28*(3), 32–36.

Lomicka, L., & Lord, G. (2007). Social presence in virtual communities of foreign language teachers. *System, 35*(2), 208–228.

Lomicka, L., & Lord, G. (2011). Podcasting—past, present and future: Applications of academic podcasting in and out of the language classroom. In B. R. Facer & M. Abdous (Eds.), *Academic podcasting and mobile assisted language learning: Applications and outcomes* (pp. 1–20). Hershey, PA: IGI Global.

Lomicka, L., & Lord, G. (2012). A tale of tweets: Analyzing microblogging among language learners. *System, 40*(1), 48–63.

Lomicka, L., Lord, G., & Manzer, M. (2003). Merging foreign language theory and practice in designing technology-based tasks. In C. M. Cherry (Ed.), *Dimension 2003* (pp. 37–52). Valdosta, GA: SCOLT Publications.

Long, M. H., & Crookes, G. (1992). The approaches to task-based syllabus design. *TESOL Quarterly, 26*(1), 27–56.

Long, M., & Robinson, P. (1998). Focus on form: Theory, research and practice. In C. Doughty & J. Williams (Eds.), *Focus on form in classroom second language acquisition* (pp. 15–41). New York, NY: Cambridge University Press.

Lord, G. (2008). Podcasting communities and second language pronunciation. *Foreign Language Annals, 41*(2), 364–379.

Lord, G., & Lomicka, L. (2004). Using collaborative cyber communities to further teacher preparation and education: The TIFLE model. *Foreign Language Annals, 37*(3), 401–416.

Lord, G., & Lomicka, L. (2007). Foreign language teacher preparation and asynchronous CMC: Promoting reflective teaching. *Journal of Technology and Teacher Education, 15*(4), 513–532.

Lord, G., & Lomicka, L. (2008). Blended learning in teacher education: An investigation of classroom community across media. *Contemporary Issues in Technology and Teacher Education, 8*(2), 158–174.

Magnan, S. S. (2008). Reexamining the priorities of the National Standards for Foreign Language Education. *Language Teaching, 41*(3), 349–366.

Magnan, S. S. (Ed.). (1991). *Challenges in the 1990s for college foreign language programs.* Boston, MA: Heinle Cengage.

Mancing, H. (1991). Teaching, research, service: The concept of faculty workload. *ADFL Bulletin, 22*(3), 44–50.

Mason, K. (1992). Beyond the methods course: Designing a graduate seminar in foreign language program direction. In J. C. Waltz (Ed.), *Development and supervision of teaching assistants in foreign languages* (pp. 113–133). Boston, MA: Heinle Cengage.

Maxim, H. H. (2005a). Articulating foreign language writing development at the collegiate level: A curriculum-based approach. In C. M. Barrette & K. Paesani (Eds.), *Language program articulation: Developing a theoretical foundation* (pp. 78–93). Boston, MA: Heinle Cengage.

Maxim, H. H. (2005b). Enhancing graduate student teacher development through curricular reform. *ADFL Bulletin, 36*(3), 15–21.

McGrath, I. (2002). *Materials evaluation and design for language teaching*. Edinburgh, United Kingdom: Edinburgh University Press.

Medgyes, P. (1992). Native or non-native: Who's worth more? *ELT Journal, 46*(4), 340–349.

Medgyes, P. (1994). The non-native teacher. London, United Kingdom: Macmillan.

Medley, D. M., Coker, H., & Soar, R. S. (1984). *Measurement-based evaluation of teacher performance: An empirical approach*. New York: Longman.

Mintzberg, H. (1987). Crafting strategy. *Harvard Business Review, 65*(4), 66–75.

Modern Language Association. (2003). *Statement on non-tenure-track faculty members*. Retrieved from http://www.mla.org/statement_on_nonten

Modern Language Association. (2007). *Foreign languages and higher education: New structures for a changed world*. Retrieved from http://www.mla.org/flreport

Morain, G. (1990). Preparing foreign language teachers: Problems and possibilities. *ADFL Bulletin, 21*(2), 20–24.

Moyer, A., & Gonglewski, M. (1998). Surviving the leap from graduate student to language program director: Issues, challenges, rewards. *ADFL Bulletin, 30*(1), 52-58.

Mukundan, J. (2004). *A composite framework for ESL textbook evaluation*. (Unpublished doctoral dissertation). University Putra Malaysia, Serdang.

Mukundan, J. (2007). Evaluation of English language textbooks: Some important issues for consideration. *Journal of NELTA, 12*(1&2), 80–84. Retrieved from http://nepjol.info/index.php/NELTA/article/view/3432/2978

Murphy, J. M. (1992). An etiquette for the nonsupervisory observation of L2 classrooms. *Foreign Language Annals, 25*(3), 223–225.

Muyskens, J. (Ed.). (1998). *New ways of learning and teaching: Focus on technology and foreign language education*. Boston, MA: Heinle Cengage.

Niño, A. (2009). Internet and language teaching/learning; Reflections on online emerging technologies and their impact on foreign-language instruction. In R. Oxford & J. Oxford, (Eds.), *Second language teaching and learning in the Net Generation* (pp. 23–30). Honolulu, HI: University of Hawai'i, National Foreign Language Resource Center.

Norris, J. M., Davis, J. M., Sinicrope, C., & Watanabe, Y. (Eds.) (2009). *Toward useful program evaluation in college foreign language education*. University of Hawai'i at Manoa: National Foreign Language Resource Center.

Nunan, D. (1988). *Syllabus design*. New York: Oxford University Press.

Nunan, D. (2001). Aspects of task-based syllabus design. *Karen's linguistics issues: Free resources for teachers and students of English*. Retrieved from http://www3.telus.net/linguisticsissues/syllabusdesign.html

Ogeyik, M. C. (2009). Attitudes of the student teachers in English language teaching programs towards microteaching technique. *English Language Teaching, 2*(3), 205–212.

Omaggio Hadley, A. (2001). *Teaching language in context* (3rd ed.). Boston, MA: Heinle Cengage.

O'Reilly, T. (2005, September 30). What is Web 2.0? *O'Reilly Network.* Retrieved from http://oreilly.com/web2/archive/what-is-web-20.html

Oskoz, A. (2009). Using online forums to integrate the *Standards* into the foreign language curriculum. In V. M. Scott (Ed.), *Principles and practices of the Standards in college foreign language education* (pp. 106–126). Boston, MA: Heinle Cengage.

Otto, S. E. K., & Pusack, J. P. (1988). Calculating the cost of instructional technology: An administrator's primer. *ADFL Bulletin, 19*(3), 18–22.

Oxford, R., & Oxford, J. (2009). Introduction. In R. Oxford & J. Oxford (Eds.), *Second language teaching and learning in the Net Generation* (pp. 1–9). Honolulu, HI: University of Hawai'i, National Foreign Language Resource Center.

Paesani, K., & Barrette, C. M. (2005). The role of the language program director within a three-dimensional model of articulation. In C. M. Barrette & K. Paesani (Eds.), *Language program articulation: Developing a theoretical foundation* (pp. 2–20). Boston, MA: Heinle Cengage.

Paradowski, M. B. (2010). *Foreign language textbook evaluation chart.* Unpublished manuscript.

Parry, M., & Young, J. R. (2010, November 28). New social software tries to make studying feel like Facebook. *The Chronicle of Higher Education.* Retrieved from http://chronicle.com/article/New-Social-Software-Tries-to/125542

Peredo, M. W. (2000). *Directions in professional development: Findings of current literature.* Retrieved from http://www.ncela.gwu.edu/files/rcd/BE022895/Directions_In_Professional_Development.pdf

Phillips, J. K. (2008). Foreign language *Standards* and context of communication. *Language Teaching, 41*(1), 93–102. New York: Cambridge University Press.

Phillips, J. K. (2009). Strengthening the connection between content and communication. In V. M. Scott (Ed.), *Principles and practices of the Standards in college foreign language education* (pp. 29–37). Boston, MA: Heinle Cengage.

Rabbini, R. (2002). An introduction to syllabus design and evaluation. *The Internet TESL Journal, 8*(5). Retrieved from http://iteslj.org/Articles/Rabbini-Syllabus.html

Rahimpour, M. (2010). Current trends on syllabus design in foreign language instruction. *Procedia Social and Behavioral Sciences, 2,* 1660–1664.

Rava, S. (1991). Minding our business. *ADFL Bulletin, 22*(3), 51–53.

Rava, S., & Rossbacher, B. (1999). Teaching and technology: A new course for TA development. *ADFL Bulletin, 30*(3), 63–71.

Reagan, T. G., & Osborn, T. A. (2001). *The foreign language educator in society: Toward a critical pedagogy.* New York: Routledge.

Rice, A. (2011, October 27). Students push their Facebook use further into course work. *The Chronicle of Higher Education.* Retrieved from http://chronicle.com/blogs/wiredcampus/students-push-their-facebook-use-further-into-academics/33947

Richards, J. C. (n.d.). The role of textbooks in a language program. Retrieved from http://www.professorjackrichards.com/articles/role-of-textbooks/

Richards, J. C. (1990). *The language teaching matrix.* New York: Cambridge University Press.

Richards, J. C. (2001). *Curriculum development in language education.* New York: Cambridge University Press.

Richards, J. C., & Lockhart, C. (1994). *Reflective teaching in second language classrooms.* New York: Cambridge University Press.

Richards, J. C., & Rogers, T. S. (2001). *Approaches and methods in language teaching.* New York: Cambridge University Press.

Rifkin, B. (Ed.). (2001). *Mentoring foreign language teaching assistants, lecturers, and adjunct faculty.* Boston, MA: Heinle Cengage.

Robinson, P. (2009). Syllabus design. In M. H. Long & C. H. Doughty (Eds.), *Handbook of language teaching* (pp. 294–310). Malden, MA: Wiley-Blackwell.

Rosen, L. (2009). Reaching students: A hybrid approach to language learning. In R. Oxford & J. Oxford (Eds.), *Second language teaching and learning in the Net Generation* (pp. 65–84). Honolulu, HI: University of Hawai'i, National Foreign Language Resource Center.

Rubio, F., Passey, A., & Campbell, S. (2004). Grammar in disguise: the hidden agenda of communicative language teaching textbooks. *RAEL (Revista Electrónica de Lingüística Aplicada), 3,* 158–176. Retrieved from http://dialnet.unirioja.es/servlet/oaiart?codigo=1396249

Sadow, S. A. (1989). Methodologists: A brief guide for their colleagues. *ADFL Bulletin, 21*(1), 27–28.

Salaberry, R. (2001). The use of technology for second language learning and teaching: A retrospective. *The Modern Language Journal, 88,* 39–56.

Sammons, J. L. (1976). Teacher training once more: Some respectful objections. *ADFL Bulletin, 8*(2), 8–10.

Sayers, D. (1993). Distance team teaching and computer learning networks. *TESOL Journal, 3*(1), 19–23.

Schon, D. (1987). *Educating the reflective practitioner.* San Francisco, CA: Jossey Bass.

Schultz, J. M. (2005). The role of special focus sections in the articulation of language and literature courses. In C. M. Barrette & K. Paesani (Eds.), *Language program articulation: Developing a theoretical foundation* (pp. 560–577). Boston, MA: Heinle Cengage.

Schulz, R. A. (1980). TA training, supervision, and evaluation: Report of a survey. *ADFL Bulletin, 12*(1), 1–8.

Schulz, R. A. (1984). Language acquisition and syllabus design: The need for a broad perspective. *ADFL Bulletin, 15*(3), 1–7.

Schulz, R. A. (1988). Proficiency-based foreign language requirements: A plan for action. *ADFL Bulletin, 19*(2), 24–28.

Scott, V. M. (2009). (Ed.). *Principles and practices of the* Standards *in college foreign language education*. Boston, MA: Heinle Cengage.

Scott, V. M., & Tucker, H. (Eds.). (2002). *SLA and the literature classroom: Fostering dialogues*. Boston, MA: Heinle Cengage.

Sheldon, L. (1988). Evaluating ELT textbooks and materials. *ELT Journal, 42*(4), 237–246.

Shrum, J., & Glisan, E. (2005). *Teacher's handbook: Contextualized language instruction* (3rd ed.). Boston, MA: Heinle Cengage.

Shrum, J., & Glisan, E. (2010). *Teacher's handbook: Contextualized language instruction* (4th ed.). Boston, MA: Heinle Cengage.

Silva, G. V., Macián, J. L., & Mejía-Gómez, M. (2006). Peer TA mentoring in a foreign language program. *International Journal of Teaching and Learning in Higher Education, 18*(3), 241–249.

Siskin, H. J. (Ed.). (2007). *From thought to action: Exploring beliefs and outcomes in the foreign language program*. Boston, MA: Heinle Cengage.

Skehan, P. (1991). Individual differences in second language learning. *Studies in Second Language Acquisition, 13*(2), 275–298.

Skehan, P. (1998). *A cognitive approach to language learning*. New York: Oxford University Press.

Skierso, A. (1991). Textbook selection and evaluation. In M. Celce-Murcia (Ed.), *Teaching English as a second or foreign language* (pp. 432–453). Boston, MA: Heinle Cengage.

Soppelsa, E. (1997). Empowerment of faculty. In M. Christison & F. Stoller (Eds.), *A handbook for language program administrators* (pp. 123–141). Burlingame, CA: Alta Book Center.

Stepp-Greany, J. (2008, November). *Preparing future language program directors*. Presentation at the American Council on the Teaching of Foreign Languages (ACTFL) Annual Meeting and Convention, Orlando, FL.

Stoller, F. L. (1992). *Analysis of innovations in selected higher education intensive English programs: A focus on administrators' perceptions*. (Unpublished doctoral dissertation). Northern Arizona University, Flagstaff, AZ.

Stoller, F. L. (1995a). *Managing intensive English program innovations*. (NAFSA Working Paper No. 56). Washington, DC: NAFSA Association of International Educators.

Stoller, F. L. (1995b). Innovation in a non-traditional academic unit: The intensive English program. *Innovative Higher Education, 19*(3), 177–195.

Stoller, F. L. (1997). The catalyst for change and innovation. In M. Christison & F. Stoller (Eds.), *A handbook for language program administrators* (pp. 33–48). Burlingame, CA: Alta Book Center.

Sykes, J. (2009). Learner requests in Spanish: Examining the potential of multiuser virtual environments for L2 pragmatic acquisition. In L. Lomicka and G. Lord (Eds.), *The second generation: Online collaboration and social networking in CALL* (pp. 199–234). San Marcos, TX: CALICO.

Sykes, J., & Holden, C. (2011). Communities: Exploring digital games and social networking. In L. Ducate & N. Arnold (Eds.), *Present and future promises of CALL:*

From theory and research to new directions in language teaching (pp. 311–336). San Marcos, TX: CALICO.

Sykes, J., Oskoz, A., & Thorne, S. (2008). Web 2.0, synthetic immersive environments, and the future of language education. *CALICO Journal, 25*(3), 528–546.

Tajino, A., & Tajino, Y. (2000). Native and non-native: What can they offer? Lessons from team-teaching in Japan. *ELT Journal, 54*(1), 3–11.

Tapscott, D. (1999). *Growing up digital: The rise of the Net Generation*. Boston, MA: McGraw–Hill.

Terry, R. M. (1998). Authentic tasks and materials for testing in the foreign language classroom. In J. Harper, M. G. Lively, & M. K. Williams (Eds.), *The coming of age of the profession: Issues and emerging ideas for the teaching of foreign languages* (pp. 277–290). Boston, MA: Heinle Cengage.

Terry, R. M. (2009). The national *Standards* at the postsecondary level: A blueprint and framework for change. In V. M. Scott (Ed.), *Principles and practices of the* Standards *in college foreign language education* (pp. 17–28). Boston, MA: Heinle Cengage.

Teschner, R. (Ed.). (1991). *Assessing foreign language proficiency of undergraduate*s. Boston, MA: Heinle Cengage.

Thorne, S. (2010, June). *Avoiding the worst game ever: Media and emergent semiospheres*. Keynote presented at the annual meeting of the Computer Assisted Language Instruction Consortium (CALICO), Amherst, MA.

Thorne, S. (2012). Gaming writing: Supervernaculars, stylization, and semiotic remediation. In G. Kessler, A. Oskoz, & I. Elola (Eds.), *Technology across writing contexts and tasks* (pp. 297–316). San Marcos, TX: CALICO.

Thorne, S., Black, R., & Sykes, J. (2009). Second language use, socialization, and learning in internet interest communities and online games. *The Modern Language Journal, 93,* 802–821.

Tucker, C. A. (1975). Evaluating beginning course books. *English Teaching Forum, 23*(3), 355– 361.

Ur, P. (1996). *A course in language teaching: Practice & theory*. New York: Cambridge University Press.

van Compernolle R., & Williams, L. (2009). (Re)situating the role(s) of new technologies in world-language teaching and learning. In R. Oxford & J. Oxford (Eds.), *Second language teaching and learning in the Net Generation* (pp. 9–22). Honolulu, HI: University of Hawai'i, National Foreign Language Resource Center.

Waldinger, R. (1990). Training Ph.D. students to teach in college. *ADFL Bulletin, 22*(1), 20–23.

Walsh, K. (2010, August 11). Facebook as an instructional technology tool. *EmergingEdTech*. Retrieved from http://www.emergingedtech.com/2010/08/facebook-as-an-instructional-technology-tool/

Walz, J. (Ed.). (1992). *Development and supervision of teaching assistants in foreign languages*. Boston, MA: Heinle Cengage.

Warschauer, M. (1996a). Comparing face-to-face and electronic discussion in the second language classroom. *CALICO Journal, 13,* 7–25.

Warschauer, M. (1996b). Motivational aspects of using computers for writing and communication. In M. Warschauer (Ed.), *Telecollaboration in foreign language learning: Proceedings of the Hawai'i symposium* (Technical Report #12, pp. 29–46). Honolulu, HI: University of Hawai'i, Second Language Teaching & Curriculum Center. Retrieved from http://scholarspace.manoa.hawaii.edu/bitstream/handle/10125/8946/NW01.pdf?...

Wasley, P. (2008, March 14). The syllabus becomes a repository of legalese. *Chronicle of Higher Education*. Retrieved from http://chronicle.com/article/The-Syllabus-Becomes-a/17723

Weber, M. (1925/1947). *The theory of social and economic organization* (A. M. Henderson & T. Parsons, Trans.). New York: Oxford University Press.

White, R., Hockley, A., van der Horst Jansen, J., & Laughner, M. (2008). *From teacher to manager: Managing language teaching organizations*. New York: Cambridge University Press.

White, R., Martin, M., Stimson, M., & Hodge, R. (1991). *Management in English language teaching*. New York: Cambridge University Press.

Whitney, H. (2011, September 14). Simple Post-Its for teaching improvement. *The Chronicle of Higher Education*. Retrieved from http://chronicle.com/blogs/profhacker/simple-post-its-for-teaching-improvement/35863

Widdowson, H. G. (1983). *Learning purpose and language use*. New York: Oxford University Press.

Widdowson, H. G. (1990). *Aspects of language teaching*. New York: Oxford University Press.

Wilkins, D. (1976). *Notional syllabuses: A taxonomy and its relevance to foreign language curriculum development*. New York: Oxford University Press.

Williams, D. (1983). Developing criteria for textbook evaluation. *ELT Journal, 37*(3), 251–255.

Willis, D. (1990). *The lexical syllabus: A new approach to language teaching*. London, United Kingdom: Collins.

Windham, S. (2008). Redesigning lower-level curricula for learning outcomes: A case study. *ADFL Bulletin, 39*(2&3), 31–35.

Wood, D., Harms, P., & Vazire, S. (2010). Perceiver effects as projective tests: What your perceptions of others say about you. *Journal of Personality and Social Psychology, 99*(1), 174–190.

Woody, D. B. (2005). Language program articulation from the perspective of the learner: Constructing coherence through the use of a language learning portfolio. In C. M. Barrette & K. Paesani (Eds.), *Language program articulation: Developing a theoretical foundation* (pp. 131–148). Boston, MA: Heinle Cengage.

Young, J. (2011, August 28). College presidents are bullish on online education but face a skeptical public. *The Chronicle of Higher Education*. Retrieved from http://chronicle.com/article/College-Presidents-Are-Bullish/128814/

Zaro, J. (1996). Syllabus design and implications for teaching units. In N. McLaren & D. Madrid (Eds.), *A handbook for TEFL* (pp. 186–208). Alicante, Spain: Marfil.

CREDITS

Chapter 2:

Page 21: Google Mission Statement in Google Website, accessed on 22 June 2012. Used by permission.

Page 21: Wikimedia Mission Statement in Wikimedia Foundation Website, accessed on 22 June 2012. Used by permission.

Page 21: NC State Board of Education Mission Statement in North Carolina Public Schools Website, accessed on 22 June 2012. Used by permission.

Page 21: Aero Rental Mission Statement in Aero Rental website. Used by permission.

Page 33: Mission Statement Excerpt, Bucknell University, Dept. of Spanish in Bucknell University, Dept. of Spanish website. Used by permission.

Page 33: Mission Statement Excerpt, Davidson College, Dept. of German and Russian, in Davidson College Website, accessed on 22 June 2013. Used by permission.

Page 34: Mission Statement Excerpt, Dickinson College, Dept. of Spanish and Portuguese in Dickinson College Website, accessed on 22 June 2012. Used by permission.

Page 34: Mission Statement Excerpt, Illinois Valley Community College, World Languages Department in Illinois Valley Community College Website, accessed 22 June 2012. Used by permission.

Page 35: Mission Statement Excerpt, Sam Houston State University, Department of Foreign Languages in Sam Houston State University Website, accessed on 22 June 2012. Used by permission.

Page 35: Mission Statement Excerpt, University of San Diego, Department of Languages and Literatures in University of San Diego Website, accessed on 22 June 2012. Used by permission.

Page 36: Mission Statement Excerpt, University of Washington, Division of Spanish and Portuguese Studies in University of Washington Website, accessed on 22 June 2012. Used by permission.

Page 36: Mission Statement Excerpt, Western Kentucky University, Modern Languages Department in Western Kentucky University Website, accessed on 22 June 2012. Used by permission.

Chapter 3:

Page 64: Syllabus Excerpt, Lynchburg college in Lynchburg College Website, accessed on 1 June 2012. Used by permission.

Page 66: Syllabus Excerpt, University of North Texas in University of North Texas Website, accessed on 4 June 2012. Used by permission of the coordinators of the UNT elementary and intermediate Spanish Programs.

Page 66: Syllabus Excerpt, University of South Carolina German in University of South Carolina Website, accessed on 1 June 2012. Used by permission of Dr.Lara Ducate.

Page 66: Syllabus Excerpt, University of South Carolina French in University of South Carolina French Website, accessed on 1 June 2012. Used by permission.

Page 68: Syllabus Excerpt, University of Kansas, Department of Spanish and Portuguese in University of Kansas Website, accessed on 1 June 2012. Used by permission.

Page 70: Syllabus Excerpt, Western Michigan University, Department of Spanish in Western Michigan University, accessed on 1 June 2012. Used by permission.

Page 71: Syllabus Excerpt, University of Iowa, Department of Spanish and Portuguese in University of Iowa Website, accessed on 1 June 2012. Used by permission.

Page 73: Syllabus Excerpt, Michigan State University in Michigan State University Website, accessed on 1 June 2012. Used by permission.

Chapter 4:

Page 96: Textbook Evaluation Form adapted by Tammy Jandrey Hertel, Lynchburg College and Gretchen Sunderman, Florida State University. Used by permission.

Page 98: Textbook Evaluation Form, Word Press in WordPress Website, accessed on 14 November 2011. Used by permission.

Page 101: Textbook Evaluation Form, University of South Carolina German in University of South Carolina Website, accessed on 1 June 2012. Used by permission of Dr.Lara Ducate.

INDEX